Politics and the Twitter Revolution

How Tweets Influence the Relationship between Political Leaders and the Public

John H. Parmelee
Shannon L. Bichard

LEXINGTON BOOKS
Lanham • Boulder • New York • Toronto • Plymouth, UK

Published by Lexington Books
A wholly owned subsidiary of The Rowman & Littlefield Publishing Group, Inc.
4501 Forbes Boulevard, Suite 200, Lanham, Maryland 20706
www.rowman.com

10 Thornbury Road, Plymouth PL6 7PP, United Kingdom

Copyright © 2012 by Lexington Books
First paperback edition 2013

All rights reserved. No part of this book may be reproduced in any form or by any
electronic or mechanical means, including information storage and retrieval systems,
without written permission from the publisher, except by a reviewer who may quote
passages in a review.

British Library Cataloguing in Publication Information Available

Library of Congress Cataloging-in-Publication Data

The hardback edition of this book was previously cataloged by the Library of Congress
as follows:

Parmelee, John H., 1970–
   Politics and the Twitter revolution : how tweets influence the relationship between
political leaders and the public / John H. Parmelee and Shannon L. Bichard.
      p. cm.
   1. Communication in politics—Technological innovations—United States.
2. Political leadership—Technological innovations—United States.   3. Public relations
and politics—United States.   4. Twitter.   I. Bichard, Shannon L., 1973–   II. Title.
   JA85.2.U6P37 2011
   320.97301'4—dc23   2011031112

ISBN: 978-0-7391-6500-3 (cloth : alk. paper)
ISBN: 978-0-7391-6501-0 (pbk. : alk. paper)
ISBN: 978-0-7391-6502-7 (electronic)

♾™ The paper used in this publication meets the minimum requirements of American
National Standard for Information Sciences—Permanence of Paper for Printed Library
Materials, ANSI/NISO Z39.48-1992.

Printed in the United States of America

NC
320.973
P24J
P759
C.2

Contents

JOLIET JUNIOR COLLEGE LIBRARY
JOLIET, IL 60431

Acknowledgments

I am grateful to all those people who had a hand in creating the data on which this book is based. Thank you to those people who tweeted the online survey to their followers; to those who filled out the survey; and especially to those who took the extra time to participate in the interviews. A special thank you goes to my wife, Amy, who served as an editor and adviser; and to our son, Scott. In addition, a research grant from the University of North Florida's Office of Academic Affairs provided financial support. I want to express gratitude to Robert Denton, the editor of the Lexington Studies in Political Communication, for taking on this book idea.

—John H. Parmelee

I wish to express my appreciation to the following individuals for their support and encouragement while writing this book. First, to Tom Johnson for his mentoring and for being an example of what an academic should be. Also, to Austin Sims for his countless hours coding tweets. I am eternally grateful to my husband, Rob, and our boys, Caleb and Colton, for their patience as Mommy went off to work (especially on weekends). I thank my parents, Red and Nancy, for inspiring me to always work hard and to dream big. I thank God for giving me the strength and determination to complete this academic adventure.

—Shannon L. Bichard

Chapter 1

Introduction

The Importance of Twitter in Politics

In any given week, political leaders send thousands of messages, called *tweets*, to millions of people who choose to follow them on Twitter. The messages that are tweeted give a glimpse of how Twitter is influencing campaigns, governance, and the relationship between political leaders and the public. The following examples (taken from the second week in May 2011) show the range of how Twitter is used by political leaders. Some politicians direct followers to timely policy information, while other politicians interact with followers to improve government services or share personal thoughts.

The following are tweets from five politicians. While these messages are short, the maximum length on Twitter is only 140 characters.

From John Boehner, the Speaker of the U.S. House of Representatives:

- SpeakerBoehner: House votes today on two American Energy Initiative bills that will boost #americanenergy, help create #jobs http://j.mp/jh1FEo

From John Kasich, the governor of Ohio:

- JohnKasich: As the Dispatch notes, our budget stops kicking the can down the road and starts bringing Ohio back: http://goo.gl/46Myy

From Sam Adams, the mayor of Portland, Oregon:

- MayorSamAdams: I want to follow up: when & where? RT @bkerensa Saw guy getting jumped: took police almost 20 minutes to respond #pdx @portlandpolice

From Orrin Hatch, a U.S. senator from Utah:

• OrrinHatch: Here's the river flow tracking for those of you in No. UT, concerned about flooding in your area. http://bit.ly/g2pLtI #utpol #utah

From Cory Booker, the mayor of Newark, New Jersey:

• CoryBooker: "Peace is not merely a distant goal that we seek, but a means by which we arrive at that goal." ~ MLK #NewarkPeace

Political tweeting raises many questions for those who study political communication. For example, to what degree do political tweets influence followers' political views and behavior? The tweets from Boehner and Kasich were clearly meant to influence followers' opinions on political issues and politicians. Boehner's tweet linked readers to a website with energy policy information, and Kasich's tweet linked followers to an Ohio newspaper editorial praising Kasich's budget proposal. But how successful are such tweets? Do followers have certain characteristics that make some followers more easily influenced than others? Who can be most easily influenced may rest on characteristics such as demographics, ideology, interest in politics, trust in government, and followers' motives for using Twitter. To measure the impact of tweets, it is possible to find these connections by constructing a detailed profile of the people who choose to follow political leaders on Twitter. Measuring the impact of tweets also means comparing the effects of political tweets with more traditional forms of political influence: friends, family, acquaintances, and co-workers. Are tweeted messages from political leaders (whom most followers have usually never met) more or less politically influential than messages that are communicated by family or acquaintances?

It is also important to know the degree to which political leaders use Twitter to *interact* with followers, rather than to merely *broadcast* to them. The tweet from Adams (following up on a constituent's comments about a crime) is just one example of how Twitter can facilitate a closer and helpful connection between government and the people. Hatch's tweet, which linked to a Salt Lake City television news website that had local flooding information, is an instance in which Twitter allows leaders to aid constituents in real time. The inspirational quote in Booker's tweet leads to other questions: How do political leaders present themselves in their tweets, both politically and personally? Which types of presentations are most desirable to followers? This book aims to answer these questions and others about political tweets.

Now is a good time to examine how Twitter is used in politics. In the five years since Twitter's inception, Twitter has enjoyed an exponential increase in popularity that compares only to social networking sites such as Facebook and YouTube. Twitter is used by more than 175 million people worldwide, and more than 30 billion tweets have been sent (Carlson, 2011; Penner, 2010; Ostrow, 2010a). Politicians are increasingly using it, too. Today, the president and most governors, members of Congress, and mayors of large metropolitan areas have Twitter accounts. President Barack Obama has the most Twitter followers of any political leader, with more than 7 million. Other political leaders tend to have between 10,000 and 100,000 followers, though some governors, mayors, and other officials have more than 1 million followers. The number of followers that a political leader has varies considerably and often does not depend on the size of the leaders' constituency. For example, the mayor of New York (which has a population of 8 million), has about 83,000 followers. In comparison, the mayor of Newark, New Jersey (which has a population of less than 300,000), has more than 1 million followers.

When political leaders and their followers engage on Twitter, they are part of the power and promise of Web 2.0, which refers to websites and social networking platforms that enable users to create their own content and share it with other users. Just one example of Web 2.0 is the video-sharing site YouTube, a service where anyone can post video messages to be seen, commented on, and forwarded by millions of viewers literally overnight. In terms of politics, the participatory and interactive nature of Web 2.0, including Twitter, has the potential to promote a more open exchange of ideas across a wide audience concerning key issues. Most new communication technology, such as Web 2.0, has been touted at one time or another as the hope for strengthening democracy. On the other hand, of course, if people follow and interact with only those leaders with whom they agree politically, Twitter may be harmful for democracy (by further enabling people to block out diverse views). Whether Twitter strengthens or weakens democracy is a question that will be addressed in this book. The section that follows will review Twitter's brief history, its jargon and applications, how it has been used for campaigning and governing in the United States and abroad, and what past research has found about its effects.

A TWITTER PRIMER

Twitter was created in 2006 by a team of programmers who had worked in blogging and podcasting. The San Francisco-based company is the largest microblogging service and the third-largest social networking site (behind Facebook, and YouTube; Hitwise, 2011). Twitter allows users to send and receive short messages via mobile phone, e-mail, instant messaging, and the Web. The messages are supposed to be based on the theme "What's happening?"

TWITTER'S FEATURES

While Twitter messages can be only 140 characters, a lot can be communicated in that small space. Tweets can include links to websites that provide additional information. Political leaders often use this linking function to direct followers to sites such as the following:

• online news sites or blogs that validate their policies
• websites for their campaign or an ally's campaign
• petitions
• photos of themselves on the job
• government-based sites that provide services to constituents

The following is an example of a tweet from Massachusetts Governor Duval Patrick that includes such a link:

• MassGovernor: Before grabbing your helmet, learn how the rules of the road have changed. http://cot.ag/dCnemg

Clicking the link sends the user to an official Commonwealth of Massachusetts site that explains a new law regarding vehicle safety. As can be seen in this example, a link's Web address often is shortened on Twitter to save valuable space.

Hashtags are another important aspect of political tweets. A *hashtag* is a word or abbreviation (designated in a tweet by the "#" sign) that can be searched on Twitter's website. The tweets of anyone who includes that hashtag are grouped together on Twitter. Hashtags have political value because political leaders, or anyone else, can spark dialog on an issue by giving the issue a hashtag in their tweets. Twitter users can search the hashtag, see what has been said about the issue, and they can also contribute to the conversation. The following tweet from the White House Twitter account shows how hashtags are used:

• whitehouse: President Obama: "the long battle to stop the leak and contain the oil is finally close to coming to an end" "#oilspill

Clicking (or searching for) the hashtag "#oilspill" directs users to hundreds of tweets from a wide cross-section of people who are talking about the 2010 British Petroleum (BP) oil spill in the Gulf of Mexico. Often, those tweets include additional links to websites and hashtags, which allow users to learn and discuss even more about BP, oil drilling, and the environmental impact of the spill.

Leaders also can spread their influence beyond their band of followers if they are included on "lists" that are made by Twitter users. Any user can create a list, which is simply a grouping of other Twitter users that is based on some commonality: a hobby, a musical taste, or an interest in politics. Users who click a list that is labeled, say, "influential political leaders," see a stream of tweets from the leaders on that list, regardless of whether the users are followers. Also, users can add leaders to a list even if the users are not the leaders' followers.

Tweets can be seen by anyone, with two exceptions. The sender can block that function. Or, the sender can send a direct message, called a *DM*, which is a private correspondence. Political leaders almost always leave their tweets public, as this technique helps them spread their message as far as possible. Tweets also can be shared, called *retweeting* (RT), by anyone. Followers can retweet political leaders' tweets, and leaders can retweet followers' tweets. Followers who retweet a political leader's message can create a snowball effect that allows a leader to communicate with a larger audience than they could assemble on their own. For example, South Carolina Senator Jim DeMint had about 38,000 followers in the summer of 2010—but because of retweeting, DeMint could have had his tweets seen by as many as 100,000 Twitter users (Klout, 2010). As a result, some leaders will include the phrase "please RT" in their tweets, hoping they will be retweeted generously. When political leaders retweet the messages of others, leaders tend to retweet ideas or links that bolster whatever points the leaders wish to make. In addition, leaders who regularly retweet followers' tweets can demonstrate publicly that they listen to and value their followers' opinions.

Another way for political leaders to show that they interact with followers, or anyone else on Twitter, is to mention them in their tweets. Leaders do this by putting "@username" in their tweet, as can be seen in the following tweet from Arizona Senator John McCain:

- SenJohnMcCain: Check out @leiboaz's report on my stimulus report-beware coked out stimulus monkeys! http://www.azfamily.com/video/?sec=528732&id=100158134

Clicking @leiboaz directs users to the Twitter account of television commentator David Leibowitz. The Web link connects to a video of Leibowitz criticizing that taxpayer funds were going to research the effects of drugs on monkeys.

Political leaders also can be on the receiving end of mentions from follow-ers, or anyone else. Positive-mentions can increase a leader's exposure on Twitter and attract additional followers. Twitter also has a reply feature that lets leaders react to questions or comments that they receive. A reply also can be called an "@reply." Twitter shorthand for a mention is "@mention." As with mentions, replies help a leader seem interactive, especially to the user (the person who is being replied to). A reply looks similar to a mention, except the "@username" appears at the beginning of the tweet. Another dif-ference deals with who sees a reply. While mentions by a leader are sent to all of a leader's followers, a reply is sent only to those who follow both the leader and the user getting the reply.

TWITTER'S AUDIENCE

While past research has not examined the demographic makeup of those who follow political leaders on Twitter, there are data on the people who use Twit-ter. The United States has by far the most users, with 51 percent of the total. Brazil, the United Kingdom, and Canada are next, with 9 percent, 7 percent, and 4 percent of users, respectively (Sysomos, 2010c). Women use Twitter slightly more than men (Saleem, 2010), though men use it more to find politi-cal news (Abraham, Morn, and Vollman, 2010, p. 13). In terms of age, 18- to 34-year-olds are the largest users, with 35- to 49-year-olds in second place. The majority of users have children and an undergraduate or graduate degree. In addition, only about 10 percent of users follow more than 50 people; the vast majority follow 10 people or fewer (Carlson, 2011; Saleem, 2010). This fact suggests that followers are quite selective in choosing what people to follow. It also implies that the "followed" can have a significant amount of influence on their followers.

Twitter is not mainly a venue for young people, but rather a place for an older, more professional audience. A study by the consultancy firm Trend-stream found that about 80 percent of Twitter users work in information tech-nology, professional services such as law and accounting, financial services, education, or in government. The study's conclusion suggests that Twitter is ideal for political leaders who want to reach an influential audience: "Regu-lar Twitter users are educated, tend to be in their 30s and hold a position of responsibility, all of which means that Twitter is good for engaging decision makers" (Global Web Index, 2010, p. 4).

Since its founding in 2006, Twitter's popularity and use has skyrocketed. The service went from about 5 million users at the end of 2008 to 75 mil-lion users one year later (Saleem, 2010). In addition, users are becoming increasingly active. Users went from sending 1 billion tweets a month in the fall of 2008, to 2 billion tweets per month during the summer of 2010. According to media commentator Jolie O'Dell (2010), "Twitter's growth curve is clearly accelerating." Twitter is considered important enough that the Library of Congress is archiving every public tweet since the company's inception (Raymond, 2010).

The growth in users and activity has lead to companies creating tens of thousands of applications to be used with Twitter. Among the most popular applications are websites run by firms such as Twellow, which provides a phonebook of Twitter users; Twitterfall, which finds keywords and hashtags and provides an up-to-date display of what's being tweeted about them; and Trendistic, a service that shows hashtag trends. TweetDeck is a service that allows users to organize those they are following into convenient groupings; this service is so popular that it was purchased by Twitter in 2011. Other sites, such as Klout and Twitalyzer, measure the influence and interactivity of Twitter users. In addition, Twitter has applications that integrate their service with LinkedIn, a professional networking site, and Facebook, the world's largest social networking site. According to technology journalist Ben Parr (2010a), a former Facebook company insider, the ability to send tweets and follow friends on Facebook "could be huge: it brings existing Facebook connections into the Twitterverse, which is likely to spur new levels of engagement and growth."

Some applications are designed especially to help political leaders and followers to be more influential (and influenced). The website TweetCongress displays the tweets of all congressional members, shows trending keywords and hashtags, and provides a directory to find which members tweet and how frequently. TweetCongress calls its site "a grass-roots effort to get our men and women in Congress to open up and have a real conversation with us" (About this site, 2010). GovTwit, which focuses on the tweets of government agencies, has many of the same features as TweetCongress.

Twitter's early success also has come with some problems. The service has occasionally crashed due to the high volume of tweets. Also, hackers have had some success in hijacking user accounts. The most high-profile example came in January 2009, when hackers were able to send a phony tweet from the account of then-President-elect Obama (Tessler, 2010). Other people simply set up a Twitter account and pretend to be somebody famous. As a result, Twitter now does "verified accounts" for celebrities and other high-profile users, including political leaders. This process requires a background check to establish the authenticity of the user. Despite some setbacks, Twitter has grown considerably since its founding and it attracts an audience that political leaders find valuable.

PAST TWITTER USE IN POLITICS AND GOVERNANCE

The rapid rate at which political leaders have gotten emeshed in Twitter is due (in part) to the success that Obama's presidential campaign had in using it and other forms of social media. By showing the potential of social networks to mobilize and connect with voters, communicate ideas, and fundraise, Obama's social media team provided a blueprint for other political leaders to follow (Hendricks and Denton, 2009). Obama was not the only 2008 presidential candidate to have a Twitter account, but he used it more strategically than his competition. During the Democratic primary, for example, Hillary Clinton also used Twitter to get out the word on her candidacy. But her campaign did not take the extra step of following those users who followed her, which is considered impolite by many Twitter users. Obama, on the other hand, followed those who followed him. According to business-strategist blogger Jason Oke, Obama's strategy showed that his social media team "understands the grammar of social media. Clinton is basically using Twitter as another broadcasting medium; Obama is using it as a tool for connecting with people on an individual level" (quoted in Tapscott, 2009, p. 252).

Shortly after Obama was inaugurated, only 69 members of Congress had Twitter accounts. Just three months later, that number had nearly doubled, to 134 (Ventsias, 2009). As of May 2011, 387 members of Congress were on Twitter, according to TweetCongress's website. Some members have multiple Twitter accounts—one for campaign advocacy and another for information about their congressional activities. It is not only young members or the newly elected who see the value of Twitter. Members who have been in Congress for decades also see the opportunities of the service. Ike Skelton, a Missouri congressman since 1977, was in his seventies when he joined Twitter during the 2010 congressional election. He did so in an effort to better connect with his constituents (Associated Press, 2010). To help politicians and government employees to better tap Twitter's potential, former congressional staff member Adam Sharp was hired as Twitter's Washington liaison (Parker, 2011).

How much political leaders use Twitter varies greatly. Some leaders can go weeks between tweets, while others send an average of three to five tweets a day. There is one question that is hard to answer: Who really writes the tweets, the leaders or their staff? Most leaders won't say, and it would be hard to verify. Obama surprised some Twitter users when he admitted at a town hall meeting that he has never done his own tweeting (Milian, 2009). Arnold Schwarzenegger, when he was governor of California, directed what went into each message; but he let his staff type and send the tweets (Jones, 2010). Some political leaders note in their tweets which messages are written by staff and which come from them personally (Fabian, O'Brien, and Viebeck, 2010).

Other political leaders are adamant that all their tweets come from them, as can be seen in the following exchange in which the then San Francisco mayor Gavin Newsom is asked about the authenticity of his tweets:

- GavinNewsom: Yes I Do!! RT @mandymarks: Excited to meet @Gavin-Newsom in the morning...I'm curious if he tweets his own tweets?

THE CONTENT OF POLITICAL TWEETS

What goes into leaders' tweets? There is research on that question. So far, the findings suggest that political leaders use tweets primarily to broadcast information about their policies and their personality. Interacting with followers is a secondary priority. One analysis (Golbeck, Grimes, and Rogers, 2010) of more than 6,000 tweets of members of Congress showed these results:

> Congresspeople are primarily using Twitter to disperse information, particularly links to news articles about themselves and to their blog posts, and to report on their daily activities. These tend not to provide new insights into government or the legislative process or to improve transparency; rather, they are vehicles for self-promotion. (p. 1612)

Political leaders at the state level also focus heavily on disseminating information to followers about themselves and about their issues. A case study of one particularly prolific tweeter, Minnesota State Representative Laura Brod, found mentions of policy issues to be the most frequently occurring category of tweet. In second place were tweets she made that dealt with what the study called "personal life and musings" (Ostermeier, 2009, p. 1).

Those politicians who are particularly successful at using Twitter make an effort to have more than one-way communication with followers. By replying to and retweeting followers' tweets, leaders are able to create a conversation on Twitter that keeps existing followers satisfied and attracts more followers (Sternberg, 2009). That strategy is one reason why Newark's Mayor Booker has more than twice as many followers as there are residents in the city he runs. Booker's tweets often include two-way communication with followers, and he does not focus solely on policy. A study by Donia (2010) found that his tweets are designed to meet the needs of a busy social media audience:

> Mayor Booker realizes that there are literally hundreds of thousands of people reading what he says on a daily basis and they likely give his page or profile a quick scroll before moving on to something else, so his information has to captivate them, if even for a few seconds. He is able to captivate them by

mixing up his types of posts—not just events or quotations—but also links, videos, pictures, and stories. (p. 4)

Some other political leaders conduct two-way communication on Twitter. Congressman Michael Burgess of Texas invited the public to ask questions via Twitter during a health policy forum that was being broadcast online (Viebeck, 2010). In another example, to field questions about budgetary issues, Democrats conducted a "Twitter town hall" in which members of Congress responded to comments sent to the hashtag #AskDems (Benderly, 2011).

The "personality" of the writing in political tweets can range considerably. Some messages are formal and read like short press releases, such as the following from New York Mayor Michael Bloomberg:

• MikeBloomberg: Dangerous heat forecast for NYC this weekend. For info on cooling centers call 311, visit http://nyc.gov/oem or follow @ notifyNYC

Others tweets have a homespun, personal style. Missouri Senator Claire McCaskill is an exemplar of this approach, as can be seen in her response to a followers' tweet:

• Clairecmc: Yes @tigeranniemac that was me at Target in the soap aisle. You shoulda said hi. Was with my daughter Lily. We're very friendly.

Still others' tweets include humor or sarcasm to get the point across. Senator John McCain, who has long been known for fighting what he sees as wasteful federal spending, uses sarcasm frequently when tweeting about such spending:

• SenJohnMcCain: $1,427,250 for genetic improvements of switchgrass—I thought switchgrass genes were pretty good already, guess I was wrong.

Sometimes the content in political tweets has gotten political leaders in trouble, and the following are some famous illustrations of that fact. For example, New York Congressman Anthony Weiner was forced to resign after he tweeted a lewd photo (Fahrenthold and Kane, 2011). Michigan Congressman Peter Hoekstra caused a security risk when he tweeted that his congressional delegation had just landed in Iraq (de Vise, 2009). Missouri Senator Claire McCaskill had to apologize after being criticized, even by her own mother, for tweeting on the House floor during Obama's first State of the Union address (Oliphant, 2009). Problems sometimes arise because of the speed and ease at which leaders can send a tweet, combined with the desire to make their followers feel connected.

THE CONTENT OF GOVERNMENT AGENCY TWEETS

Twitter is not just used for political campaigning. Federal and state agencies employ the microblog for many of the same reasons that politicians do: It is a quick way to transmit information and to interact with interested parties. There are many examples. For instance, during the BP oil spill in the Gulf of Mexico, the Environmental Protection Agency (EPA) regularly tweeted about how it was responding to the crisis (Howard, 2010). The Centers for Disease Control and Prevention (CDC) uses Twitter to keep followers up-to-date on outbreaks and to provide tips to avoid getting sick. The Federal Emergency Management Agency (FEMA) provides updates on heat advisories and the approach of hurricanes. The National Oceanographic and Atmospheric Administration (NOAA) educates students about oceans. The National Park Service (NPS) notifies followers about park discounts. The U.S. Geological Survey (USGS), which is tasked with monitoring earthquake activity, uses Twitter to help pinpoint seismic activity. By watching for tweets with words such as "earthquake," the USGS can better understand where the shaking is happening.

Those people who do business with government agencies find that Twitter allows them to interact with government officials more directly and quickly than before, which helps with tasks such as scheduling meetings and bidding on government contracts (Radick, 2010). The directory on the website Gov-Twit makes it easy to find which federal, state, and local officials have Twitter accounts. The GovTwit directory is at 3,000 accounts and counting. The site also lets users search for keywords, or hashtags, that relate to their business with the government.

Local governments are increasingly using Twitter to educate people and make services more efficient. San Francisco's 311 nonemergency line is connected to Twitter, so that residents can report potholes or other problems that require assistance (Farrell, 2009). In New York, @notifyNYC alerts followers to road closures, fires, water main breaks, and other emergency events.

REASONS TO TWEET

Tweeting serves several purposes for political leaders. The main purpose is that Twitter allows leaders to communicate directly to a mass audience.

Politicians are always looking for ways to get their message across without having it filtered and potentially altered by others, such as news media. Twitter, along with other social networks, can fill that need. That reason is why many inside and outside politics, such as former House Speaker Newt Gingrich, encourage its use: "Using Twitter to bypass traditional media and directly reach voters is definitely a good thing" (quoted in Oliphant, 2009, p. 2). Some political leaders are unable to get as much press coverage as they desire, or go through periods of limited power. Spreading the word on Twitter is essential for these politicians. One media consultant noted that Republicans (GOP) used Twitter far more than Democrats in the months after Obama's inauguration solidified Democratic control of the legislative and executive branches of government. Because the GOP's power was at low ebb, they found that their ideas and issues were not being covered; thus Twitter became an alternate venue to disseminate their message (Ammah-Tagoe, 2009). In addition, strategic use of Twitter can increase the amount of press coverage that a politician gets. Journalists often follow the politicians they cover, so tweets that include newsworthy information can lead to a story in traditional media outlets (Donia, 2010).

Tweeting can serve to mobilize action. Many political tweets include requests for followers to take some action, such as contributing to a campaign or signing a petition. A leader's tweet followers are an ideal group to contact to take part in such action because they may be more likely to be motivated to do what they are asked than the average person. The very act of choosing to be a follower suggests a significant interest and commitment to that leader.

The rise of the Tea Party is one case study of how Twitter can be used to mobilize political activists. Members of the Tea Party (whose main cause is to reduce federal spending) are part of a movement that has little centralized authority and is spread across the country. Yet without the organizational structure and resources of a major political party, they have staged numerous large protests and elected candidates to office. Sarno (2009) found that Tea Party members' use of Twitter was instrumental in their ability to share ideas on how to build up the movement and attract people to their protests:

> Much of the sharing is now facilitated by the fast-growing messaging site Twit-ter, where today the keyword "teaparty" was one of the most frequently used terms. Users sent out a flurry of updates about attendance, links to photos on Flickr and Photobucket, and videos on YouTube and other sites.

Mobilizing activists to sign petitions is regularly done on Twitter. Act.ly is one such site that has found success among progressives who want to sway political leaders. After creating a petition on act.ly and tweeting it, anyone who receives the petition can "sign" it by retweeting. The petition tweets are then sent via Twitter to the political leaders being targeted. Leaders can respond to the petitions if they choose. Speed and the ability to reach out to many people are two great advantages of using Twitter for political petitions (further, it is free). "You can go from outrage to petition idea to people signing in about 2 minutes," according to Gilliam (2009), the site's creator. "There is huge potential to tweet change." One environmental interest group used the Twitter petition concept to pressure Massachusetts Senator Scott Brown to vote its way on pending energy legislation (Havey, 2010).

Speed of idea dissemination is why many politicians use Twitter. When the then House Speaker Nancy Pelosi wanted to call back Congress early from a recess to vote on Medicaid and education funding, she broke the news on Twitter. In the modern 24-hour news cycle, there is no faster way to transmit information. According to journalist Michael O'Brien (2010),

> Her office said they opted to use Twitter to break the news, instead of a conventional press release, because of the intense interest in the vote. "We wanted to get the word out quickly on the decision that the House will be voting to keep teachers on the job. The Senate cloture vote was a major topic that was being followed closely on Twitter, the blogs, online news site, newspapers, TV, and wires," said Nadeam Elshami, a spokesman for the speaker. "So that is why we used Twitter, and we e-mailed the news release within minutes."

Twitter is used differently by the major political parties. Republicans took an early lead over Democrats in terms of joining Twitter, tweeting frequently, and attracting followers (Ammah-Tagoe, 2009; Buley, 2010). In Congress, for example, the list of members who send the most tweets per day includes few Democrats. The Democrats also lag behind Republicans when it comes to the number of followers and amount of influence. Republicans hold 70 of the 100 most influential congressional Twitter accounts (Jerome, 2010). However, the Democrats are beginning to use Twitter more. In fall of 2009, fewer than 60 Democratic members used Twitter; but 156 used it as of the summer of 2011. In comparison, 229 Republican members tweet.

Those people who consider themselves politically conservative have "taken" to Twitter more quickly than those who call themselves liberal or progressive. One way to measure ideologically based tweeting is to look at the use of hashtags that are popular with liberals and conservatives. Liberals often use the hashtag #p2, which stands for "Progressive 2.0." In contrast, conservatives use the hashtag #tcot, which means "Top Conservatives on Twitter." Hashtags are politically important because all tweets that include a certain hashtag appear together on Twitter's site; for example, tweets using the #tcot hashtag are grouped with each other on Twitter's site. In this case, conservatives from across the country can see what other conservatives are saying, continue the conversation by replying to a tweet, or disseminate a particularly interesting tweet to others by retweeting. The following example is from Minnesota Congresswoman Michele Bachmann. It shows how the #tcot hashtag appears in a tweet:

• MicheleBachmann: Time to get spending under control because doubling taxes shouldn't even be an option: http://tiny.cc/toh0j #tcot

While the #tcot hashtag has been used more than the hashtag #p2, there are several liberal websites, such as TweetProgress, that are trying to change that situation (Fabian, 2009). TweetProgress provides a directory of progressives on Twitter and encourages others to join and use the #p2 hashtag. Tracy Viselli, who is a co-founder of TweetProgress and the #p2 hashtag, said there are ideological differences in how Twitter is used. "I think we've always seen ourselves as different from conservatives on Twitter," Viselli said. "Tweet-Progress is not built around there being an elite like #tcot is. We want everyone to join the progressive fold and help us get our message across" (quoted in Fabian, 2009). A conservative version of TweetProgress' website is TCOT Report. While both websites encourage the use of their respective hashtags (also they provide a live, streaming feed of all tweets that include their tag), differences exist in how the websites are designed. The TCOT Report features more than tweets. For example, the website takes a holistic approach to its ideological cause by including links to news stories, conservative blogs, and conservative think-tanks. It invites conservative users of the site to contribute news stories as citizen journalists.

   The use of Twitter by politicians, government agencies, and political activists is quite varied in terms of types of tweets and reasons for tweeting. But why do people follow such tweets? How much influence do those tweets have on followers? These intriguing questions have not yet been widely researched.

INTERNATIONAL POLITICS USE TWITTER

While the United States has the most Twitter users, other countries are increasingly using the microblog. Three of the six cities with the most Twitter users are outside the United States: London, England; São Paulo, Brazil; and Toronto, Canada (Sysomos, 2010c). Hundreds of politicians tweet in Germany and Japan, as do cabinet members in Chile. Venezuela's president,

Hugo Chavez, has more than 700,000 followers. Political leaders abroad use Twitter for many of the same reasons U.S. politicians do. A content analysis by Golbeck et al. (2010) found that tweets from the British parliament were nearly identical to U.S. congressional tweets in terms of using tweets more to transmit policy positions than to interact with constituents. In Chile, opposition leaders use Twitter to get their message out because they have trouble getting news media coverage. In a similar illustration, the GOP used Twitter in 2009 and 2010, when they were in the minority in the House and Senate (The Economist, 2010). Like many American political leaders, Russian President Dmitri Medvedev sometimes uses his tweets to show a personal side. When Medvedev visited Obama at the White House in June 2010, he tweeted his followers a link to a photo of the view from his hotel window (Shear, 2010).

Twitter use during political uprisings in Egypt, Iran, and Moldova provide three case studies of how the microblog can inform and mobilize activists. Moldova is an Eastern European country that was once part of the Soviet Union. Twitter enabled organizers to turn out more than 10,000 people to protest alleged voter fraud by the ruling Communist Party during the country's April 2009 parliamentary elections. Protesters used the hashtag #pman to disseminate information with each other. They also used the tag to communicate their cause to mass media and anyone around the world who was sympathetic to their situation (Berry, 2009). The hashtag stands for Piata Marii Adunari Nationale, the public square in the country's capital city where the protests took place. The protest also shows the unintended consequences of Twitter's ability to mobilize thousands to take action. While the organizers wanted a peaceful gathering, the crowd quickly became too large to control, and government buildings were ransacked and burned.

Just two months after Moldova's unrest, there was another example of the use of this media. In this case, supporters of Iranian-opposition candidate Mir-Hossein Mousavi became concerned that there had been vote-rigging by the government during the presidential election. Iranians and others used the hashtag #iranelection as a place to discuss election fraud, the protests that ensued, and the government's crackdown on the protesters. Twitter was considered so useful to the opposition movement that the U.S. State Department asked the company to delay some of its scheduled maintenance. The maintenance would have made tweeting in Iran more difficult (Morozov, 2009). Another hashtag that was widely used was #neda, which referred to Neda Agha-Soltan, whose death during the protests was broadcast around the globe. In addition, Twitter was used to spur more media coverage of Iranian voting irregularities and the government's rough treatment of protesters. Those who wanted more coverage by networks such as Cable News Network

(CNN) vented their criticism with tweets that included the hashtag #cnnfail. Shortly afterward, CNN's Iranian coverage increased significantly, though it is unclear whether the critical tweets were the reason (Taylor, 2009). In Egypt in 2011, the protesters who forced President Hosni Mubarak to step down also were aided by the mobilizing power of Twitter and other social networks. The hashtags used included #Jan25 (derived from the first day of the protests) and #Egypt (Banks, 2011).

While Twitter was useful to protesters in Egypt, Iran, and Moldova, it is important to note that the microblog is not the most strategic medium for some kinds of political activity. For example, because anyone can see hashtags, the tags are thus inappropriate for transmitting protest tactics that government authorities would want to know about. What Twitter is quite good for, according to *Time's* technology journalist Lev Grossman (2009), is spreading ideas quickly and in a way that is difficult to suppress:

> Twitter didn't start the protests in Iran, nor did it make them possible. But there's no question that it has emboldened the protesters, reinforced their conviction that they are not alone and engaged populations outside Iran in an emotional, immediate way that was never possible before. . . . Totalitarian governments rule by brute force, and because they control the consensus worldview of those they rule. Tyranny, in other words, is a monologue. But as long as Twitter is up and running, there's no such thing.

BUSINESSES USE TWITTER

There are some similarities in how companies and political leaders tweet. But many small and big businesses have found success by using Twitter in ways that go beyond how most politicians use it. Political tweets tend to be used as one-way transmissions of leaders' personal and political views. Businesses, however, are embracing the two-way communication opportunities of the microblog. They are finding that their efforts are benefiting them in ways that they had not anticipated. One type of two-way interaction is soliciting customers' opinions. Pepsi, for instance, asks its followers to give their advice on the company's existing beverage products, as well as on new product launches. Tweeted responses are used by Pepsi to make improvements. According to the company's director of global social media, Bonin Bough, "Twitter is the only medium where we can have a two-way continuous dialog about the brand" (quoted in Milstein, 2010a). In a sense, Twitter acts for Pepsi as a free focus group, with participants who are easy to find and eager to offer detailed opinions. Pepsi is so committed to Twitter, that employees are asked to create and use a personal account so that they can learn about the microblog and discover other ways it can be used to help the company.

Answering customer service tweets is another form of interaction at firms such as Pepsi, Dell, and JetBlue airlines. Dell, a computer company, has more than 100 Twitter accounts devoted to answering questions and solving problems that consumers have. Dell has found that quick and helpful responses on Twitter contribute to a loyal customer base. But originally, the company thought of Twitter as merely a one-way communication tool to talk about products and offer discounts. Dell soon realized that customers expected more. Customers wanted to contribute their ideas about how the company could better serve them (Milstein, 2010b).

Large companies are not the only firms taking advantage of the interaction capabilities of Twitter. Small businesses use the microblog to improve and grow by engaging their followers (Comm, 2010). Some restaurants, for example, ask their followers for advice concerning what should be on the menu (First, 2009). Twitter is a natural fit for small businesses. Such companies are accustomed to finding most of their customers through word-of-mouth communication, and Twitter is an electronic form of word of mouth (Jansen, Zhang, Sobel, and Chowdury, 2009; Miller, 2009).

In addition to using Twitter for two-way contact with customers, small and big businesses also use tweets for one-way communication, such as transmitting updates about products and services, and offering coupons. Dell, which often tweets deals that are exclusive to their followers, credits the microblog with generating $3 million in revenue (Milstein, 2010b). Most businesses use Twitter for marketing because it is free, easier to set up than a website, and tweets spread the word about the brand from anywhere. Businesses (like politicians) have found that sharing personal insights in their tweets is more productive than using a hard-sell approach. Donna Bordeaux, whose South Carolina certified public accountancy firm makes regular use of Twitter, said:

> Our Tweets are a combination of business and personal comments. If you always post about business, you seem like you are always wearing the "selling" hat. Twitter and other forms of social media are really for awareness-building rather than direct sales. To be authentic, you really have to show all facets of yourself. (quoted in Pinkston, 2009)

One reason why businesses of all sizes have made the effort to use Twitter for one-way and two-way communication is because so many customers and potential customers use the microblog to guide their purchasing decisions.

Almost 70 percent of daily Twitter users follow at least one brand (Stewart and Rohrs, 2010). Another reason businesses reach out to their followers is that research shows that Twitter users represent a unique and commercially useful demographic. Using surveys and focus groups, researchers Stewart and Rohrs found that "the individuals who do use Twitter are the most influential online consumers that exist—a key audience for most modern marketers" (p. 14). Twitter users are especially influential because they are eager to share their opinions in other forums, both online and offline. More than 70 percent of daily Twitter users regularly publish in blogs, and 61 percent comment on news websites. As a result, say Stewart and Rohrs, "the collaboration and sharing that happens on Twitter affects all other areas of the Internet, providing fodder for blog posts, product reviews, and living room conversations alike" (p. 14).

Research to date has examined the followers of business tweets more than the followers of political tweets. As a result, it is unclear how similar the two groups are, in terms of using the microblog for two-way communication and expecting the ones they follow to do the same. It also would be helpful to know if the followers of political tweets are as influential at spreading the word about politicians and policies as business tweet followers are about "talking up" a brand.

TWITTER WITHIN THE LARGER CONTEXT OF SOCIAL MEDIA, BLOGS, AND POLITICS

Twitter is part of the large phenomenon that is considered social media. Such media include websites such as Facebook, MySpace, and YouTube. Political leaders employ various types of social media to campaign and govern. For example, the White House uses YouTube to interact with people during major events. Obama used YouTube to answer people's policy questions after the 2010 State of the Union address, and his press secretary took YouTube questions after the president's Oval Office address regarding the BP oil spill (Ehrlich, 2010). Other political leaders use their Facebook pages to let their constituents know how they voted on legislation and to explain the reasons why they voted "yes" or "no" (Silverman, 2010). While there is a long history of politicians using mailings to serve the same function, sites such as Facebook allow leaders to communicate instantly and in a way that seems more intimate and responsive. For campaigning purposes, candidates can create their own channel on YouTube, complete with videos of speeches and ads, and thumbnails of the videos to help viewers navigate the site. Campaigns also can track how many times the videos are being watched (Van Grove, 2010).

Campaigns often make use of the social nature of social media. Those politicians who are successful are able to communicate and influence an audience that is far larger than the audience that could have been reached through traditional media (such as a television ad or an op-ed column in a newspaper). According to online consulting strategist Julielyn Gibbons, one effective social media strategy is for a politician to simply ask his or her supporters to help spread the word:

> Some of the tactics that we used included asking supporters to change their Facebook profile picture and Twitter avatar to the campaign logo days before the election, posting and sharing campaign ads and messages on YouTube, encouraging supporters to share on their Facebook walls, [and] creating and spreading a hashtag when folks tweeted about the campaign. (quoted in Silverman, 2010)

Having people share information and opinions online with friends, or even strangers, in the manner described by Gibbons is electronic word-of-mouth communication. This tactic can be highly influential (Steffes and Burgee, 2009). Success also can be achieved by having messages on one social media platform connect to the other platforms that the leader is using. So campaign tweets can link to, say, the candidate's YouTube channel or Facebook page, and their Facebook page can include links to the candidate's Twitter account and YouTube channel (Silverman, 2010).

Political leaders now consider social media vital to many aspects of the job. Leaders use social media to appear transparent to their constituents by explaining votes and answering questions. Campaigns use social media to influence their supporters into providing free advertising. While it might seem strange that leaders have taken so quickly to social media sites (given that most of these sites have existed for only a handful of years), the reason is simple: The websites' popularity is too big to ignore. As an illustration of this fact, Facebook (which started in 2004) has 600 million members worldwide. Videos on YouTube (which began in 2005) are viewed 2 billion times a day (Carlson, 2011; Ostrow, 2010b; Weeks, 2010). Further, the popularity of social media continues to grow. The average social media user spent almost 70 percent more time on such sites in 2010 than in 2009 (Nielsen Wire, 2010).

Political blogs also have benefited from significant growth and increased political influence. Blogs have had to evolve during the last five years as a result of the rise of social media. There are 133 million blogs, the most popular being *The Huffington Post* (Catone, 2010). Political blogs usually include a combination of personal commentary, original reporting, and multiple links to traditional news media sites. Blogs on the political left, such as *The Huffington Post,* and on the right, such as *RedState*, increasingly affect the national agenda on a wide range of political issues. Because social media sites often are designed to encourage brief comments, blogs are focused more than ever on providing an in-depth discussion on issues. According to the Pew Research Center (2010), each type of media has distinct advantages. Their studies showed that Twitter is best at delivering breaking news and information, while blogs are proficient at sparking sometimes-heated debate. The visual nature of YouTube allows it to transcend language barriers and enjoy a universal appeal. These findings suggest that political leaders would do well to learn the unique strengths of each type of media and then find ways to capitalize on these strengths.

Gender plays a role in how social media is used. Women use social media more than men. This situation is true not just in the United States, but also worldwide; and the gender gap for most social media is increasing. The gender gap of Twitter use is less pronounced (Abraham, Morn, and Vollman, 2010). Facebook and photo-sharing sites such as Flickr are especially valued by women. Almost 40 percent of young women say that they consider themselves Facebook addicts, and almost 60 percent of young women say that they spend more time interacting with people online than in person (Parr, 2010b).

As social media continues to grow in size and influence, many people wonder what effect it will have on society and democracy. While some research suggests that a society's reliance on social media can positively influence civic engagement (Johnson, Zhang, Bichard, and Seltzer, 2010; Zhang, Johnson, Seltzer, and Bichard, 2010), several negative effects are also apparent. One fear is that social network users will continue spending more time interacting remotely with people rather than face-to-face, a trend that could inhibit users' "in person" social skills. Negativity is also prominent on such platforms. People seem more willing to express negative views (or even attack others) because of their increased sense of anonymity (Chambers and Bichard, in press; Papacharissi, 2004) Another concern is that social networking sites and blogs encourage users to isolate themselves politically. Thus they are rarely exposed to views that challenge their own (Anderson and Rainie, 2010; Johnson, Bichard, and Zhang, 2009). Whether concerns about political isolation applies to Twitter use is something that needs to be studied.

THE IMPACT OF TWITTER: RESEARCH RESULTS

Now that billions of tweets are being sent by more than 100 million people worldwide, some researchers and companies are devoted to measuring the ways in which Twitter use influences politics and other facets of society. One of the most difficult aspects of this research work is determining what constitutes "influence" on Twitter. There are many possible definitions of the concept of influence. In terms of politics, for example, one measure of influence is to simply count the number of followers that leaders have and then conclude that those politicians with the most followers have the most influence. By that measure, Obama's 7 million followers make him the most influential leader. However, this measure ignores many important features of Twitter that, if used effectively, can increase a leader's influence. Features such as retweeting, replying, and linking to URLs are especially useful to examine. For example, a leader with 10,000 followers may be able to spread his or her ideas further than a leader with 20,000 followers, depending on how actively the two leaders' messages are retweeted by followers. In addition, leaders who often reply to followers' tweeted questions and comments can create an appreciative and loyal group of followers who may be more willing to fulfill leaders' requests for action. One of those actions is clicking links; these links direct followers to websites that a leader deems politically useful. Such links often are embedded in a leader's tweets.

Because of the different ways in which influence can be measured, some social media analytics companies (such as Sysomos, Twitalyzer, and Klout) have examined the concept of influence by using a variety of definitions. For instance, Sysomos (2010a) looked at the Twitter influence of political leaders such as Obama, celebrities such as Britney Spears, and news organizations such as *The New York Times*. Sysomos found that a follower count is not as meaningful a measure of influence as one would think. Sysomos's calculation of influence, which is called an *authority ranking*, was based on several factors, including these characteristics: number of followers, frequency of updates, and retweets. By this measure by Sysomos, Obama has less influence than *The New York Times,* even though the news organization has far fewer followers than the president. In another example, in measuring the amount of replying that leaders do to followers' tweets, Twitalyzer found that many politicians, including senators McCain and McCaskill, took more time to address questions and comments than Obama (Grindley, 2009). Klout has still other ways to measure the impact of leaders on the microblog. One of Klout's calculations of influence is called *true reach*, a measure that reveals how many of a leader's followers are paying attention to the tweets they receive. Another Klout calculation of influence is called a *network influence score*, which takes into account that some followers are more important to a leader than other followers. Some followers are highly influential in terms of who follows them and how engaged they are. A leader whose network of followers is highly influential is likely to find Twitter a more valuable political tool than a leader with followers who have a low network influence score.

Keith Urbahn is chief of staff at the office of former Defense Secretary Donald Rumsfeld. Urbahn is one of the best examples of why follower count does not equal influence. Before the White House had formally announced that U.S. forces had killed terrorist Osama Bin Laden, Urbahn found out about the raid and tweeted the news to his mere 1,016 followers:

- keithurbahn: So I'm told by a reputable person they have killed Osama Bin Laden. Hot damn.

According to an analysis by the firm SocialFlow of more than 14 million tweets posted in the hours prior to the official announcement of the raid, "the rate at which Keith's message spread was staggering" (Lotan and Gaffney, 2011).

Academic research into Twitter's influence confirms many of the findings from the analytics companies, including the idea that follower count is not the most important measure of influence (Huberman, Romero, and Wu, 2009). An analysis of 1.7 billion tweets from 54 million users found that the most-followed people on Twitter were not the most influential in terms of getting retweeted or mentioned in tweets (Cha, Haddadi, Benevenuto, and Gummadi, 2010). On the other hand, those people whose tweets were focused on a single topic were successful at gaining influence. The study's researchers concluded that "the most connected users are not necessarily the most influential when it comes to engaging one's audience in conversations and having one's message spread" (p. 4). These results suggest that political leaders who want to be influential on Twitter should not worry about their follower count. Instead, they should make the effort to tweet about a limited number of topics that are of interest to their followers.

Research into the impact of Twitter also covers the content of the billions of messages found on the microblog. Such research reveals why Twitter is a valuable tool for measuring public opinion. The sentiments expressed in tweets regarding political issues can be as accurate a measure (of public opinion) as is found with traditional telephone surveys. One study analyzed 1 billion tweets from 2008 through 2009 and found that on issues such as consumer confidence and presidential approval, opinions expressed in the tweets matched survey findings on the same topics (O'Connor, Balasubramanyan, Routledge, and Smith, 2010). This result suggests that Twitter users should not be considered an unusual subset of the general population, but rather a group whose opinions are (at least collectively) fairly mainstream and representative.

Business-related research into tweeting patterns also has significance for the study of political tweets. Researchers have found that microblogging often is used as electronic word-of-mouth communication, which is part of the "buzz" (or "viral") marketing that is used extensively in advertising. Of the 150,000 tweets analyzed by Jansen et al. (2009), almost 20 percent talked about a brand, and nearly 20 percent of those did so in a way that expressed an opinion about the brand. Most mentions were positive, but one-third of the mentions were negative. The authors conclude that "the microblogging medium is a viable area for organizations for viral marketing campaigns, customer relationship management, and to influence their eWOM branding efforts" (p. 2184). It is crucial to realize that Twitter is a form of word-of-mouth communication (called WOM or eWOM), because there is an extensive body of research that shows how word-of-mouth communication is highly persuasive, even more so than TV advertising. People often make decisions on what to think, what to buy, or what actions to take based on WOM or eWOM from friends, family, or even complete strangers (Katz and Lazarsfeld, 1955; Schindler and Bickart, 2005; Steffes and Burgee, 2009). Because Twitter is used for WOM purposes, companies or political leaders can harness that persuasive power to affect decision making in terms of buying products or voting for candidates.

Other textual analyses of tweets show how Twitter can be used to measure the mood of the country on any given day and in various regions. An analysis of more than 300 million tweets from 2006 to 2009 found that people tend to be happier in the early morning, the late evening, and on the weekends. In addition, West Coast residents display more happiness than those on the East Coast (Mislove, Lehmann, Ahn, Onnela, and Rosenquist, 2010).

In addition to tweeting reflecting users' moods, it also can affect how users feel. Preliminary research suggests that Twitter use elevates levels of oxytocin, a hormone that stimulates empathy and trust, while decreasing anxiety. Magnetic Resonance Imaging (MRI) scans and an examination of blood samples taken before and during tweeting showed that users experience a pleasurable emotional state that is similar to the feeling one gets during face-to-face contact with friends (Penenberg, 2010). Such a finding helps explain why microblogging has become so popular, so quickly. Users spend time on Twitter not only because it helps them accomplish tasks related to business or politics, but because it feels good. It is also interesting that the absence of physical contact does not interfere with a user's feeling connected on an emotional level to other users. Because users are in a positive emotional condition, the tweets that they receive may influence their behavior or thoughts more easily in various aspects of their lives, including politics.

WHAT THIS BOOK WILL SHOW ABOUT POLITICAL TWITTER USE

While much is known about the uses and users of Twitter, there are many questions that still need to be answered, especially in the areas of how the microblog is used in politics and how it affects the relationship between leaders and the public. The research questions of this book are discussed in detail in later chapters. These topics concern the act of following political leaders and the followers, and the influence and content of tweets.

WHO FOLLOWS POLITICAL LEADERS ON TWITTER—AND WHY?

Research shows that followers who use Twitter for general purposes are from an older and more professional demographic than those who use other forms of social media (Global Web Index, 2010). But no studies have examined the demographic makeup of those who follow political leaders on Twitter. This lack of studies is important because certain demographic and psychographic groups, such as those who are highly educated and interested in politics, are potentially more politically influential and valuable to leaders than other groups. Even more fundamental is to discover what types of people and organizations are considered to be political leaders who are worth following. Certain individuals, such as elected public officials, are an obvious choice of who might be worth following. But to what degree do followers choose to follow people who fall outside that narrow definition? Today some of the most politically influential people hold no office. Al Gore (a former U.S. vice president) and Sarah Palin (a former candidate for U.S. vice president) are two good examples. Gore is arguably more powerful today in terms of environmental politics than when he was vice president. As a private citizen, Palin has reached a larger audience and influenced the national agenda more than when she was governor of Alaska.

In addition to finding out who is being followed, it also would be helpful to know what motivates users in choosing which political leaders to follow. Do they follow leaders primarily as a means to receive political information? If so, that would be an information-seeking motive. Or do they follow leaders because they want to interact with leaders or fellow political junkies? If so, that would be a social and self-expressive motive. Further, does a follower's motivation affect how much influence a leader's tweets have?

HOW INFLUENTIAL ARE POLITICAL TWEETS?

Political leaders tweet for many reasons, including going over the heads of the mass media (such as television) to reach the public. By tweeting, they wish to generate media coverage. At other times, these leaders want to mobilize their political "troops" of followers to take action on their behalf. Leaders could suggest to followers a wide variety of actions: take part in a petition or protest, read a recommended blog post or news story, spread the word to others to vote for a candidate, or support legislation. Spreading the word is especially easy on Twitter because of its features such as retweeting, mentioning, hashtags, and website linking. While previous research has found that Twitter users are eager to share opinions (Stewart and Rohrs, 2010) and often do so regarding brands they like or dislike (Jansen et al., 2009), it is not clear whether followers of political tweets are as willing to spreading the word about politicians and policies. Because there is no research on how influential political tweets are on followers, it is impossible to know how often followers take actions that are requested by leaders. In addition, it is not clear how much influence political tweets have on shaping followers' political views. Is that influence greater than more traditional sources of political influence, such as friends, family, and co-workers? It may even be that the influence of political tweets varies depending on a follower's ideology or demographic makeup.

DOES POLITICAL TWITTER USE INCREASE
EXPOSURE TO DIVERSE VIEWS?

The act of following political leaders needs more study. While the average Twitter user follows ten people or fewer (Saleem, 2010), it is not known if followers of political leaders are that selective. Furthermore, no one has discovered what criteria followers use to select political leaders. Followers may seek leaders from a variety of political perspectives, or they may limit themselves to only those leaders whose views reinforce their ideology. The best scenario for a democratic society would be for followers to use Twitter as a tool to expand their understanding of various sides of key political issues. On the other hand, Twitter use that fuels political isolation would suggest that the microblog can be harmful to democracy.

WHAT IS THE CONTENT OF POLITICAL TWEETS?

Past analyses of political tweets have found that leaders mostly do one-way transmitting of policy information and personal musings, and they do not really interact with many followers except in the case of a few leaders (Golbeck et al., 2010; Sternberg, 2009). Businesses, on the other hand, are heavily involved in two-way communication with customers on Twitter (Milstein, 2010a). It would be interesting to discover which type of tweeting is preferred by followers of political leaders. Do political followers feel they are mainly getting one-way communication from leaders? To what degree do followers desire two-way interaction with political leaders on Twitter?

The style of writing found in tweets also needs examination, especially the style of those tweets written during campaigns. The tone of tweets can be formal, personal, or even sarcastic. What is not understood is how followers react to these various styles of writing. Do followers prefer a formal or personal style, or a mixture of the two? Also, what writing styles are used primarily in an election campaign, when leaders most need their followers? How do those styles portray leaders' policies and personality? The influence of leaders is often a function of how engaged they are in terms of retweeting, replying, and mentioning. Thus it is important to find out to what degree leaders' campaign tweets reflect this level of engagement.

THEORETICAL PERSPECTIVES

This book examines the use of political tweets from six theoretical perspectives: uses and gratifications, word-of-mouth communication, selective exposure, framing, innovation characteristics, and the continuity-discontinuity framework.

The theoretical perspective of uses and gratifications is used to uncover which motives drive people to select various types of media (such as television, cell phones, and the Internet). This perspective also shows the degree to which those motives influence how people are affected by media (Kaye and Johnson, 2002; Papacharissi and Rubin, 2000; Ruggiero, 2000). This theory helps reveal which people follow political leaders on Twitter, why they follow. Looking at their motives for following—how do these motives affect how political tweets impact them?

Word-of-mouth communication, which includes recommendations (online, via phone, or in person) from family, acquaintances, and strangers is studied because research shows that such communication can be highly persuasive (Brown and Reingen, 1987; Granovetter, 1973; Steffes and Burgee, 2009).

Because political tweets from leaders and followers are a form of word-of-mouth communication, Twitter's persuasive power can be measured and compared with other, more traditional forms of word of mouth.

Some researchers study selective exposure. They measure the degree to which people use mass media to block out diverse views, a behavior that is harmful for democratic societies (Iyengar and Hahn, 2009; Sunstein, 2001). These researchers examine the political following patterns of Twitter users. The scientists want to discover how much the microblog is expanding or limiting users' exposure to a variety of political perspectives that could make them better citizens.

Framing theory is used to understand the content of political tweets and how such messages portray leaders' policies and personalities. Framing theory examines themes embedded in media content. Themes influence how viewers interpret (and are affected by) that content (Entman, 1993; Parmelee, 2003; Scheufele, 1999).

Researchers try to understand why some innovations become popular while others do not. They have found that successful innovations are compatible with users' needs, have a relative advantage over competitors, are not complex, and are easy to observe and try out (Rogers, 2003, pp. 229–264). While Twitter has enjoyed remarkable popularity so far, it still needs to be determined if the microblog possesses the characteristics of successful innovations. Another way to understand Twitter's significance as an innovation is by using Robertson's (1971) continuity–discontinuity framework. It categorizes innovations on a scale ranging from continuous (meaning innovations that cause only minor behavioral changes) to discontinuous (innovations that spark major shifts in behavior). Exploring Twitter in this framework can show where the microblog fits within the larger context of past innovations (such as personal computers and cable television).

HOW USING MANY METHODS CAN REVEAL TWITTER'S INFLUENCE IN POLITICS

Because there are so many questions that need to be answered regarding political Twitter use, it would be impossible to rely on a single research method. This book's research uses four methods: surveys, in-depth interviews, content analysis, and frame analysis. These methods are used in a way that allows each method to answer certain research questions. The techniques also elaborate on the findings from the other methods. Take, for example, the survey method. There are advantages to conducting surveys of people who follow political leaders on Twitter. Such surveys can find out about who follows political leaders and what motives they have for following. This method benefits from the use of large sample sizes and provides data observation from a variety of respondents. The quantifiable nature of the data obtained allows for statistical inferences. Such inferences offer insightful information regarding the intensity and varied use of Twitter in the political sphere. However, the survey method, like every method, has inherent weaknesses that limit its ability to give full answers. That is because surveys rely on closed-ended questions, which limit the number of possible answers that a respondent can give. While there are many benefits to asking closed-ended questions, survey findings may miss key information. To be sure, in terms of finding out who follows political leaders and why, closed-ended questions can discover what kinds of political leaders participants do follow (and what motivates participants to follow). But the survey's list of possible responses may fail to include many of the kinds of leaders or motivations that a participant finds important. While it is true that surveys usually include an "other" (or "fill-in-the-blank") response that allows participants more leeway in their answers, this option still can miss information. Kaye (2007), who uses surveys to research online political information gathering, encourages the addition of a qualitative approach. Kaye's rationale is because the "fill-in-the-blank procedure does not allow for in-depth discussion, as do interviews, where the researcher can probe for deeper meaning and respondents can further explore their motivations" (p. 143). In-depth interview questions, which are open ended and qualitative, encourage participants to provide as many responses as they need, in their own words. Consider the example of who follows political leaders and why. In-depth interviewers can ask participants to give their personal definition of who (or what) qualifies as a political leader. Participants also can more comprehensively discuss which motives drive them to follow leaders.

In addition to surveys having the restriction of being closed ended, survey questions also are based on predetermined operational definitions of terms. In this book, terms and concepts (such as having a *social motivation* or an *information-seeking motivation* to follow leaders) are defined in ways that are based on past studies. However, such definitions demand, as Pauly (1991) puts it, "consistency of denotation and absence of connotation. The language of everyday life, however, is lushly metaphorical, wildly contradictory, willfully connotative, and cynically strategic. What can researchers hope to know of human communication if their methods ban the play of meanings?" (p. 6). By examining in-depth interview comments (along with the survey findings), this book provides a deeper understanding of how followers define terms such as *social motivations* and *information-seeking motivations*.

Complementing surveys with in-depth interviews can provide added insight regarding how much influence political tweets have on followers.

This method shows whether the leaders they follow help to increase exposure to diverse political views. In-depth interviews can explore the ways in which political tweets influence followers, as well as how followers define the term *political diversity*. But the open-ended nature of the method cannot numerically measure (as surveys can) which influences are the strongest or the amount of diversity that followers strive for on Twitter.

As previously mentioned, this book uses the methods of content analysis and frame analysis. (The term *frame* means dominant themes.) These techniques delve into the content of political tweets and what such messages say about the leaders who sent them. Quantitative content analysis yields data based on predetermined categories and themes from prior research. While these data are valuable, a qualitative frame analysis is the best method to add depth and reveal additional themes that may emerge. By using both techniques, the content can be explored more holistically.

Several research designs were used in this book. Chapters 2, 3, and 4 combine survey and in-depth interview data to examine the motives for following political leaders, the persuasive power of leaders' tweets, and the effects on democracy of following leaders. These chapters use a mixed-methods design known as *sequential explanatory*. This design is sequential because the data were gathered and analyzed in separate phases. It is an explanatory method because the survey came first in the sequence. This strategy allows the in-depth interview findings to explain and elaborate on the survey findings. Chapter 5 does not mix methods; this chapter is a qualitative exploration of the roles that political Twitter use play in users' lives, and how users view Twitter as an innovation. Chapter 6 combines frame analysis and content analysis, while focusing on the framing in tweets. This mixed-methods design, called *concurrent triangulation*, is ideal when two methods are being conducted at the same time to "confirm, cross-validate, or corroborate findings" (Creswell, Plano Clark, Gutmann, and Hanson, 2003, p. 229). To understand more about how the methods complement each other, it is important to discuss next how the data were gathered.

HOW THE SURVEY AND IN-DEPTH INTERVIEW DATA WERE GATHERED

Participants were recruited by asking political leaders to tweet to their followers to take an online survey (this survey was then used for this book). Leaders were contacted via letter, e-mail, tweet, and direct message. A diverse ideological range of leaders was contacted: Democrats, Republicans, conservatives, liberals, moderates, independents, Libertarians, and leaders connected with the Tea Party. Some leaders had more than 1 million followers; other leaders had a few thousand followers. Those leaders who were contacted were monitored on Twitter to see which ones tweeted a link to the online survey. The leaders who tweeted the link included a mix of public officials, organizations that provide political information, and political activists. The leaders' titles are current to when they tweeted the survey. The following list shows the leaders who tweeted the link: Mufi Hannemann, Democrat, mayor of Honolulu, Hawaii; Sam Adams, Democrat, mayor of Portland, Oregon; Michael Patrick Leahy, publisher of the *TCOT Report*, a conservative website, and one of the founders of the #tcot hashtag; TweetCongress, a nonpartisan website that encourages people to interact with members of Congress on Twitter; Justin Sayfie, publisher of *Sayfie Review,* a news website on Florida politics; Ezra Klein, a *Washington Post* blogger; Doug Mataconis, of the Libertarian blog *Below the Beltway*; Christopher Hayes, Washington editor of *The Nation*; John Bambenek, a conservative writer and policy adviser; Larry Sabato, the director of the University of Virginia's Center for Politics; John C. Drew, a political scientist and consultant; Jordan Raynor, president of Direct Media Strategies; Danny Glover, conservative blogger and editor of @tweetwatch; Katie Harbath, digital strategist at the National Republican Senatorial Committee; Nansen Malin, a member of the Washington State Republican Party's executive board and national political director for Smart Girl Politics; eStampede.org, a site that describes itself as a political information network and social media for Republicans; and Billy Hallowell, a journalist and conservative advocate.

Once tweeted, the link to the survey was retweeted multiple times. In addition, the survey link appeared on Democratic and progressive hashtags (such as #dems, #dnc, #p2, and #pfla); Republican and conservative hashtags (such as #gop, #rnc, #tcot, and #teaparty); and other political hashtags (such as #libertarian, #centrist, #2010, #vote2010, and #sayfie). Many of the in-depth interview participants in this study also tweeted the survey link to their followers.

As a result of these recruiting efforts, 436 people completed the survey from August to November, 2010. Past research indicates that it is not uncommon for Internet surveys to obtain lower numbers of participants due to fear of spam or issues of confidentiality (Cook, Heath, and Thompson, 2000; Sills and Song, 2002). The consent statement at the top of the online survey informed participants of their rights, which included the right to stop at any time and the assurance that their answers would be confidential to the extent provided by law. To ensure that people taking the survey met the requirements of this study, participants were notified (in the consent statement) not to take the survey unless they followed at least one political leader on

Twitter and were at least 18 years old. Participants were told that a "political leader" could be a person or a political organization, and that the word *following* meant that they chose to get the leader's Twitter messages sent to them. In addition, one question in the survey had participants give their age and another question asked how many political leaders they followed. These questions were asked so that anyone who answered that they were under 18 or noted that they followed no political leaders could be dropped from the study. Ten participants were dropped as a result, which left 426 completed surveys. To guard against anyone submitting a survey more than once (by accident or on purpose), a "thank you" message appeared after they hit the "submit" button. Further, the computer system (meaning the system that the online survey was on) allowed participants to submit only once on the Internet account to which they were registered.

The survey included 16 questions, which could be answered in total in about ten minutes. The questions dealt primarily with issues that will be discussed in the next three chapters: the uses and gratifications of following political leaders on Twitter; how political tweets act as a form of word-of-mouth communication; and the degree to which political Twitter use promotes selective exposure and selective avoidance. Question items were adapted from past research in order to develop appropriate measures and indices for the constructs under scrutiny. After the survey data were gathered, the results were analyzed using the SPSS computer package (an IBM data software). Of course the participants in the study did not make up a random sample. Thus generalizing the survey's results to the larger population of political Twitter users is more difficult—it is almost impossible to do random sampling on specialized Internet and social network audiences (Ancu and Cozma, 2009; Kaye and Johnson, 2002; Stafford, Stafford, and Schkade, 2004).

Those followers who took part in the survey had the opportunity to be interviewed in-depth. At the end of the online survey, participants were asked to click the e-mail address of one of the authors of this book if they were interested in taking part in an interview. Those who e-mailed received additional information, including consent information. Participants were informed that they could refuse to participate at any time. In addition, as a way of protecting their privacy, participants were asked to choose a pseudonym. They would be identified by this pseudonym during the data analysis stage and in the findings. The participants filled out a brief demographic form.

The 18 in-depth interviews that were completed were enough to reach saturation (a point that occurs when no additional themes can be found). Each phone interview lasted about 30 minutes, though some interviews were done via e-mail if that method was the participant's choice. There were nine main open-ended questions (known as *grand tour questions*) that extensively explored how and why participants use Twitter for political information. Many of the questions focused on the same topics as the survey questions (uses and gratifications, word of mouth, and selective exposure), so the respondents' lengthy answers could add depth to the closed-ended survey findings. Follow-up questions (called *probes*) were asked when it was necessary for participants to clarify or expand on some of their answers (McCracken, 1988). The interview data included the transcribed audiotapes of the phone interviews and printouts from the e-mail interviews. These data were then analyzed qualitatively to find common themes. The data were examined using a grounded theory and constant comparative approach (Glaser and Strauss, 1967). In this technique, a list of common themes emerged through an initial coding process in which information from the transcripts and e-mails was organized into categories. Both of the authors of this book engaged in this process separately, and then we reviewed each other's themes to find commonalities. The University of North Florida's Institutional Review Board approved the protocol for the survey and the in-depth interviews. None of the participants received compensation.

HOW THE CONTENT ANALYSIS AND FRAME ANALYSIS DATA WERE GATHERED

For the content analysis and frame analysis, all tweets were collected from candidates in 12 competitive 2010 races from October 1 to November 2. The races included those for the U.S. Senate in Alaska, California, Connecticut, Florida, Kentucky, Missouri, Nevada, and Pennsylvania; and for governor in California, Florida, Ohio, and South Carolina. These races were selected because they were competitive, but also because these in these races the candidates represented a variety in terms of ideology, gender, and age. The candidates also showed a variety of "political insider versus political outsider" standings. Content analysis of the tweets by SPSS software reviewed the types of appeals that were being used, how candidates used tweets to portray their issues and personalities, and how those appeals and portrayals connected to dominant themes (called *frames*). The tone of the tweets' content was also evaluated, as was the level of interactivity featured. The frame analysis uncovered which major themes candidates used in their tweets. A qualitative analysis of the tweets' keywords, phrases, sources of information, and moral evaluations (Entman, 1993, p. 52) allowed the themes to emerge from the data.

OVERVIEW OF THE NEXT CHAPTERS

Chapter 2 investigates why people use Twitter for political information. This chapter has a "uses and gratifications" perspective. It employs surveys and in-depth interviews to show what motives people have for following political leaders' tweets. The chapter will discuss whether social or information-seeking motivations are greatest among followers, and how other factors (such as an interest in politics and trust in government) influence motivations and Twitter use.

Chapter 3 looks at the impact of political tweets when used as word-of-mouth communication. This chapter uses surveys and in-depth interviews of followers to reveal to what degree they take actions that are requested in political leaders' tweets. The chapter examines how influential political tweets are at shaping the political views of followers.

Chapter 4 takes on the selective exposure debate. This controversy suggests that people seeking political information sometimes engage in ideological selectivity. Do they avoid sources that provide a counterpoint to their political views? Surveys and in-depth interviews are examined to show how and why followers of political tweets use Twitter to broaden or narrow their exposure to political views that differ from their opinions.

Chapter 5 delves into the interviews to find out how Twitter has changed the followers' lives politically. The chapter explores the roles and value of political Twitter use. It shows how the microblog can be viewed as an innovation.

Chapter 6 uses a content analysis and frame analysis of tweets from the 2010 campaign to understand how candidates frame their issues and their personalities on Twitter.

Chapter 7 summarizes Chapters 1 to 6 and discusses the implications of all the findings.

Chapter 2

Why People Use Twitter for Politics

The Uses and Gratifications of Following Political Leaders' Tweets

What motivates people to follow political leaders on Twitter? What do those motives say about the influence that Twitter has on the political process? Research is lacking in these areas, but the answers are fundamental to understanding how Twitter impacts the relationship between political leaders and the public. People's main motivation may be informational. If so, this reason would suggest that followers use leaders' tweets primarily as a news source to keep up-to-date on key issues and candidates. Such a finding would reinforce comments by one Twitter executive who said that tweets are news and that Twitter should not be considered a social network (Perez, 2010). However, if social or expressive motives are what drive people to follow political leaders, Twitter should be seen in a different light.

Social or self-expression motives suggests that followers are not merely one-way receivers of information but rather that they are engaged in two-way communication (which includes sharing political tweets with their followers and replying to leaders they follow). Self-expression motives, in particular, imply a need to communicate personal opinions and critique. Another possibility is that followers have a guidance motive, meaning that they depend on tweets from political leaders to guide their decisions on how to vote and what position to take on an issue. Such a finding would show Twitter to be even more influential than political leaders have hoped it could be. The opposite might be true if followers primarily have an entertainment motive, which would suggest that followers often use political tweets for fun and do not take them seriously.

Equally fundamental for a study on political leaders' tweets is to discover how followers define what constitutes a political leader. While the most obvious (and narrow) definition is that a political leader is an elected public official, it may be that people choose to follow all sorts of individuals and groups. Revealing the types of individuals and groups that most followers consider political leaders can show where political power really resides among Twitter's more than 100 million users. In addition, it is important to know what types of people follow political leaders in terms of demographic factors (such as age and gender); and psychological factors (such as ideology, interest in politics, and trust in government). It may be that some demographic factors determine the motives followers have, or perhaps shape the definition of who is a political leader, all of which might also affect the influence of political tweets.

What is the best way to find out people's motives for following political leaders? It would also be good to know the degree to which demographic and psychological factors trigger followers' motives and patterns of use. One method is to examine the act of political following through the lens of the "uses and gratifications" theory. The benefit of this theory is that it reveals why people use various types of media and it shows how they use the media.

USES AND GRATIFICATIONS

The uses and gratifications framework is considered ideal for studies that examine new technology, including the Internet and social networks (Ancu and Cozma, 2009; Kaye and Johnson, 2002, 2006; Papacharissi and Rubin, 2000; Ruggiero, 2000; Park, Kee, and Valenzuela, 2009). Uses and gratifications research assumes people are active users of media, and clearly Twitter is made for active use. Unlike other mediums, such as television, where viewers are generally passive receivers of information, Twitter users can be actively engaged in the information they receive by replying to it, tweeting about it, or retweeting it. Uses and gratifications theory is based on the idea that media use is goal-oriented. In terms of political Twitter use, it is logical to assume that people have a goal in mind when they make the effort to seek out and follow political leaders' tweets. Crucially, the theory assumes that people have motivations to use media, and that those motives can influence people's media use patterns as well as the effects of that use. So, for example, Twitter users who have a social motive to follow political leaders on Twitter might use the microblog differently and be influenced by the tweets differently than those users who have informational or entertainment motives.

It also is important to note that motives are not necessarily the first step in the process. In some cases, social, psychological, and demographic factors can determine what motives people have, which, in turn, affects what media people use (Parmelee and Perkins, 2012). In other cases, social, psychological, and demographic factors can directly influence media use and media effects, independent of motivation (Haridakis and Rubin, 2003). To better understand the power that motives and factors have on media use and media effects, it is useful to review what other studies have found in these areas.

THE MOTIVES PEOPLE HAVE FOR USING MEDIA

There are a handful of motives that people usually have in their use of media for finding out political information or other types of information. Such studies (Ancu and Cozma, 2009; Johnson, Kaye, Bichard, and Wong, 2008; Kaye, 2005, 2007; Kaye and Johnson, 2002, 2004, 2006; Ko, Cho, and Roberts, 2005; Papacharissi, 2002; Papacharissi and Rubin, 2000) have indicated several key motivations. These motivations are listed here in alphabetical order:

- Convenience: People want to obtain information from media that are easy to access.
- Entertainment: The information obtained is meant to be used for amusement and relaxation.
- Self-expression: This motivation concerns a person's engagement and the expression of personal opinions (such as communicating support or criticism).
- Guidance: In this case, the person gathers information in order to help guide a decision, such as what product to buy or which candidate to support.
- Information seeking: In this case, people gather information intended to keep them generally knowledgeable and up-to-date on various issues.
- Social utility: People want the information that they obtain to assist them in their social interactions, such as when they have discussions with friends or acquaintances.

In addition, people have different motives for using different types of media. In terms of seeking political information, people go to some types of media primarily to satisfy information-seeking needs and to other venues to satisfy social-utility needs. Users of chat rooms, electronic bulletin boards, and social networking sites tend to have social motivations. In comparison, users of blogs and the Internet tend to have more information-seeking motivations (Ancu and Cozma, 2009; Kaye and Johnson, 2006).

No previous study has investigated which motives drive people to follow political leaders on Twitter. Interestingly, past research into the uses and gratifications of using blogs and social networking sites provides conflicting suggestions as to what the motives for Twitter use might be. On the one hand, Twitter shares many of the features of social networking sites such as Facebook and MySpace in terms of interactivity and the social nature of the experience. Studies have consistently shown that social networking sites in the United States and other countries are used primarily with a social motive in mind, whether the users are college students (Balaban and Baltaretu, 2010; Bumgarner, 2007; Park, Kee, and Valenzuela, 2009; Raacke and Bonds-Raacke, 2008) or the general population (Ancu and Cozma, 2009). Studies also suggest reliance on social media leads to more socially related outcomes, such as increased civic engagement (Johnson, Zhang, Bichard, and Seltzer, 2010; Zhang, Johnson, Seltzer, and Bichard, 2010).

If Twitter is another form of social networking, then followers of political leaders probably have a social motive to do so, because that is the main motive for visiting candidate profiles on MySpace (Ancu and Cozma, 2009; Postelnicu and Cozma, 2008). On the other hand, Twitter is a microblog, which suggests that blogs are a closer cousin to Twitter than social networking sites. Blogs are used mainly from an information-seeking motive (Kaye, 2005; Kaye and Johnson, 2006), so people also may follow political leaders on Twitter with that motive. A third possibility is that Twitter use is more closely related to talking or texting on a cell phone. If this situation is true, then the interpersonal communication motives that drive talking and texting on cell phones (Auter, 2007; Jin and Park, 2010) likely account for Twitter use.

Three recent articles on the uses and gratifications of general Twitter use yielded three different results. One study found that Twitter users primarily have "a need for an informal sense of camaraderie, called connection, with other users" (Chen, 2011, p. 755). A separate study, however, found that the need to connect with others was not a key motive for continuing to use Twitter (Liu, Cheung and Lee, 2010). Finally, other researchers found that entertainment is a key motive for using Twitter (Coursaris, Yun, and Sung, 2010). It could also be that the prime motive for following political leaders on Twitter is one that is unique and has yet to be studied.

HOW TO FIND PEOPLE'S MOTIVES FOR POLITICAL TWITTER USE

The search for a complete list of user motivations for media use has relied mostly on quantitative methods, such as surveys. There are many good reasons why uses and gratifications studies frequently use surveys. Surveys can gather hundreds, even thousands, of people's responses to questions about their motives to, say, use the Internet for political information. If those people are part of a randomly generated sample, the findings can be generalized to the millions of people who use the Internet for political information. Even when the sample is not randomly selected, surveys have still provided much insight into people's motives for using the Internet, blogs, and social networking sites for political information (Ancu and Cozma, 2009; Johnson, Kaye, Bichard, and Wong, 2008; Kaye, 2005; Kaye and Johnson, 2002).

Another advantage of using surveys comes from the nature of how survey questions are asked. With a survey, each motive that is being sought by the researcher can be given a preset definition, or operationalization, that is often borrowed by the researcher from previous studies. Using definitions from past research allows for a more direct comparison of results from study to study. While there are no previous surveys on the motives for following political leaders on Twitter, plenty of surveys have been done on the motives for gathering political information from at least somewhat similar media. For example, the social-utility motivation has been defined using statements such as "to give me something to talk about with others" and "to use as ammunition in arguments with others" in a study of why people use chat rooms and instant messaging for political information (Kaye and Johnson, 2004, p. 210).

One study on why people use the Web for politics used the statement "to keep up with main issues of the day" to define information-seeking. That study used the phrase "to help me decide how to vote" to operationalize guidance (Kaye and Johnson, 2002, p. 61). The motivation of self-expression (although measured with respect to personal home pages) included items such as "to tell others a little bit about myself" (Papacharissi, 2002, p. 357). Kaye (2005) measured self-expression on blogs with statements such as "to make my opinions known" (p. 85).

Finally, entertainment and convenience motives include definitions such as "it is entertaining" and "it is cheaper," respectively, in research into why people use the Internet generally (Papacharissi and Rubin, 2000, p. 186). Participants in these surveys were then asked to what extent they agreed with the statements. Their choices were limited to five possible responses, ranging from "strongly agree" to "strongly disagree." Using such closed-ended questions enables researchers to precisely measure what participants consider motives in terms of the most important and least important.

Of course surveys have certain built-in limitations. As such, researchers must use other methods to obtain a comprehensive understanding of the topic under study. For example, while there are many benefits to asking closed-ended survey questions, the number of possible responses from participants is limited. As a result, the findings may miss key information. In terms of studying Twitter, closed-ended questions can ask what motivates participants to follow political tweets. But the list of statements (such as "to use as ammunition in arguments with others" or "to help me decide how to vote") may fail to include the motivations participants find important. While surveys usually include an "other" or "fill-in-the-blank" response that allows participants more latitude in their answers, this option still can miss information. Kaye (2007) argues that in-depth interview questions are better than fill-in-the-blank survey questions at exploring the many possible motivations that may exist (p. 143).

In-depth interview questions are open-ended and qualitative, thus encouraging participants to provide, in their own words, as much of a response as they need. In addition, the open-ended nature of in-depth interviews includes the ability to ask one or several follow-up questions (called *probes*), so that participants can expand on any initial answers that need to be clarified. As a result, Ruggiero (2000) argues that "communication researchers should be encouraged to employ uses and gratifications more frequently in conjunction with qualitative methodologies" (p. 26). Researchers who have done so have found qualitative methods (such as in-depth interviews and focus groups) to be quite insightful, not only as stand-alone methods but also as a way to enhance the meaning of survey results. Schaefer and Avery's (1993) examination of the motivations for watching late-night comedy television used survey questionnaires and focus group interviews to "combine the strength of survey data with the richness of depth interviews" (p. 271).

Qualitative methods also have been used to explore people's motivations for using the Internet and social networking sites. In-depth interviews by Kayahara and Wellman (2007) found that recommendations from friends and family often triggered a person's motives to search for online cultural information. Focus groups by Balaban and Baltaretu (2010) discovered the dominance of social motivations when Romanian students use social networking sites. In terms of the study discussed in this book, allowing in-depth interview participants to talk at length, usually from 30 minutes to an hour, made it possible for us to discover new insights into the motives for using Twitter for political information.

HOW SOCIAL, PSYCHOLOGICAL, AND DEMOGRAPHIC FACTORS INFLUENCE MOTIVES AND MEDIA USE

It is important to identify what motives people have for following political leaders on Twitter. These motives are complex. For example, studies have shown that motives tend not to happen in isolation but rather they are associated with several factors. These factors (which can be social, psychological, and/or demographic) often trigger or inhibit communication motivations, affect media use, and influence the effects of media use. Social factors, such as problems with parents, can trigger entertainment motivations (Leung, 2007). Psychological factors, such as shyness or a fatalistic attitude about one's life, can trigger escape motivations (Finn and Gorr, 1988; Rubin, 1993). Having a fatalistic attitude also can make one less likely to have information-seeking motivations (Haridakis and Rubin, 2003). In addition, psychological factors have been found to shape people's media choices. One study found that the psychological desire to "fit in" caused international students at U.S. universities to watch American television shows rather than use the Internet (Yang, Wu, Zhu, and Southwell, 2004). In terms of influencing the effects of media use, psychological factors can either trigger motivations that lead to certain effects or influence media effects directly. Haridakis and Rubin (2003) found that the psychological factors of feeling control over one's life predicted aggressive attitudes in those who view television violence. Those attitudes often were independent of communication motivations or the viewer's level of exposure to television violence.

In terms of research on how people gather political information, there are a number of demographic and politically based psychological antecedents that predict certain motives for using social networking sites, chat rooms, electronic bulletin boards, blogs, and the Web. These factors also are linked to which types of media people use for political information.

DEMOGRAPHIC FACTORS

Studies on political information gathering show that personal characteristics such as age, gender, education, and income are associated with certain motives (such as information seeking, social utility, entertainment, and guidance) and linked with patterns of political media use. For example, Ancu and Cozma (2009, p. 576) found that the younger people were, the more likely they were to have information-seeking and guidance motives to visit candidate profiles on MySpace. Older people used MySpace more for entertainment. Another study found that being young also predicted using chat rooms for political information seeking and guidance, as well as using bulletin boards and electronic mailing lists for political guidance (Kaye and Johnson, 2004, p. 217). A person's education, however, has less consistent influence on communication motives. While having an advanced education makes one more likely to have information-seeking and guidance motives to use MySpace for politics (Ancu and Cozma, 2009, p. 576), other research indicates that more educated people are less likely to have a guidance motive to engage in general Internet use for political information (Kaye and Johnson, 2002, p. 65). Well-educated people also tend not to have a social-utility motive to use the Internet for politics.

Demographic factors influence which types of media people employ for political information. Men are more likely than women to use the Internet in general, and blogs in particular, for political knowledge (Johnson, Kaye, Bichard, and Wong, 2007; Johnson, Zhang, Bichard, and Seltzer, 2010; Kaye and Johnson, 2006, 2002; Pew Research Center, 2003). Youth use bulletin boards and electronic mailing lists for political information (Kaye and Johnson, 2004). Income is associated with using bulletin boards and electronic mailing lists. Those with lower incomes (in relative terms, rather than in absolute terms) rely more on bulletin boards, electronic mailing lists, and chat rooms for political information (Kaye and Johnson, 2006). On the other hand, having a higher income predicts using blogs for politics (pp. 159–160). Finally, while higher education is associated with using blogs, lower education correlates with using chat rooms (p. 155). While much is known about the influence of demographic factors on people's motives and media choices, it is not clear which demographic factors are associated with following political leaders on Twitter (or the motives to do so).

POLITICAL FACTORS

There are a number of political variables, such as self-efficacy, trust in government, interest in politics, and likelihood of voting, that influence motives to gather political information. *Political self-efficacy* is a term meaning people's belief in their ability to understand key issues and affect the political process. This factor predicts both information-seeking and guidance motivations to use the Web for political information (Kaye and Johnson, 2002, p. 64). So the more confident people are that they can make a difference politically, the more they use the Web to seek political information and look to the Web for guidance. Having trust in the government also predicts that a person will use the Web with an information-seeking motive, while the desire to vote predicts that a person will use the Web for convenience (Kaye and Johnson, 2004, pp. 214–215). Interestingly, having a lack of trust in the government predicts having a self-expression motive to use blogs (Kaye, 2005, p. 89). A high interest in politics predicts having a social-utility motive for using the Web for politics (Kaye and Johnson, 2002, p. 64). In addition, having an interest in politics positively correlates with using blogs for information-seeking purposes (Kaye, 2005, p. 84).

Political attitudes influence motivations for media use. Those people with a strong interest in politics are more likely to use the Web for political information, compared to those people with a weak interest (Kaye and Johnson, 2002; Pew Research Center, 2003). Political interest also is associated with those people who use blogs for politics (Kaye, 2005). However, it is unknown to what degree political attitudes influence the motives for following political leaders on Twitter. It is unknown whether certain factors make one more likely to choose Twitter as a place for "engaging with" political information.

RESEARCH QUESTIONS ANSWERED IN THIS CHAPTER

There are several research questions to be answered regarding who follows political leaders on Twitter and why followers do so. These questions are based on what is known about political information gathering via the Web, social networking sites, blogs, chat rooms, bulletin boards, and electronic mailing lists. This chapter examines the answers to such questions from survey and in-depth interview data. The research questions were designed to reveal information such as the following: Who are political Twitter users? To them, who are our political leaders? What motivates them to follow leaders? How are their motives and use of Twitter influenced by demographic and political factors? The eight research questions of the study discussed in this book are as follows:

- Question 1: What are the characteristics of the participants in the sample in terms of demographics (gender, age, race, income, education) and political variables (interest in politics, political efficacy, trust in government, past voting, likelihood of voting, party registration, and political ideology)?
- Question 2: To what degree do Twitter users in the sample follow individuals who are currently elected officials, individuals who are not currently elected officials, or political organizations?
- Question 3: What are the most important motives, to those in the sample, for following political leaders on Twitter?
- Question 4: Do the motives (of those in the sample) for following political leaders on Twitter differ for those following currently elected officials only (versus all others)?
- Question 5: How strongly does each of the motives for following political leaders on Twitter correlate with demographic and political variables?

- Question 6: Do demographic and political variables predict people's motives for following political leaders on Twitter?
- Question 7: Do people's motives for following political leaders on Twitter influence the amount and/or type of political leaders they select to follow?
- Question 8: Who are considered political leaders on Twitter?

METHODS USED TO ANSWER THE RESEARCH QUESTIONS

Survey

The online survey was conducted among Twitter users during the 2010 election cycle. Participants were recruited with direct solicitation and snowball techniques, resulting in 436 completed surveys. The final sample included a total of 426 respondents after deleting those indicating that they did not follow at least one political leader on Twitter or were under the age of 18.

Measures

The motives for following political leaders on Twitter were examined using a 20-item index that was, in part, derived from previous uses and gratifications research on information gathering and political information gathering (Ancu and Cozma, 2009; Kaye and Johnson, 2002, 2004; Kaye, 2005; Ko et al., 2005; Papacharissi and Rubin, 2000).

Political efficacy and trust in government were gauged using statements from Ancu and Cozma (2009), Kaye (2005), and Kaye and Johnson (2002, 2004). To illustrate, statements for political efficacy included "I have a good understanding of the important political issues facing the country," and "I am better informed about politics and government than most people." The 2-item additive index had a Cronbach's alpha of 0.76. (One reverse-coded item, "People like me don't have any say about what government does," had to be deleted due to low reliability scores.) A single item was used to indicate trust in government: "Most leaders are devoted to service." While a multiple-item index would have been ideal, these two measures lacked sufficient reliability scores: "Politicians never tell us what they really think," and "I don't think public officials care much about what people like me think." Responses to all statements regarding motives, political efficacy, and trust in government were measured on a 5-point scale from 1 (strongly disagree) to 5 (strongly agree).

A 10-point scale was used to measure other variables, such as interest in politics (1 = a very low interest; 10 = a very high interest), likelihood of voting in the 2010 election (1 = a very low likelihood; 10 = a very high likelihood), and political ideology (1 = conservative; 10 = liberal). Past voting behavior was determined by asking respondents if they voted in the 2008 general election. The party registration question included choices for Democratic, Republican, Independent, "other," or "not registered to vote." Finally, respondents were asked demographic questions such as their age, gender, race, income, and education.

Data Analysis

Data analysis of the questions proceeded in several steps. First, frequencies and mean scores were used to answer Questions 1 and 2, which deal with participants' demographic and political characteristics, and the types of political leaders participants follow. To address Question 3, a principal-components factor analysis (with varimax rotation) was then used to extract and interpret possible motivational factors. Identified items were then summed and averaged to form multidimensional indices representing motivations for following political leaders on Twitter. Question 4 compares the motives of those people following elected officials only, with those people following a broad range of political leaders. The data were assessed using an independent samples *t*-test. Question 5 concerns how the motives correlate with demographic and political variables. This question was answered using correlation analyses. Questions 6 and 7 involved multiple regression. Hierarchical regression analysis was conducted to identify demographic (first block) and political antecedent (second block) predictors of motivation. Motives also were analyzed as independent variables predicting the amount and the type of political leaders followed on Twitter. The results of the survey are shown in Tables 2.1 through 2.5. Table 2.1 shows why people followed political leaders on Twitter. Table 2.2 shows *t*-tests comparing motivation mean scores for those people following only currently elected officials, versus all others. Table 2.3 lists the Pearson Correlation Matrix for motivations, with the participants' demographics. Table 2.4 illustrates the Pearson Correlation Matrix for people's motivations and political attitudes. In Table 2.5 is seen the hierarchical regression analyses that predicts why people follow political leaders on Twitter.

In-depth Interviews

Participants were asked several open-ended questions to answer Question 8 and to confirm and expand upon the survey results associated with Questions 2 and 3. The research questions deal with which people the followers see as political leaders and what motives they have for following those leaders.

During the in-depth interviews, additional follow-up questions (called *probes*) were asked when there was a need to more clearly understand participants' thoughts as to whom they follow and why they follow them. The in-depth interviews included these questions: "What types of people or organizations do you consider to be 'political leaders' when you choose to follow political leaders on Twitter?" "What is your primary motive for following political leaders on Twitter?" "In what ways do you find following political leaders on Twitter to be a social activity?" "In what ways do you find following political leaders on Twitter to be an information-seeking activity?"

RESULTS

Survey

The survey's results indicated that various uses and gratifications serve as significant motivators for following political leaders on Twitter. The motives for following leaders on Twitter included these factors: social, entertainment, expression, guidance, and convenience. An assortment of participant characteristics indicated some similar and some disparate attitudes with respect to politics and those political leaders selected to be followed on Twitter. For the most part, respondents were very politically active and interested in political matters. They also tended to follow a wide variety of political leaders in and out of office, as well as political organizations. Relationships were revealed denoting key demographic and political antecedents for motivations, as well as predictive associations. The following section details the specific findings for each of the research questions.

Characteristics of Participants

Question 1 focused on the characteristics of the survey participants in terms of demographic and political variables. The sample yielded a fairly balanced mix of demographic and political backgrounds, with some outliers identified. The participants' characteristics are congruent with past research of similar Internet-savvy and politically active individuals (Ancu and Cozma, 2009; Johnson, Zhang, Bichard, and Seltzer, 2010; Kaye and Johnson, 2004, 2006; Salem, 2010).

With respect to demographics, the analysis revealed that 57.1 percent of the respondents were male, while 42.9 percent were female. In terms of age, 40.9 percent of the survey participants were in the age range of 25–40 years old. Thirty-one percent of the respondents were between the ages of 41 and 60. Only 23.5 percent of those in the sample were between the ages of 18–24.

Respondents reported moderate-to-high household income levels, with 25.7 percent making more than $100,000. The average income fell into the $65,000–$100,000 range. Also, 85.9 percent of the sample identified themselves as Caucasian, 2.6 percent African American, 4.7 percent Hispanic, 1.6 percent Asian, and 5.2 percent "other." Survey participants were on the high end of the education spectrum, with 69.7 percent reporting a bachelor's or graduate degree.

Political attitudes were assessed. The respondents showed high amounts of political interest ($M = 9.1$ on a 10-point scale; $SD = 1.5$) and political efficacy ($M = 4.6$ on a 5-point scale; $SD = 0.60$). Similarly, voting behavior was strong among the sample, with 93.4 percent indicating that they had voted in the 2008 general election, and most asserting a high likelihood that they would again vote in 2010 ($M = 9.5$ on a 10-point scale; $SD = 1.8$). They demonstrated moderate levels of trust, with 42 percent noting somewhat-to-strong disagreement with the statement "leaders are devoted to service," and 38.2 percent noting somewhat-to-strong agreement with the trust statement. The sample included a mix of party representation, with 50.5 percent Democrat, 22.8 percent Republican, 15.5 percent Independent, and 11.3 percent "other" or "not registered." Ideological leanings were moderate, with a slight skew toward liberal ($M = 6.5$ on a 10-point scale, with 10 being liberal; $SD = 3.2$). Roughly 60 percent of the sample fell into the "moderate liberal to strong liberal" category.

Description of the Political Leaders Followed

Question 2 assessed the degree to which Twitter users in the sample followed elected officials, political organizations, and those people not currently holding an elected office. Survey participants reported a high propensity to follow all of these categories. The highest percentage followed current elected officials (at 88.6 percent). This situation is true for all demographic groups and ideological leanings. For example, 91.9 percent of those respondents indicating a strong liberal ideology chose to follow elected officials. Similarly, 87.8 percent of those respondents indicating a strong conservative ideology also chose to follow elected officials. A comparable majority of the survey respondents also indicated following the tweets of political organizations (at roughly 71 percent).

Some differences did emerge with respect to participants choosing to follow political leaders who were not currently in office. Overall, 70.2 percent of the sample indicated following people who were not in office. This situation was most pronounced among those respondents identifying themselves as Republicans (82.5 percent) and those respondents with a strong conservative ideology (85.1 percent). By comparison, 63.3 percent of the Democrats in the sample (and 62.5 percent of those respondents espousing a liberal ideology) specified following people not currently in office.

Motives for Following Political Leaders on Twitter

Question 3 investigated the degree of importance attributed to each of the motivations revealed for following political leaders on Twitter. The 20 items measuring motivational variables were factored by principal-components analysis and items were assigned to factors if loadings were above 0.60. These three items were deleted due to insufficient loadings: "To find specific political information," "To keep up with issues of the day," and "For unbiased viewpoints." The remaining 17 items loaded into five factors. The factors included the following:

1. Social utility
2. Entertainment
3. Self-expression
4. Information/Guidance
5. Convenience

Together, these five factors accounted for 69.27 percent of the variance in motivations for following political leaders on Twitter. (See Table 2.1.)

Social utility emerged as the first factor, accounting for 14.46 percent of the variance, with items loading under it having a Cronbach's alpha of 0.80. Four items loaded under the social-utility factor. These values indicate that social motivations are the primary impetus for following political leaders on Twitter, with the most pronounced motivation being "something to talk or tweet about with others."

The motivation factor of entertainment was a close second, accounting for 14.36 percent of the variance. The index of three items achieved a Cronbach's alpha of 0.87. Item loadings for this factor were high across the board, indicating that the respondents viewed following political leaders as a way of passing time, entertainment, and having fun.

The third factor revealed a self-expressive desire among survey respondents. The factor explained 13.85 percent of the variance. The four items were combined to form an index of self-expression (Cronbach's alpha = 0.77). The strongest items loaded show a preference for engagement, communication, and even for critique of political leaders. Those following political tweets with this motivation apparently view Twitter as an opportunity to voice their opinions.

Table 2.1 Motivations for Following Political Leaders on Twitter

I follow political leaders on Twitter...	Factors				
	1	*2*	*3*	*4*	*5*
Factor 1: Social Utility					
To give me something to talk about with others.	0.774	0.224	0.009	0.160	0.062
To give me something to tweet about with others.	0.806	0.203	0.242	–0.083	0.071
To use as ammunition in arguments with others.	0.644	0.028	0.155	0.199	0.163
To retweet the information I receive with others.	0.669	0.116	0.343	–0.034	0.107
Factor 2: Entertainment					
To pass time when bored.	0.169	0.834	0.000	0.075	0.077
Because it is entertaining.	0.125	0.864	0.092	0.071	0.243
Because it is fun.	0.217	0.798	0.148	0.121	0.245
Factor 3: Self-Expression					
To engage in discussion with the political leader.	0.027	–0.115	0.769	0.155	0.081
To communicate support for the political leader.	0.294	0.135	0.653	0.177	0.010
To criticize the political leader.	0.125	0.140	0.759	–0.042	–0.004
To communicate with supporters of the political leader.	0.296	0.092	0.667	0.203	0.088
Factor 4: Information/Guidance					
To find out more information about the political leader.	0.014	0.202	0.234	0.667	0.249
To help me decide about important issues.	0.120	0.034	0.055	0.897	0.161
To help me decide how to vote.	0.084	0.057	0.134	0.874	0.084
Factor 5: Convenience					
To access information quickly.	0.096	0.046	0.092	0.129	0.824
Because the information is easy to obtain.	0.108	0.224	0.012	0.181	0.846
Because the information is cheap to obtain.	0.153	0.315	0.037	0.149	0.751
Eigenvalue	5.43	2.16	1.92	1.15	1.12
Variance Explained	14.46	14.36	13.85	13.43	13.17

Note: N = 426.

The next factor that emerged from analysis involved a combination of previously designated information-seeking and guidance motivations. Past research also has combined items for information seeking and guidance (Ancu and Cozma, 2009). This grouping of three items accounted for 13.43 percent of the variance and had a Cronbach's alpha of 0.84. The strongest loadings imply that these motivations derive from a need for help regarding decisions related to issues (and to voting in particular).

The final factor, convenience, explained 13.17 percent of the variance in motivational factors, with a Cronbach's alpha of 0.84. Three items were combined to form the index. The items reveal that followers regard Twitter as a valued tool for quick, cheap, and easy access to information in the political sphere.

Differences in Motivations for Those Following Only Elected Officials

Question 4 investigated possible motivational differences for those people choosing to follow on Twitter currently elected officials alone, versus those people following a mix of political leaders on Twitter. An independent samples t-test was conducted, and results indicate some significant differences (see Table 2.2). There was a significant difference in the scores for social-utility motivations between those following only elected officials (M = 2.5, SD = 0.99) and all others (M = 3.1, SD = 1.0); $t(399) = -3.66$, $p < 0.01$. This finding suggests that when respondents only follow those people who are elected officials, the respondents are less likely to have social-utility motivations. The same is true for the motivations of entertainment, $t(396) = -3.49$, $p < 0.01$, and self-expression, $t(401) = -2.40$, $p < 0.05$. Ultimately, those respondents who follow only elected officials differ significantly from all other respondents, because they are less likely to be motivated by social utility, self-expression, and entertainment.

Relationship among Motives and Demographic or Political Variables

Various relationships among motivations and demographic variables can be noted in response to Question 5 (see Table 2.3). Correlation analysis indicated gender, age, and education were all associated with varying motivations for using Twitter to follow political leaders. The strongest correlation coefficient denoted a relationship between younger respondents and entertainment motivations ($r = -0.29$, $p < 0.01$). Younger respondents also had a weak—but significant—correlation with social-utility motivations ($r = -0.14$, $p < 0.01$). Other significant relationships were those with lower education and motivations of self-expression and information/guidance ($r = -0.15$ and -0.13 respectively, $p < 0.01$), although the coefficients were quite weak. Findings

**Table 2.2   *T*-tests Comparing Motivation Mean Scores for Those
Following Only Currently Elected Officials, versus All Others**

Motivation	Mean (SD)	t
Social Utility		$t = -3.66**$
Follows only elected	2.5(0.99)	
Follows others	3.1(1.0)	
Entertainment		$t = -3.49**$
Follows only elected	2.9(1.2)	
Follows ethers	3.5(1.1)	
Self-expression		$t = -2.40*$
Follows only elected	2.4(0.90)	
Follows others	2.8(1.1)	
Information/Guidance		$t = 1.18$
Follows only elected	3.6(0.98)	
Follows others	3.4(1.2)	
Convenience		$t = -0.884$
Follows only elected	3.8(0.97)	
Follows others	4.0(1.0)	

Note: $*p < 0.05$; $**p < 0.01$.

also specify that females have a significant relationship with the information/ guidance motivation ($r = 0.15$, $p < 0.01$).

A correlation analysis was performed with motivations and a variety of political variables (see Table 2.4). The results indicate several significant relationships with respect to factors such as social, entertainment, self-expression, and convenience. Political interest had a significant relationship with social ($r = 0.19$, $p < 0.01$), entertainment ($r = 0.16$, $p < 0.01$), self-expression ($r = 0.14$, $p < 0.01$), as well as convenience ($r = 0.11$, $p < 0.05$) motivations for following politics on Twitter. Similarly, efficacy had a prominent connection to motivations such as social ($r = 0.14$, $p < 0.01$), entertainment ($r = 0.11$, $p < 0.05$), self-expression ($r = 0.11$, $p < 0.05$), and convenience ($r = 0.12$, $p < 0.05$). Conservative ideology ($r = -0.14$, $p < 0.01$) and lower trust ($r = -0.10$, $p < 0.05$) appeared to relate to self-expressive desires when following leaders on Twitter. On the other hand, higher levels of trust ($r = 0.19$, $p < 0.01$) and a more liberal ideology ($r = 0.14$, $p < 0.01$) correlated significantly with entertainment motives.

Predicting Motives for Following Political Leaders on Twitter

Question 6 assessed the predictive power of demographic and political variables on motivations for following political leaders on Twitter. (See Table

Table 2.3   Pearson Correlation Matrix for Motivations and Participant Demographics

	Age	Race	Income	Edu.	Social	Entert.	Self-Expr.	Info/Guid.	Conven.
Demographics									
Gender	−0.023	−0.044	−0.100*	−0.052	0.064	0.067	0.042	0.152**	0.035
Age		0.122*	0.235**	0.107*	−0.138**	−0.288**	−0.002	0.034	−0.073
Race			−0.023	−0.054	0.051	0.040	−0.008	−0.022	−0.009
HH income***				0.156**	−0.011	−0.053	−0.041	−0.061	0.001
Education					−0.018	0.025	−0.151**	−0.129**	0.034
Motivations									
Social utility						0.303**	0.409**	0.124*	0.207**
Entertainment							0.111*	0.128**	0.353**
Self-expression								0.253**	0.101*
Info/Guidance									0.286**

Note: Female was coded higher for Gender. Caucasian coded higher for Race.
*$p < 0.05$; **$p < 0.01$; ***HH = Household.

Table 2.4 Pearson Correlation Matrix for Motivations and Political Attitudes

	Ideol.	Trust	Efficacy	Vote Likely	Past Voter	Dem.	Rep.	Social	Entert.	Self-expr.	Info/ Guid.	Conven.
Political Att.												
Pol. Interest	-0.068	0.009	0.559**	0.078	0.063	-0.048	0.074	0.191**	0.159**	0.141**	-0.049	0.110*
Ideology		0.261**	-0.137**	-0.013	0.032	0.696**	-0.698**	0.005	0.137**	-0.136**	-0.081	-0.044
Trust			0.014	0.006	-0.026	0.224**	-0.137**	0.085	0.185**	-0.096*	-0.079	0.048
Efficacy				0.112*	0.030	-0.049	0.098*	0.141**	0.110*	0.107*	-0.042	0.123*
Vote likely					0.591**	0.180**	0.055	0.088	-0.057	0.072	0.012	-0.027
Past voter						0.154**	0.009	0.074	-0.010	0.032	-0.028	-0.094
Democrat							-0.548**	0.075	0.081	-0.085	-0.030	-0.020
Republican								0.030	-0.076	0.133**	0.056	0.050

Note: Liberal was coded higher for Ideology. Party identification was represented as three dummy variables with Independents/other serving as the reference group for Democrat and Republican.
*p < 0.05; **p < 0.01.

2.5.) The most pronounced impact involved demographic and political influence on the motive of entertainment. The demographic block accounted for a 10.5 percent variance, while the combined blocks of demographic and political variables explained a 16.2 percent variance in entertainment motives for following politics on Twitter. This impact was primarily due to age ($b = -0.20$, $p < 0.01$) and political interest variables ($b = 0.13$, $p < 0.01$).

Specific demographic variables did have an interesting influence on motivations for following political leaders. Female respondents were more likely to exhibit information/guidance motivations ($b = 0.12$, $p < 0.01$). Those respondents of a younger age were more likely to have the motives of social utility ($b = -0.20$, $p < 0.01$) and entertainment ($b = -0.40$, $p < 0.01$) for following politics on Twitter. Educational backgrounds had a different influence, with higher education predicting information/guidance motivations ($b = 0.07$, $p < 0.05$) and lower education predicting self-expression motivations ($b = -0.21$, $p < 0.01$).

Political antecedents were investigated for their influence on each of the five motivational factors. Minimal significant results emerged. Findings indicate that political interest predicts several motivations for following leaders on Twitter, including social utility ($b = 0.14$, $p < 0.01$), entertainment ($b = 0.13$, $p < 0.01$), and self-expression ($b = 0.09$, $p < 0.05$). The last finding of significance was that those respondents who did not vote in the last general election were more likely to have convenience motivations ($b = -0.54$, $p < 0.05$) for following politics on Twitter.

Predicting the Amount and Type of Political Leaders Followed on Twitter

Question 7 addressed the impact of motivations (for following political leaders) on the amount and/or type of leaders selected to follow. Multiple regression was performed to investigate the predictive nature of each motivational factor. The findings reveal that in this survey, motivations are a significant predictor of the number of leaders followed on Twitter ($p < 0.001$). Motivations explained 10.2 percent of the variance in the number followed. Specifically, followers with the motivations of social utility ($b = 0.21$, $p < 0.001$) or self-expression ($b = 0.17$, $p < 0.001$) followed a larger number of political leaders on Twitter.

Data analysis was performed to identify the influence of motivations on the type of political leaders selected. Results indicate that motivational factors only significantly explained the variance for those respondents on Twitter following Democrats ($R^2 = 4.2$ percent, $p < 0.001$) or liberals ($R^2 = 6.5$ percent, $p < 0.001$). Specifically, those respondents motivated by social utility or entertainment were more likely to follow Democrats (b = 0.06, $p < 0.001$) and liberals (b = 0.08, $p < 0.001$). Twitter users with self-expression motivations

Table 2.5   Hierarchical Regression Analyses Predicting Motivations for Following Political Leaders on Twitter

Independent Variables	Social Utility B	Social Utility SE	Entertainment B	Entertainment SE	Self-expression B	Self-expression SE	Information/Guidance B	Information/Guidance SE	Convenience B	Convenience SE
Demographics										
Gender (female coded higher)	0.15	0.11	0.19	0.11	0.07	0.11	0.34	0.12**	0.16	0.10
Age	−0.20**	0.07	−0.40**	0.07	−0.07	0.07	0.07	0.08	−0.09	0.07
Race (Caucasian coded higher)			0.22	0.16	−0.20	0.15	−0.13	0.17	−0.07	0.15
	0.14	0.15								
HH*** Income	−0.01	0.05	0.01	0.05	−0.07	0.05	−0.07	0.06	−0.01	0.05
Education	−0.02	0.06	0.04	0.06	−0.21**	0.06	−0.16	0.07*	0.03	0.06
R^2(%) =	2.9*		10.5**		3.4*		4.7**		0.9	
Political Antecedents										
Political interest	**0.14	0.04	0.13**	0.05	0.09*	0.05	−0.03	0.05	0.08	0.04
Ideology (Liberal coded higher)	−0.01	0.03	0.05	0.03	−0.01	0.03	−0.03	0.03	−0.02	0.03
Trust	0.04	0.05	0.08	0.05	−0.07	0.05	−0.06	0.05	0.05	0.05
Efficacy	0.12	0.11	0.12	0.11	0.06	0.11	0.02	0.12	0.15	0.10
Vote likelihood	0.02	0.04	−0.03	0.04	0.04	0.04	0.01	0.04	0.02	0.04
Past voter	0.27	0.27	0.17	0.29	0.09	0.28	−0.10	0.30	−0.54*	0.27
Democrat (not Ind/other)	0.15	0.15	−0.22	0.16	−0.03	0.15	0.14	0.17	0.04	0.15
Republican (not Ind/other)	0.12	0.17	−0.06	0.18	0.31	0.18	0.11	0.19	0.09	0.17
Incremental R^2(%) =	6.7**		5.7**		5.2**		1.2		4.7*	
Total R^2(%) =	9.6**		16.2**		8.6**		5.9*		5.6*	

Note: Party identification was represented as three dummy variables with Independents/other serving as the reference group for Democrat and Republican.
*$p < 0.05$; **$p < 0.01$; ***HH = Household.

were less likely to follow Democrats (b = –0.05, $p < 0.05$) or liberals (b = –0.05, $p < 0.05$).

In-depth Interviews

Comments from the interview participants confirm and expand upon what was found in the survey, especially regarding Questions 2 and 3. Those questions sought to measure the degree to which certain individuals and groups are followed as political leaders, and what motives are the strongest for following them. As was also seen in the survey, in-depth interview participants reported following a mix of elected officials, those who are not currently elected officials, and political organizations. In addition, those interviewed shed light on just how diverse their definition is of the term *political leader* (which answers Question 8). To these participants, the categories of "not currently elected officials" and "political organization" include the following: former elected officials, candidates for office, current or past political appointees, bloggers, pollsters, radio talk show hosts, cable television news show hosts, political journalists/columnists, academics, think-tanks, political action committees, and civic organizations. Those not mentioned as political leaders include friends and family. These findings make it easier to understand who is politically influencing the in-depth interview participants. Also, the finding provides a clearer picture of where participants are drawing the political information that they then share with others.

In terms of the motives for following political leaders, both the survey takers and the in-depth interview participants indicated factors such as social utility, entertainment, self-expression, information/guidance, and convenience. There are two benefits to having had interview participants talk about their motives. One advantage was that participants' comments matched the many statements used in the survey to define and measure the five motives. This result helps confirm that the survey statements did accurately reflect the motives that they were supposed to. Also, the interview responses gave a much more detailed description of the motives than the survey could. For example, the survey measured social utility using statements such as "I follow political leaders on Twitter to give me something to tweet about with others." In contrast, the open-ended nature of the interviews allowed participants to offer examples of *how* they use leaders' tweets as a source for their own tweets. The section that follows elaborates on the interview findings.

Characteristics of Participants

The 18 people who participated in the in-depth interviews were drawn from the 426 people who took the survey. Because of this strategy, the in-depth interview findings provided a deeper understanding of the survey results. However, note that the two groups of people did not share a completely similar demographic and political profile. The demographic forms that the in-depth interview participants filled out indicate that the sample has more of a gender balance than the survey sample, with a 50–50 split between males and females in the interviews. The sample also included more Republicans and fewer Democrats in the in-depth interviews than in the survey. Republicans accounted for 38.8 percent of the in-depth interview participants, Democrats were at 33.3 percent, and the rest identified as Independent, "other," or "not registered to vote." The demographic profiles of the survey takers and in-depth interview participants are more similar when it comes to their age, ethnicity, income, and education. The average age for those in the in-depth interviews was 42; and most participants (78 percent) were white. The average annual income was between $65,001 and $100,000, and 78 percent had a bachelor's degree or a graduate degree.

Description of Political Leaders Followed

All but one participant followed at least one elected official. Such officials included governors, mayors, those in state legislatures, and members of Congress. However, most participants followed both elected officials and those without elected power. Michael, 58, was one of the few participants who relied primarily on elected officials:

> Normally, I would say members of Congress, occasionally a candidate for Congress or Senate, there are a few administration officials that use Twitter for their official functions.... But I rely most on members of Congress. I'd say that's probably 75 percent to 80 percent of my political use of Twitter is with members of Congress.

On the other end of the spectrum, Dana, 36, was the only participant to follow no elected officials:

> Dana: I'm a master's student in social work right now, and I'm somebody who reads a lot, so I tend to avoid actual elected leaders. I'm naturally pretty questioning of who's putting out the tweets, so I lean more towards academics and certain commentators who I've read previously and I agree with them or think they make valid arguments. So I'm probably leaning more toward an academic bent. They might not be an actual elected political leader, but they're someone who is involved in the political discourse.
> Interviewer: Do you follow any elected officials?
> Dana: Umm. Let me pull up my Twitter. [pause] I don't think I do. I haven't come across anyone who's an elected leader who's tweeting anything that I really felt, "OK, now I need to follow this person."

JOLIET JUNIOR COLLEGE LIBRARY
JOLIET, IL 60431

It was far more common for participants to list (as political leaders worth following) a wide variety of elected and nonelected individuals, as well as organizations. Nonelected individuals included those appointed by elected officials. Political appointees are crucial to follow, according to Steve, 28, because important political information often comes from people in the federal or state bureaucracy:

> I would consider political leaders to be any Twitter account for any elected or appointed leaders—especially a member of Congress, state legislature, or any person in an executive office or a bureaucratic position. These people must answer to the public, and if they are going to communicate via Twitter, there's a chance that communication could be newsworthy. I follow probably dozens of people like this.

John, 34, also follows political appointees, but for a slightly different reason than Steve. John said that the political power that appointees wield make their tweets essential viewing:

> Mostly political candidates, elected officials, people who are appointed—for example, if they're appointed by the president or they're the chairman of the Ways and Means Committee. So the people I consider political leaders are those who have some influence on public policy. I would consider them a political leader if they are a part of the political spectrum, and maybe a future candidate, and if they have influence on public policy.

In addition to political appointees, candidates for office were mentioned as one kind of nonelected individual who has political power. James, 33, said that people who are likely to be candidates for high office are political leaders:

> For me, it's like three categories: There's elected officials or presumptive candidates, like Mitt Romney, for example, or the president, for example. And then there are policy leaders; so I follow, like, Ezra Klein or policy-wonky people. And then think-tanks.

Romney also is a former elected official, which is another type of political leader who is followed. Nancy, 53, said she follows one former elected official because she believes others consider that person important: "I follow Sarah Palin because the conservative right considers her a political leader, even though she has left office and plays kind of peek-a-boo with the press."

Many participants named individuals who work for news organizations as political leaders. Jon, 25, said most of his political leaders fall into this category:

I follow a wide variety of politically related people and organizations on Twitter. Many of these are actual politicians or candidates for office, but the vast majority is political journalists or media organizations that focus primarily on politics. I follow these accounts in particular because they tend to be the best at relaying information and providing new insight into the latest news.

Other participants said political commentators and journalists occupy a smaller (but still significant) place on their list of political leaders. Jeff, 29, said that those people who report on politics or provide commentary on politics for news organizations are political leaders because they can set the political agenda:

Types of people I consider leaders are (a) elected officials and nominees for elected office, and (b) organizations, pundits/bloggers, and journalists known for political reporting, commentary, and activity who have a sizable impact on the discourse. While I follow many other political thinkers and people who may not fit this, I believe staying in tune with these people is important for my ability to stay informed both regarding news and the way the proverbial wind is blowing.

Cecily, 52, also believes news media outlets can shape public opinion. So in addition to "conservative Republican leaders," she said that she follows "people who are able to have a media platform and come out publicly and say that government needs to follow the Constitution." Media platforms include news magazines, talk radio, and cable news networks such as Fox, MSNBC, and Current TV. Some participants, such as Nathalie, 74, follow political commentators from cable networks to help in scheduling where they will get other political information:

I do follow Keith Olbermann. He kind of gives you a heads up on what he's going to do with his show. And to that extent where there's going to be a heads up for something that's coming along, like Rachel Maddow, that's very useful to me in planning my viewing, such as it is.

Esta, 65, follows political journalists and commentators on Twitter because of the power they exercise in more traditional media venues, such as national newspapers. One *New York Times* columnist is Esta's particular favorite:

I choose folks that I like, folks that I read; and I enjoy Frank Rich, for instance. I choose to follow him because I agree with much of what he says in his op-eds.... Especially in this day and age, *journalists* (although I use the term loosely), I think those that espouse their own ideas either in print or on television, or the radio, in addition to people who hold office, are important to follow.

Participants mentioned political organizations and civic groups as political leaders. To Ed, 36, organizations are political leaders when they influence legislation. He said, "Anything ranging from political action committees or candidates committees to nonprofits: anyone who has an interest in legislation or who can affect the journey of any piece of legislation." Others, such as Carole, 44, were fairly selective in their definition of what makes a political organization:

> I consider any organization that's main focus is political to be a political organization, like the League of Women Voters, the Republican Party, the Democratic Party, etc. I don't actually qualify the Tea Party in this yet. I think they need to get less fractional for me to consider them a group.

In terms of how participants defined political leaders, perhaps the most expansive definition came from Brett, 30:

> As an anarchist, I consider everyone to be a political leader. Even if nothing that someone says is overtly political, I sincerely believe that the personal and the political are (or should be) identical; and that there are political meanings and consequences to everything that people say. I do recognize some people as having much more political power than others, though, and I'd include in that category people with power in the media as well as in government.

Social, Expressive, and Entertainment Motives for Following Political Leaders

Participants' comments indicate they have many motives for following political leaders on Twitter, including social utility, entertainment, self-expression, information gathering, guidance, and convenience. In addition, their comments are helpful in understanding how participants define the motives, especially the motive of social utility and self-expression. Participants talked about social utility in terms of using leaders' tweets as fodder for their own tweets, while self-expression motives involved following leaders in order to engage with those leaders, the leaders' followers, and other politically interested individuals.

Regarding social utility, John is one of many participants who are motivated to follow political leaders because the information in leaders' tweets is a valuable resource to pass along to others:

> I'm following pretty much the global arena. And I can retweet that, you know, some of the new laws that have been passing in the European Union or what's going on in Pakistan or what's going on with the recently elected prime minister of Australia, or what's going on even locally. . . . I'm using Twitter for

information; not only I'm getting information, but I'm selecting some of the things that I like, whether it's a current law, whether it's a bill being passed, or whether it's an informational study that comes from the Department of Defense or the Department of State. . . . I kind of put in my own analysis and then put a link.

John's statement also shows that social utility means more to him than merely retweeting a leader: He often comments on the information he passes along. Jeff, too, shares information from leaders' tweets while adding his perspective:

Knowing what my leaders are doing in somewhat real-time assists me in getting the word out to like-minded people and helps me react to those situations when appropriate in an easier way than waiting for a newspaper or blog post to report it.

To Michael, social utility means following political leaders because their tweets help him maintain political relationships: "I have some friends who have the same interests, and I'll occasional retweet [political leaders] or bring things to their attention. So in that regard it's just fostering friendships, it's part of the normal discourse of a relationship." For Jon, social utility relates to following political journalists rather than elected officials: "I enjoy co-opting journalists' takes on news and passing on that insight to others when political discussion comes up." Carole's social utility motive involves searching leaders' tweets for information that will be useful to members of an organization that she is a part of:

I do use it for information, as I am part of a group that puts on debates. I go to other debates and speeches. I also follow what [political leaders] are saying in hopes of finding questions that are not just their talking points.

Self-expression motives were discussed in terms of participants' desire to tell the leaders they follow what they think, as well as communicate with the leaders' followers. Brett said what he most wants is to engage in discussion with political leaders:

I guess my main motive is to engage with them. I consider everyone on Twitter part of the same conversation. . . . A powerful person's tweets ought to be an opportunity to respond to them directly and have at least some chance of being heard.

Sometimes participants respond to leaders with positive comments, but other times the engagement is critical. Dana is one who likes to "nit-pick and mock certain leaders for things they say that are outright ridiculous."

Cecily said her self-expression motive is so strong that it affects which leaders she follows: "I only follow political leaders if they follow me back. I don't follow any politician (Democrat, Republican, Independent) who doesn't want to hear what I have to say." By following political leaders who follow her, Cecily ensures that all of her tweets appear in those leaders' Twitter streams.

Another aspect of self-expression is interacting with political leaders' followers. One way to do this is by replying to a leader's tweet. The reply is seen by anyone who follows both the leader and the sender of the reply. For example, Jon regularly makes use of this feature:

> I like to respond to various politicians' and journalists' tweets, knowing that many of my friends also follow the same accounts and will therefore see my responses. I enjoy talking to other people and asking them if they saw so-and-so's tweet, and what did they think?

Because the information in tweets is searchable by anyone, comments made about leaders can potentially be seen by an even larger number of politically interested Twitter users.

Entertainment motives were important in getting participants to follow political leaders. Nancy, for instance, said that it is good to scan leaders' tweets "if you're bored," while Steve said that he gets a lot of "fun" out of some leaders' tweets. Michael's entertainment motive is directed toward following members of Congress:

> There are certain members who I have greater respect for or less respect for, and I'm always interested in seeing what they're saying about something. Reading tweets of members who are sitting in the Congress during, say, the State of the Union speech, giving their snide comments. It's funny. There's no substance to it, but it's entertaining. I would say it's more of a prurient interest rather than a real substantive interest.

However, it would be inaccurate to suggest that all of those followers with an entertainment motive are focusing on tweets that are devoid of political substance. For example, Nathalie said that even tweets that are presented in a funny way often contain valid political points:

> There are some really interesting characters that have something to say and some of them are couched in comedic terms, but not inaccurate. So that's gives me a chuckle, because if you look at some of the stuff that's going on, laughing is the only remedy.

Information/Guidance and Convenience Motives for Following Political Leaders

Participants mentioned being motivated to learn as much as they could about political leaders and the key issues being discussed. Jim, 42, said, "It's sort of like an old-fashion teletype wire service. It's a running stream of consciousness, that's what I use it for." As with most of the other participants, Nathalie's informational motive comes from her very high interest in politics:

I am fascinated to the point that I think of myself as a news junkie. I don't tweet out anywhere near as much as I receive because I discovered that it was a great way to get pretty much clued into everything that was happening.

In addition, the need for followers to gather political information was often rooted in a desire to have that information to help them in their political decisions. Amanda, 23, said that leaders' tweets are especially useful in guiding her political beliefs because of the firsthand nature of the information:

I primarily follow political leaders because I am able to get news directly from the source, without having to receive it through the filter of a news organization. When a new piece of information is tweeted by a political leader, I am getting it fresh and unadulterated, and am able to form an opinion about it on my own, rather than someone else, like the news media, skewing the information in a way that they want to report it.

Similarly, John wants political information straight from the source: "Following political leaders allows me to have direct access to the information posted by political leader, instead of following traditional newspapers." Esta's informational motive comes from a lack of trust in any one political source:

I want to learn about all sides of an issue and to be well-informed. . . . I truly, truly believe that it's very difficult to get just the facts, and I think that the broader the net that you throw out to get information, the more you get some idea of really what's happening.

The information in tweets has guided some participants, such as Carole, to the extent of altering their political opinions:

The thing I like most is that people on either side will post links to interesting blogs or articles or sometimes facts about a past bill or race that you might not know about. I read information from both parties and any group who is writing about something I am interested in. A lot of times they will mention stuff that

I might have never considered before. Sometimes it will even make me change my mind about a position, even though I thought I had thoroughly researched it.

One important aspect of the information/guidance motive is the desire for political insight. Participants said that they wanted an insider's perspective of politics and, therefore, followed leaders to get a deeper understanding of what the leaders are really thinking and doing. Nancy said, "I follow political leaders on Twitter because I feel it gives me insight to their true agenda and ideology." James said, "My primary motive for following political leaders on Twitter is to learn what political leaders are thinking and reading—what influences the influential." Jon said the insight he gets from tweets helps him better detect political spin: "My primary motive for following political leaders on Twitter is to read about what they want the public to believe about them and their record." For Steve, political tweets provide insights that he cannot get elsewhere: "It's a great way to have access to statements of politicians that otherwise I wouldn't have access to. In some situations, it also provides a strong glimpse into what life is like for a politician."

Twitter is easy to use, so it is not surprising that people are motivated by convenience to use it. Political information can be found fairly quickly. Dana said that the "relatively instant information" she gets is the key reason that she follows leaders on Twitter:

> In the last six months since I really started using it regularly, it's kind of become one of my morning news sources that I just automatically check. Especially for things that are in my area of interest, with like global affairs and migration studies and things like that, it's scanning through what I should be reading, what I would have missed.

Cecily, too, is drawn to the timely information. In addition, her motive to follow political leaders comes from the unobtrusive way that information on Twitter can be accessed at any time. "I work and cannot watch news or listen to radio at various times during day and night. The Twitter app on my phone allows me to have instant news," she said.

CONCLUSION AND DISCUSSION

Looking at the findings from the survey and in-depth interviews, a pattern emerges as to what motivates people to follow political leaders on Twitter. The survey found that (in order of importance) the motives of political Twitter users include social utility, entertainment, self-expression, information/

guidance, and convenience. Social utility was the strongest motivation and suggests that followers are, indeed, interested in two-way communication sharing and dialogue. This result aligns with past studies of social networking sites (Ancu and Cozma, 2009; Balaban and Baltaretu, 2010; Bumgarner, 2007; Park, Kee, and Valenzuela, 2009; Raacke and Bonds-Raacke, 2008). The remaining motivational factors were fairly equal in their impact on respondents. Also, the survey found differences with respect to followers of current elected officials. Those choosing to follow only elected political leaders were less likely to be driven by social, expressive, or entertainment motivations. Additional differences also were noted when looking at specific demographic and political variables, and the predictive influence of those variables.

During the in-depth interviews, people confirmed the survey finding that social utility, entertainment, self-expression, information/guidance, and convenience are the motives for following political leaders on Twitter. Equally as important, the interviews did not reveal any other motives that the survey should have addressed. Participants' comments also provided detailed descriptions of various aspects of each motive. In doing so, it is easier to understand how each motive acts to drive people to follow political leaders. For example, the survey measured the information/guidance motive with statements such as "To find out more information about the political leader," but the interview participants went one step further and defined which types of information they wanted to find out. One type of information—political insight—involved following political leaders to get an insider's perspective of what the leaders are thinking and feeling, and what influences them. As a result, those political leaders whose tweets include insider details may be better at attracting, keeping, and influencing followers because followers are often motivated to find political insight.

Results from the in-depth interviews and surveys also indicate that most political Twitter users follow a variety of political leaders. Interviews found that the political leaders followed on Twitter include current elected officials, former elected officials, candidates for office, political appointees, political commentators, political parties, political action committees, and think-tanks. The list did not include other types of individuals such as friends and family. These findings suggest that future studies on the political influence of Twitter need to take into account which types of individuals and organizations wield political power on the microblog.

These survey results show the relative value of each motive. Such results say a lot about the kind of influence that Twitter has on the political process. Two of the top three motives—social utility and self-expression—involve a desire on the part of followers to engage in two-way communication, either by passing on leaders' information to others or engaging in conversations with the leaders. Consequently, Twitter's political appeal and influence come mostly from how it is used socially. It should be noted, however, that this conclusion applies less to those who follow only currently elected officials than to those who follow a mix of elected officials, candidates, appointees, commentators, and political organizations. The relatively low ranking of the information/guidance motive (which involves followers being one-way receivers of information rather than two-way communicators) suggests that followers usually want more than timely political briefs from their leaders. However, the information/guidance motive should not be thought of as unimportant as this motive was not rated greatly lower than motives such as self-expression.

What is the meaning of the popularity of the entertainment motive? One interpretation is that those with this motive follow political leaders simply for fun, and that they do not take leaders' tweets seriously. In-depth interviews provide an alternate explanation. When directly asked "What is your primary motive for following political leaders on Twitter?" not one participant used any words that denoted entertainment. The entertainment motive was always mentioned as secondary to other motives, such as social and informational. It may be that the need for political entertainment stems from followers' heavy exposure to serious (and sometimes depressing) political news. As one interview participant, Nathalie, said, "If you look at some of the stuff that's going on, laughing is the only remedy." Seen from this perspective, the entertainment motive's high ranking does not indicate that political leaders' and their tweets are usually laughed at, and, therefore, lack credibility and influence. Instead, the entertainment motive is secondary to followers' social, expressive, and informational motives and is a defense mechanism against being overloaded by information that is politically sobering.

It is worthwhile to see the relative value of each motive. Political leaders could make use of this information. For example, two of the top three motives involve actions such as passing on leaders' information to others and engaging in conversations with leaders. Leaders who want to increase their two-way communication with followers could use several methods: replying to followers' comments, soliciting followers' advice on political matters, retweeting, mentioning followers in their tweets, and interacting by using hashtags that their followers frequent.

Many of these two-way techniques already are being used by businesses. Pepsi asks for followers' advice on beverage products, and Dell (a computer company) has more than 100 Twitter accounts that are devoted to answering followers' questions and solving their computer problems (Milstein, 2010a).

Survey findings regarding followers' motives also help to put political Twitter use in a larger context. Comparisons now can be made among Twitter, blogs, and social networking sites. Politically speaking, the results suggest that Twitter is more akin to social networking sites such as Facebook and MySpace, and less similar to blogs, because past research shows that blogs are used mainly for information-seeking motives (Kaye, 2005; Kaye and Johnson, 2006). In contrast, social networking sites are used for social utility (Ancu and Cozma, 2009).

In addition, the survey findings add to other studies on Twitter uses and gratifications. The high ranking of social utility and self-expression motives among followers of political leaders is similar to one study of general Twitter use, which found that users have "a need for an informal sense of camaraderie, called connection, with other users" (Chen, 2011, p. 755). Also, the popularity of the entertainment motive among followers of political leaders matches results from Coursaris, Yun, and Sung (2010), who found that entertainment is a key motive for using Twitter.

There were several noteworthy survey results regarding demographic and political variables that interact with followers' motives. Political interest and younger age predicted motivations that were primarily social or entertainment driven. This finding conflicts with Ancu and Cozma (2009), who found that older individuals used MySpace with more entertainment motives. This difference may be due to the increased amount of features available on MySpace. Other studies also have noted that younger age groups tend to use online platforms more for information-seeking (Kaye and Johnson, 2004). The current findings suggest that Twitter use is different and may be used by younger age groups in a unique way.

Self-expression motivations were primarily among the less educated, but still politically interested. Past research has noted that less educated individuals are motivated by social utility in Internet platforms (Kaye and Johnson, 2002). Perhaps political interest and measures of efficacy are more important indicators guiding individuals to express their opinions in a more social arena.

Female participants and those with higher education appeared to use Twitter politically to fulfill information/guidance motivations. This result aligns with past research (Ancu and Cozma, 2009) noting that higher education predicts information-seeking and guidance motivations.

Finally, motivational desires for convenience were predicted solely by those choosing not to vote in the 2008 election. This finding possibly indicates that individuals who are less engaged politically have a strong desire for easy access to political leaders and their communications. They may be less involved in the overall political process, yet willing to follow leaders on Twitter simply because it is easy to do so.

Contrary to past research, political efficacy and trust appeared to have no significant influence on motivations for following political leaders on Twitter. Past analysis notes that high efficacy and trust leads to information-seeking motivations (Kaye and Johnson, 2002). Yet the current research found no significant correlation between efficacy or trust and information/guidance as a motivation for using Twitter. This lack of correlation may partly be due to the single-item measure used to measure efficacy and the fact that the overall sample indicated high efficacy with little variance. The survey sample was similarly high on measures of political interest and voting behavior.

While many past analyses note information-seeking motivations for a variety of online platforms, this study reveals that Twitter is a much more socially driven tool. What is still unknown, however, is whether the social nature of Twitter makes tweets from political leaders particularly influential on followers' political actions and beliefs. To find out more about the microblog's power of persuasion, political Twitter use needs to be examined as a form of word-of-mouth communication, which is the topic of the next chapter.

The Impact of Political Tweets When Used as Word-of-Mouth Communication

While it is important to know why people follow political leaders on Twitter, perhaps the ultimate test of Twitter's political worth is to discover what followers do with all those tweets.

This chapter will reveal answers to questions such as the following: How influential are political tweets? To what degree do followers take actions that are requested in political leaders' tweets? How much influence do political tweets have at shaping followers' political views? How does that influence compare with more traditional sources of opinion leadership, such as friends, family, co-workers, and acquaintances? This chapter will answer these and other questions by examining political tweets as a form of word-of-mouth communication (WOM). Most people engage in WOM every day. WOM simply means people passing along information to other people, whether face-to-face, on the phone, via e-mail, or on Twitter. WOM involves people communicating with others to share opinions and to make recommendations, which can cover what movies to see, what products to buy, and what political candidates to support.

Decades of studies have shown that something as seemingly simple as WOM can be more persuasive on people's buying decisions and political actions than expensive advertisements or mass media coverage (Beck, Dalton, Greene, and Huckfeldt, 2002; Goldsmith and Horowitz, 2006; Katz and Lazarsfeld, 1955). WOM can even make television advertisements more effective (Traylor and Mathias, 1983). It is for these reasons that many companies try to harness the power of WOM to create "buzz marketing" or "viral marketing campaigns" around their products. However, there has been no investigation into whether political leaders' tweets can generate viral marketing campaigns around candidates or issues. The following section examines what is known about WOM in terms of its history, applications, and effects.

A SHORT HISTORY OF RESEARCH RELATED TO WOM

The pioneering work of Katz and Lazarsfeld (1955), Lazarsfeld, Berelson, and Gaudet (1948), and Rogers (1958) revealed how influential communication between people can be. Informal conversations that people have with their friends or acquaintances often can affect their subsequent purchasing or voting choices. Katz and Lazarsfeld (1955) used the term *opinion leaders* to describe those leaders in a person's social circle whose conversations can wield that kind of influential power. Of course, not everyone in a person's social network is equally as influential. In his research on why people choose to adopt new technology, Rogers (1958, 2003, pp. 282–285) divided society into five categories: innovators, early adopters, early majority, late majority, and laggards. Rogers discovered that those people who are early adopters are the most influential at convincing people to use new technology. Early adopters are the most likely people in society to both understand the value of the technology and be eager to spread the word about it to friends, family, acquaintances, and even strangers.

Later work by Gladwell (2000) found that three types of people (connectors, mavens, and salespeople) tend to be responsible for shaping opinions and spreading trends by word of mouth. Mavens are those people who have a lot of information, whether about products or politics, that they want to share with others. Salespeople are those who are especially adept at persuading others. Connector people are social butterflies and, as a result, have a social network of family, friends, and acquaintances that is far larger than the average person. To put connectors into perspective, research indicates that the average person usually has no more than about 150 people in their social network (Hill and Dunbar, 2003). However, the rise of the Internet and social networking websites has affected the size, scope, and influence of a person's social network (Tancer, 2008).

Other research suggests that it is not just a small band of highly connected individuals who can influence opinions. Moderately connected individuals are just as willing as the highly connected to engage in WOM (Smith, Coyle, Lightfoot, and Scott, 2007). The recommendations that happen in WOM can be positive, negative, or mixed, though research indicates that negative WOM spreads faster and is somewhat more effective than positive WOM (Knauer, 1992; Park and Lee, 2009). In addition, WOM can be effective whether the recommendations come spontaneously from people or whether the recommendations are orchestrated by an outside force, such as a company (Godes and Mayzlin, 2009). In terms of political Twitter use, this last idea is especially important because it suggests that political leaders can be proactive in using their tweets to generate a lot of interest in a campaign or an issue.

There are many effects of WOM in politics. WOM affects where people go online for political information (Parmelee, Davies, and McMahan, 2011). It can increase political learning (Kennamer, 1990) and can lead to political participation (McLeod, Scheufele, and Moy, 1999). The learning that occurs can be particularly useful for democracy when WOM takes place among people of differing political views. Such conversations help people to understand views that differ from theirs and help to promote civility (Price, Cappella, and Nir, 2002).

So what are the effects of WOM, in terms of political tweets? The effects are potentially very powerful if followers regularly retweet political leaders' messages to their followers. Doing so would help leaders spread their message far wider than they could do on their own. While research has not focused on this issue in regard to political tweets, one survey of Twitter users found that 53 percent have retweeted (Smith and Rainie, 2010). Also, a study of 1.2 billion tweets found that less than 30 percent of the tweets generated a reaction, such as replying or retweeting (Sysomos, 2010b). More research is needed to discover whether replying to (or retweeting) political tweets are rare or regular effects. Even if followers rarely share political leaders' tweets via retweeting, such tweets can still have strong effects. Leaders' tweets may cause followers to look for information recommended in a tweet (such as a website or book) or to take actions that are requested in a tweet (such as sign a petition, vote, or contribute money to a candidate). At this point it is not clear how often political leaders' tweets create these kinds of effects.

WOM AND EWOM

While WOM traditionally relied on face-to-face conversations, the popularity of the Internet and the ubiquity of mobile devices have lead researchers to broaden WOM's definition. WOM can happen via cell phones, smart phones, and personal computers. Researchers also have found that these newer platforms for conducting WOM often facilitate different outcomes than are found via face-to-face WOM. For example, mobile-based WOM can elicit in a person a stronger willingness to make referrals than face-to-face WOM (Okazaki, 2009a). WOM that is conducted via electronic means of communication is called electronic word-of-mouth communication (eWOM).

There are significant differences between the nature of traditional WOM and eWOM, both in terms of convenience and reach. Thus eWOM is potentially more influential than face-to-face WOM. For example, eWOM from a mobile Internet device can occur virtually anywhere and at anytime. Because the Internet allows for asynchronous communication, senders and receivers of eWOM do not need to worry about finding the right time to interact. In addition, eWOM that happens on websites such as blogs and customer review sites can reach millions of people at once. Those people then can post public feedback in ways that broaden or reinforce the comments they read on these sites. Political tweets, which are a type of eWOM, may benefit from these advantages and features.

Research on candidate blogs found that such sites have persuasive effects when users feel that they are getting the opportunity to share and interact with the candidate and other politically interested individuals (Thorson and Rodgers, 2006). Twitter, with such features as replying and retweeting, also provides the perception of interactivity. However, not all locations where eWOM takes place are equally able to persuade. For instance, product recommendations found on personal blogs are less likely to lead to product referrals than recommendations found on independent review websites or the brand's own website (Lee and Youn, 2009). In other words, receivers of eWOM do consider where they saw the information when deciding whether to pass it on to others. As a result, those people who want to be opinion leaders need to choose carefully where they place their eWOM.

TYPES OF SOCIAL TIES

While opinion leaders can be hard to identify (Weimann, Tustin, Vuuren, and Joubert, 2007), they are found in three areas of a person's social contacts: strong ties, weak ties, and nonexistent ties. Strong ties include a person's family and friends—individuals with whom a person has close and frequent dealings. Weak ties include a person's co-workers and other acquaintances, and their interactions are far less frequent and intimate. The term *nonexistent ties* refers to virtual strangers. While one would expect that WOM from a person's strong ties could influence their behavior, actually all types of social ties are able to do so (Brown and Reingen, 1987; Friedkin, 1980; Granovetter, 1973; Steffes and Burgee, 2009).

But which type of social tie is the most influential? The answer is murky. Studies show that each tie can be better than the others, in certain situations. For example, strong ties have several advantages over weak ties, because strong ties are more available, more likely to be used as a source of information, more likely to influence decision making, and more credible in the eyes of people than weak ties (Brown and Reingen, 1987; Granovetter 1983; Wee, Lim, and Lwin, 1995).

However, weak ties are sometimes beneficial. Weak ties serve an important bridging function that allows information to travel from one group to another (Brown and Reingen, 1987, p. 350). A clear example is found in research by Stanford sociologist Mark Granovetter. In a study on how people get jobs, Granovetter (1973) found that communication from weak ties, such as an old college friend or former employer, was frequently more useful in gaining employment than communication from strong ties. Why is this true? Ironically, it is true because weak ties allow one to reach a larger audience than can be reached through one's close-knit strong ties. Furthermore, weak ties are at least as influential as strong ties when it comes to the speed of disseminating information (Goldenberg, Libai, and Muller, 2001).

In terms of nonexistent ties, research indicates that even a source who is completely anonymous can sometimes be more influential on decision making than strong or weak ties. For instance, Steffes and Burgee (2009) asked college students to identify those social ties who were the best at influencing their decisions of which professors to choose. Interestingly, anonymous comments posted on a website that rates professors were more influential to students than conversations they had with friends or academic advisers.

There are two definitions of the concept of *tie strength*. In drawing a distinction between strong and weak ties, Granovetter (1973, p. 1361) writes: "The strength of a tie is a (probably linear) combination of the amount of time, the emotional intensity, the intimacy (mutual confiding), and the reciprocal services that characterizes the tie." Walker, Wasserman, and Wellman (1994) believe that strong ties are characterized by these factors:

> (a) a sense that the relationship is intimate and special, with a voluntary investment in the tie and a desire for companionship with the partner; (b) an interest in frequent interactions in multiple contexts; and (c) a sense of mutuality of the relationship, with the partner's needs known and supported. (p. 57)

By these definitions, political leaders' tweets would almost never be considered as coming from a strong tie source. This situation is because "tie strength" refers to the nature of the relationship between the sender and receiver of a message, not whether the message was delivered on Twitter (or even face-to-face, for that matter). Unless a follower happens to be a personal friend of a leader, and they are frequently communicating and responding to one another on Twitter or by some other means, there is no mutual confiding or companionship. It is therefore more accurate to characterize political tweets as coming from a nonexistent tie, because the overwhelming majority of followers have likely never interacted with the leaders they follow. However, those leaders who are heavily involved in replying to their followers' tweets and soliciting their followers' advice might create among those followers just enough of a mutual relationship that the leader could be considered a weak tie.

Regardless of whether political tweets represent weak or nonexistent ties, past WOM research suggests that political tweets are not as influential on decision making as strong ties. On the other hand, because some eWOM research indicates that nonexistent ties can be more influential than strong ties when it comes to decision making (Steffes and Burgee, 2009), it is not clear how much power political tweets should be expected to have. Followers of political leaders' tweets need to be asked how influential those tweets are on their political views relative to other sources, such as family and acquaintances.

SOURCES: HOMOPHILOUS VERSUS HETEROPHILOUS

The influence of political leaders' tweets also may depend on the degree to which leaders and followers share similar political views. The extent to which two people share similar attributes (such as age, gender or socio-economic background) is called *homophily*. Past studies have found that people use information more when it comes from someone with a high level of homophily (a homophilous source), rather than from someone with a low level of homophily (called a *heterophilous* source; Brown and Reingen, 1987; Steffes and Burgee, 2009). Research also indicates that social media users form more connections with people who share a similar ethnicity, religion, or several other demographic and psychological factors (Thelwall, 2009).

In terms of political tweets, when a follower agrees with a leader politically, that leader is a homophilous source. When a follower disagrees with a leader politically, that leader is a heterophilous source. The expectation is that tweets from homophilous leaders are sought out more and are more influential on followers' political views than heterophilous leaders' tweets, although research is needed to confirm this assumption.

It would be interesting to know how tweets from homophilous and heterophilous leaders compare in influence to strong and weak tie sources, such as family and acquaintances. Finding out might help reveal the distinctions between homophily and tie strength, which are separate but related concepts (Steffes and Burgee, 2009). For example, someone who follows tweets from a political leader who has a similar ideology to theirs (a homophilous and nonexistent tie) may find those tweets more influential on their political views than political conversations with a parent who is ideologically different (a heterophilous and strong tie). If this assumption is true, the finding would further show that strong ties are often not the most powerful ties, especially in the age of the Internet and social networking sites.

LINKING WOM TO MOTIVATIONS, DEMOGRAPHICS, AND POLITICAL FACTORS

Research reveals that often the decision to engage in WOM or eWOM is driven by other variables, such as communication motivations, demographics, and political and psychological factors. Social motives, for example, can trigger eWOM behavior, such as communicating by e-mail, consumer opinion websites, and mobile devices (Phelps, Lewis, Mobilio, Perry, and Raman, 2004; Hennig-Thurau, Gwinner, Walsh, and Gremler, 2004; Okazaki, 2009b). Having concern for others and a need for enjoyment also can lead to eWOM (Yoo and Gretzel, 2008). No study as yet has looked for a link between people's motives for following political leaders' tweets and their political WOM behavior.

Psychological and political factors are another trigger of WOM. *Identification* refers to a person's feeling of oneness with a product or organization. This feeling exerts significant influence on engaging in positive WOM (Brown, Barry, Dacin, and Gunst, 2005). In terms of political tweets, it may be that followers who have ideological identification with a leader are more apt to take part in eWOM on that leader's behalf. In addition, those followers on the far ends of the ideological spectrum tend to talk politics the most (Pan, Shen, Paek, and Sun, 2006), which suggests that they may also tweet about politics the most.

Demographic factors have been explored for possible effects on WOM behavior (Podoshen, 2008). In some cases, for example, women are more likely than men to engage in eWOM (Phelps et al., 2004). Research connecting demographics and political WOM is lacking in this area.

QUANTITATIVE AND QUALITATIVE WAYS TO EXPLORE THE IMPACT OF POLITICAL TWEETS

WOM has been examined using many methods, with surveys being especially popular as a technique. Surveys have been used to quantitatively measure which social ties are most influential with their WOM (Steffes and Burgee, 2009), to rank which motives most trigger WOM (Okazaki, 2009b), and to gauge the degree to which demographic, political, and psychological factors act as antecedents to WOM (Phelps et al., 2004; Podoshen, 2008; Sun, Seounmi, Guohua, and Mana, 2006).

Surveys rely on a top-down approach. Researchers begin with preset definitions of the concepts that they are examining, such as what constitutes a weak, strong, or nonexistent tie. They then calculate how often they find these predefined concepts in their data. One limitation of this approach is that the findings are only as accurate as the concept definitions that the researcher brings to the study. For example, the definition of *tie strength* is particularly open to interpretation when it comes to tweets from political leaders. Most followers may consider such tweets to be coming from nonexistent or weak ties. Some followers might even say that such tweets come from strong ties. This situation is especially plausible for followers who use leaders' tweets to have *parasocial interaction*. That type of interaction refers to the illusion of intimacy that people sometimes have with celebrities and politicians (Thorson and Rodgers, 2006). Discovering followers' definitions of *tie strength* is something best-suited for a qualitative method, such as in-depth interviews. In-depth interviews use a bottom-up approach and open-ended questions. With no preset definitions in mind, interview participants are allowed and encouraged to describe in their own words the nature of the relationship they have with the leaders they follow, as well as with other sources of political information, such as friends and family.

Rather than measure or rank various aspects of WOM, qualitative methods (such as in-depth interviews and focus groups) can use open-ended questions to explore the many reasons why people engage in WOM. Answers from participants have provided marketers and academics with an expanded understanding of the theoretical framework of WOM (Palka, Pousttchi, and Wiedemann, 2009). In one eWOM study, for example, researchers wanted to find out why some pass-along e-mails get forwarded from person to person, while others do not. *Pass-along e-mail* refers to the jokes, stories, and other information that are often sent to people by mass e-mails. Focus group participants were asked to describe the pass-along e-mails they received. Participants' answers gave researchers a better idea of when and why such e-mail is forwarded or deleted (Phelps et al., 2004). One of the study's findings was that "messages that spark strong emotion—humor, fear, sadness, or inspiration—are likely to be forwarded," so message developers "should consider crafting messages consistent with those particularly viral strains that are most appropriate to their cause" (p. 345). Political tweets share much in common with pass-along e-mail: Both can be influential when forwarded (or retweeted) many times. Asking followers to describe political tweets that they have acted upon would expand what is known about why some tweets go viral and others are ignored.

RESEARCH QUESTIONS ANSWERED IN THIS CHAPTER

Because so much is unknown regarding how political tweets are used as WOM, there are many questions to be asked specific to the political arena. Much research has been done generally on WOM, eWOM, tie strength, and homophily. The research questions examined in this chapter (shown in the following list of questions and hypotheses) borrow from that general research and connect it specifically to political leaders' tweets. In this book, these questions are answered using survey and in-depth interview data. The methods used are meant to measure the effects of political tweets on followers, compare those effects with other forms of WOM, and explore the many ways in which followers are influenced by the political tweets they receive.

- Question 1: How influential are political tweets in persuading followers to engage in subsequent activity? (Actions could include the following: to reply to a political leader's tweet, to retweet a political tweet, to look for information recommended in a political tweet, or to take other actions that are requested in a political leader's tweet, such as vote or make a financial contribution.)
- Question 2: To what degree are political variables (interest in politics, political efficacy, trust in government, past voting behavior, likelihood of voting, party registration, and political ideology) and demographics (gender, age, race, income, and education) related to a follower's willingness to engage in subsequent activity?
- Question 3: To what degree are motives for following a political leader on Twitter related to a follower's willingness to engage in subsequent activity?
- Question 4: When it comes to shaping followers' political views, how influential are social ties? Social ties include these types: Friend and family (strong ties), co-workers and acquaintances (weak ties), tweets from political leaders they usually agree with politically (homophilous nonexistent or weak tie), and tweets from political leaders they usually do not agree with politically (heterophilous nonexistent or weak tie).
- Hypothesis 1: Tweets from political leaders with whom followers usually politically agree (homophilous nonexistent or weak tie) are more influential on followers' political views than tweets from political leaders with whom they usually do not politically agree (heterophilous nonexistent or weak tie).
- Hypothesis 2: Friends and family (strong ties) are more influential on followers' political views than the following other sources: co-workers and acquaintances (weak ties), tweets from political leaders with whom they usually politically agree (homophilous nonexistent or weak tie), and tweets

from political leaders with whom they usually do not politically agree (heterophilous nonexistent or weak tie).

- Hypothesis 3: Co-workers and acquaintances (weak ties) will be less influential on followers' political views than tweets from political leaders with whom they usually politically agree (homophilous nonexistent or weak tie). But co-workers and acquaintances will be more influential than tweets from political leaders with whom they usually do not politically agree (heterophilous nonexistent or weak tie).
- Question 5: To what degree are political variables and demographics related to the types of social ties that influence the political views of followers?
- Question 6: To what degree are people's motives for following political leaders on Twitter related to the types of social ties that influence their political views?
- Question 7: Do actions taken and the influence of social ties differ for those people following current elected officials only, versus all others?
- Question 8: What makes a political leader's tweet persuasive?
- Question 9: What is the nature of the relationship that participants have with the political leaders they follow?

METHODS USED TO ANSWER THE RESEARCH QUESTIONS

Survey

The effects of political tweets on followers were examined by asking respondents how often they engaged in the following activities: "reply to a political leader's tweet," "retweet a political leader's tweet," "look for information that the political leader's tweet recommended to you (for example, look at a recommended website, or blog, or book, or article)," and "take action that was requested in a political leader's tweet (for example, sign a petition, take part in a protest, vote, or contribute to a candidate)." Respondents chose one of the following answers for each item: "never," "rarely," "sometimes," "often," or "always." Their motives for following political leaders on Twitter, as well as concepts such as political efficacy and trust in government, were examined using questions that were derived from previous research (Ancu and Cozma, 2009; Kaye and Johnson, 2004; Kaye, 2005). Those definitions, as well as the survey sample characteristics, are discussed in detail in the methods section of Chapter 2 on the uses and gratifications of political Twitter use. That chapter also explains how the study defined and measured a person's interest in politics, likelihood of voting, political ideology, past voting behavior, party registration, and demographics.

The study compared the influence of political leaders' tweets with other sources of political information. Respondents were asked to rank, on a 5-point scale (1 = very unimportant; 5 = very important), "the importance that each has in influencing your political views." Their choices were the following: "friend," "family" (strong ties), "co-workers," "acquaintances" (weak ties), "tweets from political leaders who you usually agree with politically" (homophilous nonexistent or weak tie), and "tweets from political leaders who you usually do not agree with politically" (heterophilous nonexistent or weak tie). The "friend" and "family" selections were combined to form a 2-item additive index of strong ties and had a Cronbach's alpha of 0.78. The "co-worker" and "acquaintance" selections were also combined to form a 2-item index of weak ties (Cronbach's alpha = 0.79). Definitions of *tie strength* and *homophily* were based on past WOM and eWOM studies (Brown and Reingen, 1987; Granovetter, 1973; Steffes and Burgee, 2009; Walker et al., 1994).

Data Analysis

Data from the survey were examined by calculating frequencies and mean scores for each of the measures and conducting appropriate statistical analyses. Question 1 was addressed by analyzing frequency percentages for each method of active engagement. Correlation and hierarchical regression were performed to answer Questions 2 and 3 and to identify demographic (first block), political (second block), and motivational (third block) predictors of subsequent activity. Question 4 (with its three hypotheses) was addressed by looking at the order of influence for each of the social ties (frequency percentages). Correlation and hierarchical regression were used to examine Questions 5 and 6 in order to identify demographic (first block), political (second block), and motivational (third block) predictors of influential social ties. An independent samples *t*-test and ANOVA were then used to further investigate demographic mean differences. Question 7 was assessed using an independent samples *t*-test to investigate the differences in mean scores for those people following only elected officials, versus all others.

The results are shown in Tables 3.1 through 3.7. Table 3.1 shows the Pearson Correlation Matrix for demographics, political attitudes, and action items. Table 3.2 provides the hierarchical regression analyses predicting actions taken by followers of political leaders on Twitter. Table 3.3 lists the Pearson Correlations for people's motivations and action items. Table 3.4 shows the Pearson Correlation Matrix for demographics, political attitudes, and influence of social ties. Table 3.5 provides the hierarchical regression analyses predicting influential social ties for followers of political leaders on Twitter.

Table 3.6 lists the Pearson Correlations for people's motivations and the influence of social ties. In Table 3.7, t-tests results are shown that compare action and social ties influence; the table shows the mean scores for those people following only elected officials, versus all others.

In-depth Interviews

The survey questions measured how influential political leaders' tweets are on followers' actions and views. Thus the in-depth interview questions were designed to reveal what qualities of a political tweet give it such power. Specifically, the in-depth interviews answer Questions 8 and 9; and interviews elaborate on Questions 1 and 4. Question 1 asks about the influence of political tweets in persuading followers to engage in subsequent activity, such as replying to a political leader's tweet, retweeting, looking for recommended information, and voting. In-depth interview participants were asked to explain in detail what makes some political tweets so persuasive: "Think of a tweet from a political leader that really influenced you to take some action (like retweeting the information to others, or visiting a recommended Web site, or voting for a particular candidate). Please take me step-by-step through that tweet and explain what made it so influential to you."

In-depth interview participants also expanded on Question 4, which examines the influence of friends, family, co-workers, and political leaders' tweets on followers' political views. Because tie strength with regard to leaders' tweets is relatively difficult to define, participants were asked to compare such tweets with strong ties. They were asked: "What other sources of information are more or less influential on your political views? Compared to friends and family? Why?" The follow-up questions generated the most insight into the relationship that participants have with the political leaders they follow, and the effects that the leaders' tweets have on them. One probe asked, "What's the nature of the relationship you have with the leaders you follow?"

RESULTS

Survey

The results of the survey data analysis reveal that political tweets do heavily influence followers' actions. Looking for recommended information is the most common activity that followers report; the least common activity reported is replying directly to a leader's tweet. Activity varies significantly by several demographic and political variables, but the strongest relationships are noted when correlated with the followers' motivations.

Followers of political leaders on Twitter are influenced by a variety of social ties. Interestingly, tweets from political leaders with whom followers usually politically agree (homophilous tie) were as influential on followers' political views as their family (although not their friends). Further, such tweets were the most influential social tie for several demographic groups, including women, those respondents over 40 years old, and those respondents earning $100,000 or less. The following paragraphs describe each of the findings for the research questions and hypotheses under analysis.

Influence of Tweets on Subsequent Action

Question 1 addressed the influence of political tweets in persuading followers to engage in subsequent activity. The results from the survey sample reveal that respondents engage in an assortment of actions with varied intensity. The most frequent activity in response to a political tweet involves looking for specific information that the political leader's tweet recommended, such as a blog, book, or website (M = 3.5 on a 5-point scale; SD = 0.77). Over half of the respondents indicated that they often (or always) looked for information suggested by the political leader. Almost 90 percent of the sample indicated looking for recommended information at least sometimes. The next most-engaging activities involve taking a specific action such as signing a petition or voting (M = 2.7, SD = 0.99) and retweeting the political leader's message (M = 2.7, SD = 0.97). Both retweeting and taking actions garnered high numbers, with more than 60 percent of respondents indicating doing so at least sometimes. The least-frequent activity noted among the sample was replying directly to a political leader's tweet (M = 2.2, SD = 0.98). Over 64 percent of those people surveyed indicated that they rarely (to never) reply to a political leader's tweet.

Relationship between Actions and Demographic or Political Variables

Question 2 investigated the degree to which political variables and demographics were related to an individual's willingness to engage in subsequent activity. A variety of significant correlations emerged and can be viewed in Table 3.1. With respect to demographic variables, gender (female coded higher) was significantly related to the choice to retweet ($r = 0.12, p < 0.05$), to look for information ($r = 0.13, p < 0.05$), and to take suggested action ($r = 0.17, p < 0.01$). Age also appeared to have a positive relationship with choosing to reply ($r = 0.16, p < 0.01$); but age had a negative relationship with choosing to retweet information ($r = -0.10, p < 0.05$). Education had a negative relationship with almost all action items under analysis, the strongest being for retweeting a message ($r = -0.16, p < 0.01$).

Table 3.1   Pearson Correlation Matrix for Demographics, Political Attitudes, and Action Items

	Reply to Tweet	Retweet	Look for Information	Take Suggested Action
Action Items				
Reply to Tweet		0.489**	0.138**	0.346**
Retweet			0.221**	0.379**
Look for information				0.359**
Demographics				
Gender (female higher)	0.036	0.116*	0.126*	0.171**
Age	0.158**	−0.103*	0.068	0.023
Race (Caucasian higher)	−0.067	−0.091	−0.024	−0.031
HH*** income	0.019	0.001	−0.010	−0.056
Education	−0.112*	−0.160**	−0.085	−0.121*
Political Attitudes				
Political interest	0.127**	0.186**	0.122**	0.081
Ideology (liberal higher)	−0.147**	−0.066	−0.047	0.070
Trust	−0.077	0.052	0.081	0.022
Efficacy	0.090*	0.113*	0.030	−0.015
Vote likelihood	0.129**	0.085*	0.050	0.155**
Past voter	0.097*	−0.005	0.072	0.059
Democrat (not Ind/other)	−0.121**	−0.036	−0.023	0.105*
Republican (not Ind/other)	0.133**	0.127**	0.018	−0.014

Note: Party identification was represented as three dummy variables with Independent/other serving as the reference group for Democrat and Republican.
*$p < 0.05$; **$p < 0.01$; ***HH = Household.

Political attitudes were related to the choice to take action in response to a political leader's tweet (refer to Table 3.1). The strongest relationships were with the factors of political interest and likelihood to vote. Interest was significantly related to choosing to reply ($r = 0.13$, $p < 0.01$), to retweet ($r = 0.19$, $p < 0.01$), and to look for further information ($r = 0.12$, $p < 0.01$). Those respondents more likely to vote were also likely to reply ($r = 0.13$, $p < 0.01$), to retweet ($r = 0.09$, $p < 0.05$), and to take suggested action ($r = 0.16$, $p < 0.01$) in response to a political tweet. Efficacy was positively related to choosing to both reply ($r = 0.09$, $p < 0.05$) and retweet ($r = 0.11$, $p < 0.05$).

Interestingly, those respondents with a more conservative ideology and who were Republican were more willing to reply to a tweet ($p < 0.01$). Being a Republican also was significantly correlated with a willingness to retweet ($r = 0.13$, $p < 0.01$), while being a Democrat was significantly correlated with a willingness to take a suggested action ($r = 0.11$, $p < 0.05$) in response to a tweet.

The combination of both demographic and political variables was entered into a hierarchical regression analysis to determine their predictive power. Many of the previously noted correlations were weak, yet their combined impact was noteworthy when added to the regression analysis. Several factors emerged as significant predictors of the action items under examination (see Table 3.2). The demographic block accounted for 5.1 percent of the variance in taking suggested action and 4.8 percent of the variance in deciding to reply to a political leader's tweet. Gender (female) specifically remained a predictor of willingness to retweet ($b = 0.23$, $p < 0.01$) and to take suggested action ($b = 0.23$, $p < 0.05$). An older age also predicted a willingness to reply ($b = 0.15$, $p < 0.01$). Race and education were negative predictors of choosing to reply ($b = -0.31$, $p < 0.01$) and retweet respectively ($b = -.11$, $p < 0.05$). The political attitudes block similarly accounted for a 7.5 percent variance in choosing to retweet and a 5 percent variance in choosing to reply to a tweet. Political interest emerged as a significant predictor of the willingness to retweet ($b = 0.08$, $p > 05$), and trust predicted searching for more information ($b = 0.09$, $p < 0.01$).

Relationship between Actions and Motivations

Question 3 assessed the degree to which peoples' motives for following a political leader on Twitter related to their willingness to engage in subsequent activity. A correlation analysis was performed to assess significant relationships. Table 3.3 summarizes the findings. Motivations appeared to have a stronger association with action items than demographic or political variables. Social utility and self-expression motivations were significantly related to all of the action variables assessed ($p < 0.01$). Entertainment motivations were positively associated with the willingness to retweet ($r = .09$, $p<.05$) or to look for information ($r = 0.12$, $p < 0.01$). But the factor of entertainment negatively related to the willingness to reply ($r = -0.07$, $p < 0.05$). Information/Guidance motivations were related to both choosing to look for information ($r = 0.27$, $p < 0.01$) and taking suggested action ($r = 0.31$, $p < 0.01$). Convenience motivations were significantly associated with looking for more information ($r = 0.26$, $p < 0.01$) and taking specific actions suggested by a political leader's tweet ($r = 0.10$, $p < 0.05$).

Chapter 3

Table 3.2 Hierarchical Regression Analyses Predicting Actions Taken by Followers of Political Leaders on Twitter

Independent Variables	Actions							
	Reply to Tweet		Retweet		Look for Information		Take Action Suggested	
	B	SE	B	SE	B	SE	B	SE
Demographics								
Gender	0.07	0.08	0.23**	0.09	0.12	0.08	0.23*	0.09
Age	.15**	.06	−0.09	0.06	0.10	0.05	0.04	0.06
Race	−.31**	.12	−0.23	0.12	−0.07	0.11	−0.10	0.13
HH*** income	−.01	.04	0.05	0.04	−0.00	0.04	−0.01	0.04
Education	−.07	.05	−0.11*	0.05	−0.07	0.04	−0.06	0.05
$R^2(\%) =$	4.8**		3.9**		2.6		5.1**	
Political Antecedents								
Politicalinterest	0.02	0.03	0.08*	0.04	0.06	0.03	0.05	0.04
Ideology	−0.01	0.02	0.01	0.02	−0.02	0.02	0.03	0.02
Trust	0.03	0.04	0.05	0.04	0.09**	0.03	0.05	0.04
Efficacy	0.06	0.08	0.00	0.09	−0.05	0.08	−0.08	0.09
Vote likelihood	0.03	0.03	0.04	0.03	−0.02	0.03	0.06	0.03
Past voter	0.05	0.22	−0.39	0.22	0.31	0.20	−0.22	0.24
Democrat	−0.11	0.12	−0.12	0.12	−0.04	0.11	0.10	0.13
Republican	−0.00	0.13	0.20	0.14	−0.12	0.12	0.03	0.15
Incremental $R^2(\%) =$	5.0**		7.5**		3.9		4.1*	
Motivations								
Social utility	0.13**	0.04	0.34**	0.05	0.03	0.04	0.03	0.05
Entertainment	−0.07	0.04	−0.07	0.04	0.01	0.04	−0.03	0.05
Self-expression	0.47**	0.04	0.25**	0.05	0.04	0.04	0.35**	0.05
Info/Guidance	−0.06	0.04	−0.04	0.04	0.12**	0.03	0.17**	0.04
Convenience	−0.11*	0.05	−0.02	0.05	0.15**	0.04	0.01	0.05
Incremental $R^2(\%) =$	29.6**		23.9**		10.3**		20.1**	
Total $R^2(\%) =$	39.4**		35.3**		16.8**		29.3**	

Note: Female was coded higher for Gender. Caucasian was coded higher for Race. Liberal was coded higher for Ideology. Party identification was represented as three dummy variables with Independents/other serving as the reference group for Democrat and Republican.

*$p < 0.05$; **$p < 0.01$; ***HH = Household.

Table 3.3   Pearson Correlations for Motivations and Action Items

	Reply to Tweet	Retweet	Look for Information	Take Suggested Action
Motivations				
Social utility	0.284**	0.471**	0.143**	0.217**
Entertainment	−0.068*	0.086*	0.122**	0.068
Self-expression	0.564**	0.426**	0.141**	0.435**
Info/Guidance	0.056	0.062	0.266**	0.311**
Convenience	−0.076	0.074	0.264**	0.103*

Note: $*p < 0.05$; $**p < 0.01$.

Hierarchical regression was used to analyze the combined predictive power of all variables including demographics, political items, and motivational items (refer to Table 3.2). The results indicate that the motivation block accounted for more variance overall. Motivations alone explain 29.6 percent of the variance in willingness to reply, 23.9 percent of the variance in choosing to retweet, 20.1 percent of the variance in deciding to take suggested action, and 10.3 percent of the variance in choosing to look for more information in response to a tweet. The combined model including all demographic, political, and motivational factors notably explains 39.4 percent of the variance in reply, 35.3 percent of the variance in retweet, 29.3 percent of the variance in taking action, and 16.8 percent of the variance in deciding to look for more information. A few specific motivational variables stood out for their influence in the regression model. For example, social-utility motivations significantly predicted a willingness to reply ($b = 0.13$, $p < 0.01$) and to retweet ($b = 0.34$, $p < 0.01$) a political leader's message. Self-expression predicted choosing to reply ($b = 0.47$, $p < 0.01$), to retweet ($b = 0.25$, $p < 0.01$), and to take suggested action ($b = 0.35$, $p < .01$).

Influence of Social Ties

Question 4 addressed the influence of social ties in shaping followers' political views. A variety of social influences were evaluated for their impact, including friends, family, co-workers, acquaintances, homophilous political leaders' tweets, as well as heterophilous political leaders' tweets. Friends and family were combined to represent "strong ties," and co-workers and acquaintances were combined to represent "weak ties." Results indicate that strong ties are the most influential when it comes to shaping political views ($M = 3.2$ on a 5-point scale; $SD = 1.1$). Mean scores are similar when viewed

Table 3.4 Pearson Correlation Matrix for Demographics, Political Attitudes, and Influence of Social Ties

	Strong Ties	Weak Ties	Homophilous Ties	Heterophilous Ties
Influence of Ties				
Strong ties		0.567**	0.240**	0.123*
Weak ties			0.169**	0.136**
Homophilous ties				0.494**
Demographics				
Gender (female higher)	−0.001	−0.046	0.138**	0.043
Age	−0.187**	−0.076	−0.028	0.015
Race (Caucasian higher)	−0.018	−0.086	−0.011	−0.078
HH*** Income	−0.011	−0.009	−0.145**	−0.082
Education	0.030	−0.062	−0.090	−0.060
Political Attitudes				
Political interest	−0.112*	−0.029	−0.060	−0.094*
Ideology (liberal higher)	0.059	0.033	0.053	0.021
Trust	0.100*	0.127**	0.100*	0.018
Efficacy	−0.088*	−0.033	−0.059	−0.103*
Vote likelihood	−0.021	−0.029	0.073	0.084
Past voter	0.008	−0.067	0.013	0.055
Democrat (not Ind/other)	0.110*	0.072	0.131**	0.025
Republican (not Ind/other)	−0.087*	−0.086*	−0.043	−0.105*

Note: Party identification was represented as three dummy variables with Independent/other serving as the reference group for Democrat and Republican.
*$p < 0.05$; **$p < 0.01$; ***HH = Household.

distinctly (friends M = 3.2, and family M = 3.1). Almost 50 percent of the sample reported that the influence of strong ties was "somewhat" to "very" important. However, political leaders with whom respondents usually politically agree (classified as homophilous ties) were just as influential on respondents' political views as their family (both had a mean score of 3.1). The least influential of the social ties under scrutiny appeared to be the heterophilous ties, designated as those political leaders with whom respondents politically disagree (M = 2.5 on a 5-point scale; SD = 1.2).

The following analysis of hypotheses reveals the overall order of influence for all four social ties.

Table 3.5 Hierarchical Regression Analyses Predicting Influential Social Ties for Followers of Political Leaders on Twitter

Independent Variables	Influence of Social Ties							
	Strong Ties		Weak Ties		Homophilous Ties		Heterophilous Ties	
	B	SE	B	SE	B	SE	B	SE
Demographics								
Gender	−0.09	0.12	−0.12	0.11	0.19	0.12	−0.04	0.12
Age	−0.24**	0.08	−0.03	0.08	0.15*	0.08	0.07	0.08
Race	−0.00	0.17	−0.26	0.16	−0.08	0.16	−0.22	0.18
HH*** income	0.05	0.06	0.03	0.05	−0.11*	0.05	−0.02	0.06
Education	0.08	0.07	−0.06	0.06	−0.03	0.06	0.00	0.07
$R^2(\%)$ =	5.3**		2.1		4.4**		1.3	
Political Antecedents								
Political interest	−0.08	0.05	−0.02	0.05	−0.09	0.05	−0.07	0.05
Ideology	−0.05	0.03	−0.05	0.03	−0.03	0.03	−0.04	0.03
Trust	0.04	0.05	0.10	0.05	0.12*	0.05	0.06	0.06
Efficacy	−0.15	0.12	−0.10	0.11	−0.04	0.11	−0.14	0.12
Vote likelihood	−0.01	0.04	0.01	0.04	0.03	0.04	0.07	0.05
Past voter	0.10	0.31	−0.31	0.29	−0.29	0.30	0.06	0.32
Democrat	0.19	0.16	0.15	0.16	0.37*	0.16	−0.10	0.17
Republican	−0.24	0.19	−0.28	0.18	−0.06	0.18	−0.55**	0.20
Incremental $R^2(\%)$ =	2.4		2.4		3.4		3.6	
Motivations								
Social utility	0.10	0.06	0.14*	0.06	0.17**	0.06	0.05	0.07
Entertainment	0.11	0.06	0.09	0.06	0.09	0.06	0.12	0.06
Self-expression	0.03	0.06	−0.05	0.06	0.24**	0.06	0.09	0.07
Info/Guidance	0.04	0.05	0.02	0.05	0.18**	0.05	0.25**	0.06
Convenience	−0.12	0.06	−0.05	0.06	0.00	0.06	−0.13*	0.07
Incremental $R^2(\%)$ =	2.7*		2.4		15.6**		8.2**	
Total $R^2(\%)$ =	10.4**		6.9		23.3**		13.1**	

Note: Female was coded higher for Gender. Caucasian was coded higher for Race. Liberal was coded higher for Ideology. Party identification was represented as three dummy variables with Independents/other serving as the reference group for Democrat and Republican. $*p < 0.05$; $**p < 0.01$; ***HH = Household.

Hypothesis 1 asserts that tweets from political leaders with whom follow-ers agree (homophilous ties) are more influential than tweets from political leaders with whom they disagree (heterophilous ties). The results indicate support for Hypothesis 1 because the mean scores for homophilous ties (M = 3.1, SD = 1.2) are higher than that of heterophilous influences (M = 2.5, SD = 1.2).

Hypothesis 2 posits that strong ties (friends and family) are more influ-ential on political views than weak ties (co-workers and acquaintances), or tweets from homophilous and heterophilous ties. Findings support the asser-tion of Hypothesis 2 because the mean scores for strong ties (M = 3.2) are higher than all other ties examined (weak M = 2.5, homophilous M = 3.1, heterophilous M = 2.5).

Hypothesis 3 contends that weak ties (co-workers and acquaintances) are less influential than homophilous ties (agreeable), but more influential than heterophilous ties (disagreeable). Results show that weak ties indeed have a smaller mean score (M = 2.5) than the influence of homophilous ties (M = 3.1). Results also indicate equal mean scores for weak and heterophilous ties (M = 2.5). Interestingly, when the means are analyzed before rounding, they do reveal the hypothesized influence (weak M = 2.49 and heterophilous M = 2.47). Therefore, Hypothesis 3 is supported.

Relationship between the Influence of Social Ties and Demographic or Political Variables

Question 5 addressed the degree to which demographic and political vari-ables are related to the influence of various social ties. Several significant relationships were revealed (refer to Table 3.4). With respect to demographic variables, gender (females coded higher) was related to the influence of homophilous ties ($r = 0.14$, $p < 0.01$), as was household income ($r = -0.15$, $p < 0.01$). Females, specifically, were significantly more likely to be influenced by homophilous ties (M = 3.3) compared with all other influences, $t(411) = -2.82$, $p < 0.01$. Age had the strongest association and indicated a negative relationship with the influence of strong ties ($r = -0.19$, $p < 0.01$). Mean scores were the highest for homophilous tweet influence for all respondents older than 40 (for ages 41–60, M = 3.2; for 61+, M = 2.9). Homophilous tweets were significantly more influential among respondents with education levels less a college degree, $F(3, 405) = 3.47$, $p < 0.05$. Homophilous tweets also were the most influential tie for Hispanic respondents (M = 2.9) and those people with an income of $100,000 or less (less than $25,000, M = 3.3; $25,000–$65,000, M = 3.3; $65,001–$100,000, M = 3.0).

Several political attitudes were significantly related to the influence of various social ties (refer to Table 3.4). Trust was positively associated with influences from ties that were strong ($r = 0.10$, $p < 0.05$), weak ($r = 0.13$, $p < 0.01$), and homophilous ($r = 0.10$, $p < 0.05$). Political interest and efficacy had negative relationships with influences that were strong ($r = -0.11$ and $r = 0.09$, $p < 0.05$) and heterophilous ($r = -0.09$ and $r = -0.10$, $p < 0.05$), respectively. Partisanship also had some significant associations with influential ties. Democrats were positively related to influences from ties that were both strong ($r = 0.11$, $p < 0.05$) and homophilous ($r = 0.13$, $p < 0.01$). Republicans had a significant negative relationship with influences that were strong ($r = -0.09$, $p < 0.05$), weak ($r = -0.09$, $p < 0.05$), and ($r = -0.11$, $p < 0.05$).

The combined influence of demographic and political variables was entered into a hierarchical regression analysis to further investigate these variables' predictive power. A few significant predictors impacted the influence of social ties (as shown in Table 3.5). The demographic block alone accounted for a 4.4 percent variance in homophilous tie influence and a 5.3 percent variance in strong tie influence. An older age significantly predicted less influence from strong ties ($b = -0.24$, $p < 0.01$), but more influence from homophilous ties ($b = 0.15$, $p < 0.05$). Homophilous ties were significantly more influential on those people with lower household income ($b = -0.11$, $p < 0.05$). The political antecedent block revealed very few significant predictors. The factors of trust ($b = 0.12$, $p < 0.05$) and Democratic partisanship ($b = 0.37$, $p < 0.05$) predicted the positive influence of homophilous ties. Republican partisanship ($b = -0.55$, $p < 0.01$) predicted a negative influence from heterophilous ties.

Relationship between the Influence of Social Ties and Motivations

Question 6 examined the degree to which a person's motives for following a political leader on Twitter related to the types of social ties that influence his or her political views. A correlation analysis provided some significant findings (refer to Table 3.6). The influence of homophilous ties had the strongest association with all motivational variables ($p < 0.01$). The most notable factors were self-expression ($r = 0.31$), information/guidance ($r = 0.29$), and social utility ($r = 0.26$). Heterophilous ties also were related to the motivations of information/guidance ($r = 0.25$, $p < 0.01$), self-expression ($r = 0.14$, $p < 0.01$), entertainment ($r = 0.09$, $p < 0.05$), and social utility ($r = 0.09$, $p < 0.05$). The influence of strong ties (as well as weak ties) was associated with social utility ($r = 0.12$, $p < 0.01$) and entertainment motives ($r = 0.14$, $p < 0.01$; $r = 0.12$, $p < 0.05$), respectively.

Table 3.6 Pearson Correlations for Motivations and Influence of Social Ties

	Strong Ties	*Weak Ties*	*Homophilous Ties*	*Heterophilous Ties*
Motivations				
Social utility	0.122**	0.124**	0.264**	0.086*
Entertainment	0.142**	0.117*	0.156**	0.087*
Self-expression	0.041	−0.004	0.308**	0.141**
Info/Guidance	0.029	0.022	0.290**	0.251**
Convenience	−0.031	0.021	0.127**	−0.009

Note: $*p < 0.05$; $**p < 0.01$.

Hierarchical regression was used to examine the combined predictive power of all variables (including demographics, political items, and motivational items) on the influence of social ties (refer to Table 3.5). The motivation block alone accounted for a 15.6 percent variance ($p < 0.01$) in the influence of homophilous ties, 8.2 percent for heterophilous ties ($p < 0.01$), 2.7 percent for strong ties ($p < 0.05$), and 2.4 percent (n.s.) variance in the influence of weak ties. Some specific motivational variables also were significantly predictive. The social-utility motivation predicted influence from both weak ($b = 0.14$, $p < 0.05$) and homophilous ties ($b = 0.17$, $p < 0.01$). Self-expression motives predict influence from homophilous ties as well ($b = 0.24$, $p < 0.01$). Information/guidance motivations predict influence from both homophilous ($b = 0.18$, $p < 0.01$) and heterophilous ties ($b = 0.25$, $p < 0.01$). Convenience motivations predict a negative influence from heterophilous ties ($b = −0.13$, $p < 0.05$). The strongest variance explained (for the combined demographic, political, and motivation blocks) was for homophilous ties, at 23.3 percent ($p < 0.01$). Significant variance was also noted for the overall regression model, at 13.1 percent for heterophilous ties and 10.4 percent for strong ties ($p < 0.01$).

Differences in Actions and Influence for Those People Solely Following Elected Officials

Question 7 investigated the possible difference in actions and influence of social ties among those people who follow only currently elected officials, as opposed to all others. An independent samples t-test was performed, and some significant findings emerged for the action items. Respondents who chose to follow a mix of political leaders (as opposed to just elected officials) were more likely to reply to [$t(404)= −2.07$, $p < 0.05$] or to retweet

Table 3.7 *T*-tests Comparing Mean Scores for Action and Social Ties Influence for Those Following Only Elected Officials, versus All Others

Action/Influence	Mean (SD)	*t*
Reply to Tweet		
Follows only elected	1.9(0.96)	$t = -2.07^*$
Follows others	2.2(0.98)	
Retweet		
Follows only elected	2.4(1.0)	$t = -2.34^*$
Follows others	2.7(0.97)	
Look for Information		
Follows only elected	3.3(0.73)	$t = -1.41$
Follows others	3.5(0.78)	
Take Suggested Action		
Follows only elected	2.7(0.88)	$t = -0.155$
Follows others	2.7(1.0)	
Strong Ties Influence		
Follows only elected	3.1(1.3)	$t = -0.097$
Follows others	3.2(1.1)	
Weak Ties Influence		
Follows only elected	2.4(1.3)	$t = -0.745$
Follows others	2.5(1.1)	
Homophilous Ties Influence		
Follows only elected	3.3(1.3)	$t = 0.876$
Follows others	3.1(1.2)	
Heterophilous Ties Influence		
Follows only elected	2.5(1.3)	$t = 0.244$
Follows others	2.5(1.2)	

Note: $^*p < 0.05$; $^{**}p < 0.01$.

[t(401)= −2.34, $p < 0.05$] a political leader's message. There were no significant differences detected between the two groups when assessing the influence of social ties. (See Table 3.7.)

In-depth Interviews

As with the survey findings, comments from the in-depth interviews indicate that political leaders' tweets are quite influential on followers' actions and political views. The added value of the in-depth interviews for this study is that they explain why leaders' tweets have caused participants to take actions, such as clicking requested links, supporting candidates, contributing to campaigns, or retweeting. Finding out what makes leaders' tweets influential answers Question 8. Participants said political leaders are especially successful at influencing followers' actions and beliefs when a leader's tweet includes at least some of the following nine elements:

- It quickly gets to the point.
- It includes a specific call to action.
- It discusses issues that followers consider relevant.
- It includes information that is useful to followers' jobs.
- It includes links and hashtags that help followers search a topic more thoroughly.
- It provides a counterpoint to followers' beliefs.
- It discusses issues in a humorous way.
- It attempts to interact with followers.
- It includes claims that seem outrageous or incorrect.

As would be expected, tweets that include the last element on this list influence followers in ways that leaders likely do not want. The other eight elements, however, produce effects that leaders should find beneficial.

In-depth interview comments explain why followers rarely reply to a leader's tweet. Participants said there were two reasons for not replying. First, they may want to reply but they think that they will never get a response. Second, they have no desire to reply. Interviewed participants such as Michael, Esta, and Nancy said that political leaders have a reputation for not interacting with followers, which limits their desire to reply. When Michael was asked if he replies to leaders, he said: "Very seldom. I know people who do it. I know some people who do it with some success. I know more people who do it with little success." Esta said, "It's very hard, knowing that you're screaming at a wall or agreeing with a wall, and nobody is going to read it, or care, or whatever." Nancy said she is "not really convinced they read their replies, and there is very seldom a response." Other participants, such as James, simply have no interest in contacting the leaders they follow. "I'm taking what they've said and spreading it to my network," he said. "But I don't reply back or take it to the next level."

Several themes emerged from the interviews that provide insight into the relationship that followers have with political leaders, and how that relationship compares with more traditional sources in a person's social circle. These insights answer Question 9. Participants' comments show what type of social tie their leaders' tweets represent, and how the leaders' tweets compare in influence with strong social ties (such as friends and family) and weak ties (such as co-workers). With rare exception, participants have a nonexistent tie relationship with the political leaders they follow. Interestingly, though, participants often said leaders' tweets influence their political views as much (or more) than their friends and family. Comments also show a number of reasons why leaders' tweets are sometimes more influential on the followers' political views than strong or weak ties. A further explanation of these themes is given in the next few pages.

What Makes Political Leaders' Tweets Influential to Followers?

Participants said that one of Twitter's main attractions is that its simple format and 140-character messages allow followers to quickly scan a large volume of messages to find the ones that really matter to them. The tweets that speak to them politically or personally are the ones that then get read more thoroughly, acted upon, and passed on to others. However, tweets do not stand out to participants unless the messages being communicated can be easily understood during the initial scanning process. This situation means that tweets must quickly get to the point. According to participants such as Noel, vaguely worded tweets from political leaders fail to influence followers to take requested actions and/or to retweet:

> If they say, "Here's the latest photo," I say, "Photo of what? Why should I click on it? Why is it important? What is the relevancy? I don't know." So I won't click on it. But if it says something like: "Here's a photo of Michelle Obama in Anacostia in regards to her obesity program," then OK, guess what? I know what the photo is about, I'll click on it. In that sense, it has to have more information, not like, "Check me out here" or "See leaders' photo." That's what you'll sometimes see. Or, like, they'll say, "I voted on bill so and so." But it would be nice if they would provide a link and say this is what the bill is about. If I end up forwarding their links, retweeting their links, I end up having to do more legwork.

In addition to leaders' tweets being clearly worded, such tweets can benefit from the inclusion of a call to action, such as requesting that followers vote or contribute to a campaign. Cecily made a donation in a North Carolina primary race due to such a request in one candidate's tweet. She also retweeted the candidate's plea for funds. John said a tweet's call to action must be as specific as possible:

> If the message is "We want Democrats to go out and vote" or if there's a specific date, let's say, Nov. 2 in Georgia you have to go out and vote, I do retweet that because that's a date and information where people would realize that we have to do this.

While a leader's call to action is useful, participants said what matters more is for a leader's tweets to address issues that are relevant to the followers' political interests. Nancy said that she passed along information from one Obama administration tweet because the topic related to important economic changes that were impacting the political climate:

> I remember getting one from the White House about the three Detroit car companies posting a profit for the first time in many, many years. I went out and did some Googling and reading to confirm it, then tweeted this exciting news. It is exciting when we see positive things happening in this current environment, and I think we all get mired in the negative information, so I wanted to "herald" this.

Many participants said that the tweets that stood out and caused them to take action were the ones that included insight on issues that helped them to engage with others. Jon said the pragmatic messages in the tweets from Democratic Senator Arlen Specter, who had been a Republican senator for decades, persuaded him to tell his family to support Specter in the 2010 Pennsylvania primary:

> I am no longer a Pennsylvania voter, but I was born and raised in the state and my entire family votes there. As I am so politically active, my "endorsement" can go a long way toward influencing my parents' decisions on how to vote. At the time, I followed both Joe Sestak and Arlen Specter on Twitter and carefully watched their statements to determine whose values I would support. I ultimately decided to endorse Arlen Specter, despite my otherwise liberal leanings, because he was able to convince me that he was sufficiently liberal and represented the best chance to keep the seat in Democratic hands.

Like Jon, Cecily enjoys engaging with others as a result of political tweets. Cecily said that the tweets that influence her actions are the ones that deal with situations where she feels she can affect the outcome. She mentioned one tweet that prompted her to take several actions because the tweet spoke to the issue of free speech. Cecily said that conservative blogger Pamela Geller had tweeted that she had "been banned from PayPal for hate speech because of anti-Muslim terrorist tweets." Cecily then researched other groups on PayPal (an online money transfer service) that were "using their free speech to tweet anti-Semite hate speech, who are allowed to continue without threat of banishment." She canceled her PayPal account and told PayPal why she was canceling. Finally, she retweeted Geller's tweet and told her followers to cancel their PayPal accounts. The next day, Cecily received a tweet saying that PayPal apologized and re-instituted Pamela Geller's account.

Political leaders' tweets also can spur action if the messages are relevant to their followers' jobs. Amanda said one tweet that had implications for her business made her contact members of Congress, attend rallies, and retweet:

> Interviewer: Think of a tweet from a political leader that really influenced you to take some action. What made it so influential to you?
>
> Amanda: It was Congressman Boehner, and it was almost a year ago during the health care debate, and he made the statement on Twitter about how the bill would affect small businesses, and I'm right now working for a small business, and when it was laid out in the tweet, because it was so personal to me, I felt empowered to contact my representatives, not only mine, but then I started going to other states' representatives and contacting them, and I went to a couple of the rallies on Capitol Hill.
>
> Interviewer: Did the tweet include some link or something? What was the tweet asking you to do?
>
> Amanda: It didn't even ask me to do anything. Boehner said something to the effect of if this bill is passed, small businesses that have over 50 employees or something of that nature, will be forced to be on the plan. And just from that little statement, the way my company is set up, I knew that we were going to get hit with that, and, as a subchapter S corporation, it really would have been detrimental because the owners essentially put their own money into the business. That would cause the business to fail, and we don't need any more job loss in this country. So just from hearing that one fact, I took action on my own.
>
> Interviewer: Did you take other actions on Twitter?
>
> Amanda: I retweeted it, and that actually got me a lot of followers who then retweeted what I had to say.

Several participants who work in politics or who cover politics said that the tweets that stand out and elicit responses are the ones that assist them in their jobs. As a result, tweets that catch the attention of followers who are political insiders may not have as much influence on other followers. As Michael, a lobbyist, put it: "To me, a senator announcing at 10 AM that he's going to be speaking later that day on his position on a bill—to me, that's an important tweet." Michael added that tweets from politicians often get him to research their positions more thoroughly and to locate speeches that they have given in Congress. Jim, who is in marketing, said that tweets cause him to take action if the information helps him to provide better political marketing for his clients:

> I can think of one just this morning. I saw some new poll results from a political race, a congressional race, that is of some importance to a client of ours, and I immediately forwarded that and sent it to a couple of other people who would be interested, because it was odd. It was unique, but it was good news. That's basically how I use it. There's other times when there's a news story

that needs a public response from one of our clients. I'll take it and forward it around to some individuals to see if they can pursue the story even more. But that specific event (again, kind of using the whole Twitter system like a wire service) I could immediately find out about that quickly, and then we can immediately respond to it, kind of piggy-back off the story and send out our own press hit on it.

Steve, a journalist, also is affected by leaders' tweets when the information helps him do his job. He said that tweets that he deems newsworthy can influence his political coverage:

A couple of times a day, particularly during campaign season, I will visit a link on a tweet from a political leader. It's typically a news story or press release that makes that person look favorably. From there on, I decide whether the information is either worth writing a story about for my newspaper, or for my own personal political opinion about the person.

The links to websites and hashtags that are included in tweets are a vital part of Twitter's power to influence. Participants such as Nancy said that it is the "follow-up information" in links that does the most to "help with perspective and knowledge." The links can direct followers to blog posts, video clips, analysis from think-tanks, news media stories, and any other site that has in-depth information that is too big to fit in 140 characters. Ed, for instance, said that he has no problem retweeting links to information that is quite long, provided such links help him to make points to his followers:

I'm inclined at this point to support [former New Mexico Governor] Gary Johnson for president; I supported Mitt Romney in the 2008 primaries. The two candidates are very different. People that know my political involvement might be surprised if I do end up supporting Johnson, because he is quite a libertarian candidate. I recently retweeted an interview from a news station in Florida that was linked. It was 20 minutes long and really hit some critical points that could inform some Republicans why this guy is no gadfly candidate.

Including hashtags in tweets has the additional power of giving followers the opportunity to click and read a wide variety of views from others concerning the hashtag's topic. In doing so, the information in hashtags can lead to followers reinforcing or changing their views. For example, Amanda said that her opinion about plans to build an Islamic center near Ground Zero in New York was influenced by hashtags because she could "see a second-by-second update of thousands of people who are concerned about this issue." She added:

> I originally just thought to myself, "Why is this even an issue?" But then when I read about how some people are really hurt by the idea and then other people are talking about First Amendment rights, I just formed a more detailed, concise opinion on the issue.

Amanda's actions were influenced by another hashtag. She said the information on one campaign hashtag, #masen (which stands for the Massachusetts Senate), contributed to her working for U.S. Senate candidate Scott Brown in 2009.

A leader's tweet stands out and is persuasive when the information provides a counterpoint to the views of the leader or the followers. When James was asked in his interview about what can make tweets influential, James mentioned tweets from *Washington Post* blogger Ezra Klein that critiqued and linked to information regarding "A Roadmap for America's Future," a sweeping budget proposal crafted by Republican Congressman Paul Ryan. The point/counterpoint nature of the tweets drew him in:

> James: It's interesting because you have a counterpoint there. You've got Ryan, who's a conservative. You've got Ezra Klein, who's a liberal. Let's see what his perspective is on that plan. And then subsequent to that, he had a follow-up tweet in which he interviewed Ryan about it and kind of spread those out over a couple of tweets (of course, linking to the article, his blog post). That made me click through his column, his blog post, read that, which subsequently engaged me to read further on the Ryan plan, read more about what some of the issues were behind that plan.
>
> Interviewer: What was it about the nature of those tweets that made you want to click on the links and read more?
>
> James: First of all, it's the source. So with Ezra Klein, people follow him, he's got a little bit of juice—the perspective he's coming from—so it's a counterpoint. And also it was like, "Hey, here's my take on the Paul Ryan plan." Okay, very plain, very upfront about what it was. I knew exactly what I was going to click through to.

Another of Klein's tweets also influenced Nathalie. She said that as a result, she had to rethink her views about tax policy:

> Ezra Klein had a tweet today that pointed out that it may not be that important if we extend the Bush tax cuts, and he explained why. And I was so convinced that I sent it off to my e-mail list in addition to retweeting it. He had a very, very good point.

Other participants were likewise swayed by tweets that challenged their political beliefs. Carole said that political leaders' tweets "will even make me change my mind about a position, even though I thought I had thoroughly researched it." When asked for an example, she talked about tweets that altered her opinion about who should be allowed to donate to campaigns:

> One that comes immediately to mind was a discussion about people living outside an electoral area contributing to a campaign. I was pretty hard set against that as I feel it allows people to come in and buy elections. This was a discussion I watched go back and forth. Then one of the people pointed out that the Supreme Court did not make 501(c)3s [organizations that can do issue advocacy] disclose who their people were that were contributing to the campaigns even though everyday citizens did. That made me change my mind as why should regular citizens be held to a higher standard. Now, I am at the thought it should be both or neither.

Esta, like Carole, has had deeply held views changed by political tweets. Esta said that tweets from political columnist Frank Rich (which were critical of Obama administration policies) made her re-evaluate her level of support for the president:

> He casts a light on some of what Obama is doing that made me realize that it's not totally bad to not like everything he's doing. We're in such a black-and-white society that every time somebody pulled a ying, I felt like I had to yang.... It really, really opened my eyes and made me remark to it; and I use that in the back of my head when I'm remarking to journalists or political leaders.
> Interviewer: So when you're getting these tweets from Frank Rich, do you sometimes then retweet them?
> Esta: Oh, yeah. Most of the time when I read his article, I will retweet that on Twitter and put in however I felt about it.

Humor can cause a tweet to be read and acted upon, according to participants. Dana said that she "retweets things that are either good, solid information or just very witty." When Michael retweets, "more often than not it's something humorous." James said humor is especially valuable in enticing him to read tweets that concern topics that might otherwise seem dull. One example he gave was Matthias Shapiro's Twitter account @PoliticalMath, which explains "data visualizations on political topics." James said of Shapiro:

> He has just really funny, snarky stuff. It's dealing with really serious issues, something really nerdy and esoteric, but it's a witty tweet that even if you weren't interested in what that was, or understand the paper they linked to, you may click through that because it's a witty, short, snarky tweet.

A sense of engagement is an element that can cause political leaders' tweets to influence participants in ways that leaders desire. Tweets that appear to be engaging in two-way communication with followers spur participants to take notice and respond. Jeff said the interactive nature of one candidate's tweets led to support for his candidacy:

> I follow Tom Wesley, a Republican running for Congress in the Massachusetts' 2nd district. His tweets early on definitely got me more involved with his campaign early, and his interactivity with the format at the time also made me feel like part of the campaign, even though I hadn't taken on any sort of role. His continued interaction and clear work within the medium and getting the message out has helped me get more involved as a result.

Carole also has been prompted to get politically involved because of interactive tweets. She gave one example of replying to a politician who was soliciting advice from followers about an issue that has major political and economic implications:

> I think the main one was recently in regards to a congressman asking if China hacking into government systems is as big an issue as people have stated. He got a lot of responses from people who follow him on Twitter that know. I replied in regards to an incident I had heard about. I think this is a good way to get short, knowledgeable responses that then you can research. I am glad to see a politician that is not using Twitter for just press releases. It was nice that he was gathering data from a part of the public he knew would know, as his district has a lot of high-tech jobs.

There is one element in leaders' tweets that causes participants to react in ways that leaders do not desire: tweets that seem to have errors or exaggerations. Such tweets show that retweets, replies, and other actions prompted by leaders' tweets should not always be considered examples of leaders' power over their followers. Dana said she goes out of her way to be a fact-checker when she sees leaders' tweets that she believes to be erroneous:

> What gets me the most is when I see something that I, as an informed citizen, know to be outrageous. That's the thing that makes me jump and ask, "How could you possibly make that assertion?" Those are the things that grab my attention and make me want to track down the facts and understand the process of how they got to the point of actually saying something like that.

Other participants do more than check the facts. John, for example, has tweeted to his politically active followers about misleading tweets in ways that have held leaders accountable. John said that a tweet from one candidate (which linked to a television attack ad) was so upsetting that he decided to help the candidate's opponent:

> John: There was a race for attorney general here in Georgia, and there were two very powerful leaders: one a state legislator and one a district attorney. And I've known them personally, and so whom should I vote for? The state legislator, he tweeted some information that I don't think was appropriate in his ad. He tweeted his ad before it went to TV. I didn't like it. It wasn't factual. So I think I requested a response from the other candidate. So when he responded, I think that's where it not only changed my vote, it also changed how I tweeted among the folks that I know, you know, political activists and political folks who are following me on Twitter.... That changed a lot in the attorney general's election in Georgia. And, in fact, that tweet, I would say personally, that it changed a lot of minds. In fact, the legislator lost, and it went viral. It started from Twitter. I think the fire started burning and so people, you know, started retweeting that information, and it came to a point when the ads came in, people didn't really like it. That's how I think he lost half his constituency.
>
> Interviewer: So you saw this tweet, and you thought it was factually incorrect, so you tweeted the candidate being attacked and asked for a response?
>
> John: I asked the other candidate, "Is that true?" not only in a tweet fashion but also e-mailed him. He presented me some facts; in fact, called me and talked about it, and I think within a day he tweeted something.... He responded very quickly on Twitter by saying, for example, "My opponent is saying this, which is not true. Here is the video we're putting up about this person." And from there it went wild because I saw the video; it looked very factual, and spoke to him on the phone, so I retweeted that. So among all the peers I know, I requested them to retweet. So a lot of people actually flipped because of the video and tweets. They switched their votes to the other candidate.

The Nature of the Relationship between Leaders and Followers

Participants' comments indicate that followers usually have a nonexistent tie relationship with the political leaders they follow. In a nonexistent tie relationship, leaders use tweets for one-way communication to followers, but leaders avoid the kind of two-way communication with followers that could foster a sense of connection and engagement. Noel is typical of those interviewed who said that they have this type of relationship. She was asked about her relationship with the leaders she follows and she was given brief definitions of what constitutes a strong, weak, and nonexistent tie. Noel's response highlights the one-way nature of the leader/follower relationship:

> I would say nonexistent. I follow them. They have all their followers. It looks great for them, because they can say, "I have 100,000 followers." But then if you

look at their timeline, you can see there really isn't that back and forth. There isn't that call-out, you know, that talking back and forth. Sometimes you can look at their timeline, and you'll see they'll get excited, or their intern or staff person gets excited, and you'll see like three or five tweets, and then you won't see tweets for two days. And if you look at the timeline, you don't see a lot of @'s [such as replies and mentions], you just see bullet statements here and there. So, as a result, my relationship, I would say, is nonexistent. I'm on there so just in case they pass along something that's actually interesting. I may end up looking it up later on and then tweeting.

In a few cases, participants said they have a weak tie relationship with some of the political leaders they follow. For example, Nathalie said that there are some leaders she follows who will sometimes reply to her and give her a feeling of engagement:

Some, I have a sense of a weak tie. Almost without exception they are from another place. Sometimes when I shoot back my own pithy comment to somebody who has said something that I wanted to respond to, sometimes, rarely, there will be a response, or a thank you, or a pick-up on that and go somewhere with it. But for the most part, they're all strangers. It's just that some of them are not so strange as the others.

A few participants said that they had a strong tie relationship with political leaders. These participants are heavily involved in politics, usually through their job, and are personal friends with many leaders. For example, Nansen's strong tie relationship with leaders happens "on" and "off" of Twitter:

Interviewer: How much interaction do you have with the leaders you follow?
Nansen: I have a ton of interaction. Karl Rove sends me pictures of his steaks that he's grilling by private message.
Interviewer: What's the nature of the relationship you have with the leaders you follow?
Nansen: I am unique. I have a strong relationship. Without exception, the people I consider leaders in social media have sought me out. Our relationship happens a lot offline. . . . I've been in a unique position where I have a connection to political people, elected officials, but I also live in the grassroots world.

John, who also works in politics, shares Nansen's closeness with elected officials and political operatives:

Most of the time, if you know somebody personally, whether it's in the media or whether it's a politician, they will retweet what you send and reply to you. . . . For example, there's a former governor. I sent him a message about something on Twitter, and he retweeted me and said thanks for the information and, you know, "We would like to have lunch with you," and things like that. But he already knew me. I think it's very difficult for, you know, people to retweet or reply to you unless they know you.

The Influence of Leaders' Tweets versus the Influence of Family, Friends, and Others

One way to understand the power of political Twitter use is to compare the influence of political leaders' tweets with the influence of more traditional opinion leaders, such as family, friends, and other strong ties. While participants were fairly divided when it came to saying whether strong ties or leaders' tweets were the most influential on their beliefs, there was consensus on why they feel strong ties, weak ties, or leaders' tweets have such persuasive power. Participants gave several reasons why political leaders' tweets are often more influential on their political views than friends, family, and co-workers. Those people who are influenced the most by leaders' tweets said that they see such tweets as timely information coming straight from the major players on important issues. As a result, they consider leaders' tweets to be based more on fact than opinion, making the tweets more valuable. For instance, James said that the timeliness and the helpfulness of the information make leaders' tweets more influential than strong or weak social ties:

> It ranks higher for me than friends or family or co-worker. I go to the source to get information, to base my political views off of. And I think I have the tools, the expertise to do that. I don't rely on what my friends or colleagues or parents or anybody else thinks. Twitter helps me get to the primary source quicker. It's also very timely in that whatever the news of the day is, I can quickly see a bunch of different perspectives about that. And also, political leaders are thought leaders, so you get ahead of that cycle. You're ahead of that news cycle. You're ahead of the next policy cycle. You're ahead of the next policy cycle because somebody tweeted something about, you know, some report got tweeted today, and that doesn't really hit the newspapers until a month or two from now.

Noel, too, is influenced by the timeliness and informational links in leaders' tweets:

> With my family, the information there, you know, is static. I grew up with them. I know where they stand on certain things. I'm not really going to be getting any additional information from them about their political beliefs because I know what they are. It's the same with friends. They may have a little more influence because I'm engaged more regularly with them and I don't know their overall history of how their political stances changed from stage *A* to year 30. But with tweets, information gets out there quickly. You know the person's

stance, especially someone who makes good use of it, and they can provide links and stuff. So I would probably say that tweets are more important. Now, not a whole bunch because I still do a lot of research on my own. I still look at other websites, other blogs, and everything, but I would definitely say that tweets do provide me more supplemental information, so I would say that it probably is more important but not a whole bunch.

Further, those who find leaders' tweets most influential said they perceived friends, family, and co-workers to be merely sources of opinions, not facts. Nancy said, "I constantly find friends and family spouting 'talking points' or reiterating misinformation because they only have one source." John said political information from family and friends is the least influential on his beliefs:

> John: Obviously, family and friends would be the last thing because, you know, they don't influence my vote. We have a big family where we have Republicans and Democrats.
> Interviewer: Twitter is more influential than friends and family?
> John: Well, friends and family, I mean their information is . . . [pause]. It depends. Most of the time I wouldn't recommend family and friends for giving you a political analysis of something because then it becomes personal. I don't think that people who use Twitter are getting influenced by friends and family. Friends and family talk about social policy and social issues, while Twitter gives you the facts.

Ed said he finds his co-workers a particularly unreliable source for political information:

> With co-workers, I find the majority have usually been very disconnected from an in-depth understanding of politics and issues—sometimes holding unrealistic and contradictory ideas. I see my work experience as being totally divorced from political efforts.

Carole also is skeptical of information from her strong and weak social ties:

> My friends, family and co-workers might tell me something they heard, but I never take it as true unless I research it. Usually, it is something they saw on the Internet or heard in a partisan news show, and I tend not to trust that.

Some participants had another reason for not being influenced by family, friends, and co-workers: the ideological differences between themselves and their strong and weak ties. Cecily said, "I don't need friends to tell me what to think. I work in a liberal industry, so 99 percent of my peers don't agree with me anyway. My close friends love me anyway—we just don't discuss politics." Jeff said, "Family and friends are the least influential, but more because I have few friends who share my ideological leans. They act more as a dissent-ing view for me than an influential one."

On the other hand, many participants said that strong ties were more influ-ential on their beliefs than political leaders' tweets. They cited the extensive interaction they have with their family and friends as the central reason for the supremacy of strong ties. Esta said that her family "gets into depth of what's going on much further, you know. It can go on for a couple of hours of dis-cussion about something." Ed said that political engagement with his family early-on shaped his beliefs: "My family was exceptionally influential. Most of my family was conservative, excepting my parents, but growing up debat-ing my parents shaped my sense of confidence to go out there and advance my views." Nathalie added that friends and family are politically influential when they are knowledgeable and there is genuine give-and-take:

> There are really only two people who I have conversations about politics who are likely to cause me to rethink something. One is a friend who lives here in Texas who's very, very experienced, and I use him for my encyclopedia because he remembers everything. He's one of those people who reads and remembers everything. And he can persuade me to think differently on some things, and I can also persuade him to think differently about some things. He used to be very unpleasant about Nancy Pelosi, and I finally got him straightened out about that. Then my son, who's in the Foreign Service, was a reporter. He would cause me to re-examine things in the sense of looking a little more closely for the facts.

CONCLUSION AND DISCUSSION

The impact of political tweets on subsequent word-of-mouth communica-tion is an important aspect of political influence. The analysis in this chapter addresses both engagement activities prompted by tweets as well as the influence of a variety of social ties ranging from close friends to purely electronic interactions. The combined qualitative and quantitative nature of this study's inquiry allows for a thorough assessment of all the variables. The data indicate that tweets from political leaders often affect the actions of their followers. The most common action taken was looking for more informa-tion recommended by the tweet (89.2 percent of the survey sample indicated that they engaged in this activity, at least sometimes). Reactions such as retweeting also were popular, with 60.7 percent of respondents indicating having done so at least sometimes. Taking actions (such as contributing to a campaign or signing a petition) also is frequently done, with 61 percent of respondents saying they take action at least sometimes. Replying to a tweet appears the least likely activity, with only 35.4 percent of the sample indicating they had taken this step at least sometimes. The current findings imply a stronger impact of political tweets when compared with past research on general Twitter activity (Smith and Rainie, 2010; Sysomos, 2010b).

Comments from the in-depth interviews show why political leaders' tweets cause participants to take action. There are nine elements that make a political tweet more likely to be seen and acted upon, including the actions of retweeting, clicking requested links, or supporting a leader. The nine elements are clarity; a call to action; personal relevance; professional usefulness; including helpful links and hashtags; including a political counterpoint; humor; interactivity; and outrageousness. While the first eight elements produce what can be considered positive actions, such as participants telling their followers nice things about a leader's tweet, the ninth element produces negative actions. Outrageous or seemingly incorrect information in a leader's tweets caused participants to communicate unpleasant things about that leader. This finding serves as a cautionary note to political leaders. Just because leaders' tweets are influential does not mean that influence will always help leaders. As past research indicates, negative word-of-mouth, such as when participants communicate unpleasant things about outrageous tweets, can spread faster and is somewhat more effective than positive word-of-mouth (Knauer, 1992; Park and Lee, 2009).

The survey data showed that activity taken in response to political tweets varied by several demographic, political, and motivational variables. Females, for example, were more likely to retweet information or take suggested action. This result aligns with past research (Phelps et al., 2004) and may indicate that females are more likely to be opinion leaders, at least in the online sphere. Individuals with less education were also more likely to retweet information. Older respondents noted an increased likelihood to actually reply to a tweet from a political leader. Those people with more political interest and trust were more engaged in retweeting and in looking for additional information. Such individuals may be more politically active and may strive to be opinion leaders.

Motivational antecedents emerged as the most influential predictor for engaging in action in response to political leaders' tweets. Understandably, social and self-expressive motivations were the most predictive. This result aligns with past studies indicating social drivers for electronic word-of-mouth behavior (Phelps, Lewis, Mobilio, Perry, and Raman, 2004; Hennig-Thurau, Gwinner, Walsh, and Gremler, 2004; Okazaki, 2009b). Convenience and information/guidance motivations also predicted searching for information.

It is useful to know the connection between followers' motives and their likelihood of being influenced by leaders' tweets. Such knowledge can help leaders to become more influential. For example, this research shows that those respondents with self-expressive motives are especially susceptible to the influence of leaders' tweets, so leaders would do well to make an effort to attract those tweeters who have this motive. One way to attract those people with self-expressive motives is to give them what they desire, namely opportunities for two-way communication between themselves and leaders. Such communication happens when leaders reply to followers' comments and solicit followers' advice.

In the survey data regarding social ties, leaders' tweets proved to be surprisingly influential on respondents' political views when compared with more traditional strong and weak ties. Strong ties (a combination of friends and family) were the most powerful of all types of ties, a finding that was expected based on prior research (Brown and Reingen, 1987; Granovetter, 1983; Wee, Lim, and Lwin, 1995). The next most powerful tie was the influence of tweets from leaders with whom respondents usually politically agree (a homophilous but usually nonexistent social tie). These homophilous tweets were as influential as family members when it came to shaping respondents' political beliefs, even though most respondents have never met or interacted with the leaders they follow. Perhaps even more significant, homophilous tweets were the most influential social tie for demographic groups such as women, Hispanics, those people older than 40, those people earning $100,000 or less, and those people with less than a college degree. Because of this factor, political leaders have an incentive to reach out to their female followers, as well as to the other groups who rate leaders' tweets as the most influential social tie. These groups are most receptive to being influenced by leaders' tweets.

In-depth interviews revealed that most of those people in the study have a nonexistent tie relationship with the political leaders they follow. A few respondents had a weak tie relationship, and an even smaller number had a strong tie bond. The results of this research show much detail about the power of leaders' tweets, and as such these results can contribute to the research on nonexistent ties and other forms of electronic word-of-mouth communication. While it is traditionally unusual for nonexistent ties to be more influential than strong ties, the new world of eWOM makes this nonexistent-tie phenomenon more common. What was found with leaders' tweets is just another example of the persuasive ability of electronic communication from virtual strangers, and the results are similar to Steffes and Burgee's (2009) conclusion that eWOM from nonexistent ties can be more influential than strong or weak ties when making important decisions.

Those people who participated in the interviews often said that leaders' tweets influenced their political views more than (or as much as) friends and family. Participants gave several reasons why leaders' tweets where so influential, including the perceived knowledge of leaders and how similar ideologically their leaders are to them. This last point underscores for leaders the added benefits that come when their relationship with followers is homophilous (meaning that they share similar attributes), rather than heterophilous (meaning being dissimilar; Brown and Reingen, 1987; Steffes and Burgee, 2009; Thelwall, 2009).

On the other hand, those participants who said friends and family were more influential than leaders' tweets cited engagement as the main reason. The interaction and sense of a mutual relationship gave these strong ties an edge. Consequently, leaders who increase their interactions with followers may mimic a key quality that makes friends and family persuasive to many individuals.

With respect to political attitudes, the survey results showed that those people with higher levels of trust and those people indicating a Democratic partisanship were more influenced by tweets from homophilous social ties. Republicans were less influenced by tweets from heterophilous ties. Motivations had the most pronounced predictive power, with the most influence deriving from homophilous ties (tweets from leaders with whom they agree).

A few differences were noted with respect to the type of leaders followed and the subsequent actions taken. The only significant result indicated that choosing to reply or retweet was more likely for those people on Twitter who follow a mix of elected, nonelected, and organizational leaders. The influence of social ties was similar overall for those who follow all varieties of political leaders on Twitter.

Overall, political leaders' tweets have a strong impact on their followers. Many followers take action in response to tweets and these followers are influenced by the views asserted. The results of this study are a wake-up call to political leaders and those who study political communication: Tweets wield a lot of political power, and they should be taken seriously.

Chapter 4

Is Following Political Leaders Good for Democracy? Examining Political Twitter Use, Selective Exposure, and Selective Avoidance

Thus far, this book has explored why people follow political leaders on Twitter and how political tweets affect followers. Previous chapters have discussed the degree to which political tweets are successful at urging the followers to take the actions that are requested by the leaders. This chapter covers the concepts of selective exposure and selective avoidance. These aspects of Twitter use could impact our democracy.

Selective exposure refers to what happens when people seek information that reinforces their opinions. *Selective avoidance*, a less-studied phenomenon, refers to what happens when people avoid opinion-challenging information. Past research has found that these two concepts to be related but not the same (Garrett, 2009; Johnson, Bichard, and Zhang, in press; Johnson, Zhang, and Bichard, 2011). A society that avoids exposure to diverse views can be a problem for any democracy, because pluralistic societies need a well-informed population to thrive (Bimber, 1998). As Sunstein (2001) puts it, the fear is that people will use media to "hear echoes of their own voices and to wall themselves off from others" (p. 49).

Many researchers have sought to discover whether mass media promote or discourage selective exposure. The results are mixed. Some scholars make the case that people do not limit their exposure to diverse political views (Kinder, 2003; Parmelee and Perkins, 2012; Stromer-Galley, 2003; Zaller, 1992), but other evidence points to people regularly seeking their own ideological echo online and offline (Iyengar and Hahn, 2009; Stroud, 2008; Tancer, 2008). To date, selective exposure research has dealt mainly with mass media such as television, talk radio, the Internet sites of traditional news outlets, blogs, and online political discussion spaces.

Little research has been done on Twitter's possible contribution to selective exposure and selective avoidance. Knowing whether political Twitter use affects followers' exposure to differing political views would not only add to the selective exposure debate but also would show the degree to which Twitter is good for democracy. First, however, the concept of selective exposure needs to be more thoroughly described before it can be examined, given that there are two actions involved: the act of *seeking* opinion-reinforcing information and the act of *avoiding* opinion-challenging information. In addition, demographic and political characteristics of followers may influence how much they practice selective exposure and selective avoidance. To understand these ideas and other concepts as they relate to Twitter, it is useful to review what other studies have found about selective exposure and selective avoidance with other media.

THE SELECTIVE EXPOSURE DEBATE

Selective exposure theory has its roots in the theory of cognitive dissonance (Festinger, 1957). The concept suggests that people try to find a media environment for themselves in which the information coming to them supports (rather than undercuts) their beliefs. One reason people are selective in this manner is to minimize the discomfort, or dissonance, of feeling that their views are wrong. Another reason people engage in selective exposure is to maximize the positive emotions that go along with hearing information that bolsters their beliefs.

While research on selective exposure theory goes back more than 50 years, it is the current media environment that has made selective exposure one of today's most popular theories (Bryant and Miron, 2004). Much of the current research has focused on the Internet, which has features that can promote and inhibit selective exposure. In terms of aiding selective exposure, the millions of political sites on the Internet give users ample opportunity to find sources and information with which they agree. Also, many political information sites provide only one ideological perspective, further allowing users to avoid diverse views. However, these same Internet features also can reduce selective exposure. The wide variety of political sites makes it easier than ever for users to seek out information from many ideological perspectives, but only if they take the time to find and visit a diverse range of sites.

Twitter, which is accessed mostly via the Internet (Gonsalves, 2010; Taylor, 2011), is part of this phenomenon. The features that let followers receive tweets from a politically diverse range of leaders also allow followers to avoid tweets from any leader with whom they disagree.

Twitter use that contributes to selective exposure could harm people's ability to understand and deal with important political issues. Exposure to opinion-reinforcing information can make people's views more extreme, as well as make them overestimate how much the public supports their views (Wojcieszak, 2008, 2010). On the other hand, people who expose themselves to the other side of an argument often have more political tolerance and are more apt to subsequently search broadly for information (Nemeth and Rogers, 1996; Price et al., 2002).

Research on selective exposure to blog content failed to find any influence on political tolerance (Johnson, Bichard, Zhang, and Kaye, 2010). So how prevalent is selective exposure, and what exactly are its consequences? Findings from many studies suggest that there is no easy answer. While people often look for information that reinforces their political views, that behavior does not necessarily mean that they actively avoid information that challenges their beliefs.

EVIDENCE THAT PEOPLE SEEK OPINION-REINFORCING INFORMATION

Plenty of studies have shown that people seek out their own ideological echo online. In one experiment, Iyengar and Hahn (2009) found that Republicans click stories from FOX News, while Democrats click stories from National Public Radio (NPR) or CNN. FOX is more conservative in its reporting than the Columbia Broadcasting System (CBS) or NPR, two media sources that offer more liberal coverage than is found on FOX. Another study of online searching behavior found that people who visited the FOX News website also tended to select politically conservative blogs and websites just before and after going to FOX. In contrast, people who visited the CBS News website usually selected liberal blogs and sites (Tancer, 2008, pp. 46–47).

Online chat rooms, message boards, and blogs are places where people find mostly opinion-reinforcing information. People who use politically oriented chat rooms and message boards say that those online discussion groups overwhelmingly expose them to views that agree with theirs (Wojcieszak and Mutz, 2009). The situation is only slightly less extreme with blogs: "More than half (53 percent) of those who visit blogs for political information visit blogs that provide political information that they agree with, as compared to only 22.2 percent who sought out blogs that challenged their points of view" (Johnson, Bichard, and Zhang, 2009, p. 71).

Preliminary research into Twitter's connection to selective exposure indicates that people usually follow others who share their views. One study found that conservative Twitter users typically follow the Twitter accounts of major news media such as FOX News, while liberal users follow accounts such as NPR's Morning Edition (Golbeck and Hansen, 2010). The same study examined selective exposure with regard to following political leaders, but only in a limited way. Survey data using a nonrandom sample of 40 followers of members of Congress found that:

> 62.5 percent follow politicians who mostly share their political views, while only 5 percent follow politicians who mostly hold political views that oppose their own. The rest reported following a mix of both, with an average of 65 percent of the politicians they follow sharing their own views. (p. 2)

The polarization is so great, according to some researchers, that computer analysis can reveal a Twitter users' political leanings by examining which leaders they follow and who follows them (Brustein, 2011). Despite the evidence presented so far, it is not a given that political Twitter is harmful to democracy, or even that it promotes avoiding diverse views. There is a separate body of research that suggests that people do not use media to actively avoid views that challenge theirs.

EVIDENCE THAT PEOPLE DO NOT AVOID OPINION-CHALLENGING INFORMATION

Studies on how people use newspapers, television, and the Internet often show that people often seek out diverse views, or at least do not intentionally shun information that challenges their views. Research by DiMaggio and Sato (2003) into how people search websites for political information found that "as many politically attentive users went to sites that challenged their views as to sites that reinforced them, [and] even more went to sites they perceived as politically neutral, and a plurality visited a combination of sites" (p. 1). Additional studies on political website and blog use also failed to find evidence that people selectively avoid opinion-challenging information, especially among those who were highly interested in politics (Johnson et al., 2011; Johnson, Bichard, and Zhang, in press).

An analysis of more than 250,000 tweets from the 2010 U.S. congressional elections found that Twitter sometimes reduces political polarization (Conover, Ratkiewicz, Francisco, Goncalves, Flammini, and Menczer, 2011). It turns out that several of Twitter's features (such as the ability to retweet, mention other users, and discuss issues via hashtags) produce different effects. While the study found that retweets exhibit "a highly segregated partisan structure," mentions and hashtags fight polarization. Mentions are "dominated" by a "heterogeneous cluster of users in which ideologically opposed individuals interact," and hashtags are "exposing users to content they would not likely choose in advance" (pp. 1, 7).

Why would a person have the incentive to seek information that challenges his or her views? There are a number of reasons. Those people who are politically curious, politically knowledgeable, or enjoy discussing politics are likely to search for diverse views (Chaffee, Saphir, Graf, Sandvig, and Hahn, 2001). People with a high interest in politics and a strong political party preference also regularly seek opinion-challenging information (Johnson, Bichard, and Zhang, 2009; Knobloch-Westerwick and Meng, 2009). Such findings are not surprising. It makes sense that the politically active would try to learn as much as possible about the "other side." Some use the opportunity to test their allegiance to a particular position, while others want to see what their opponents are thinking so they can form a rebuttal.

Yet another reason why diverse views are so often sought is that many people are not as partisan as has been previously thought. Looking at party registration statistics, McGhee and Krimm (2009) found that "the strongest trend by far is not growing polarization but the large and pervasive increase in registered independents" (p. 345).

A BETTER WAY TO UNDERSTAND AND
EXAMINE SELECTIVE EXPOSURE

Because so many studies have found evidence that people search for both opinion-reinforcing and opinion-challenging information, a new approach has emerged to explain and measure selective exposure. Garrett (2009) began to reframe the theory by arguing that while people have powerful incentives to seek information and sources with which they agree, they also have ample reason to look for the other side of the argument. As a result, the concept of selective exposure should not be thought of as a zero-sum game in which increases in opinion-reinforcing information come at the expense of opinion-challenging information.

To make his case, Garrett examined survey data from strong and weak supporters of George W. Bush and John Kerry during the 2004 presidential campaign. Respondents were asked about their visits to politically oriented websites that were liberal, Democratic, Republican, and conservative. Not surprisingly, strong supporters of Bush were the most likely to favor Republican and conservative sites, while strong Kerry supporters preferred Democratic and liberal sites. What was surprising was that strong supporters were not less likely than weak supporters to visit sites from the opposing political perspective (pp. 686–687). These results matter because one big fear associated with selective exposure is that the more people seek their own ideological echo, the less they will want to encounter views that challenge theirs (which is selective avoidance). Selective avoidance, in turn, could lead to increased political polarization and to a society in which people do not understand (or care to understand) any opinions other than their own. Garrett's findings suggest that those fears are unwarranted, at least when it comes to using political websites:

> Contrary to prior interpretations of selective exposure theory, the data demonstrate that seeking opinion-reinforcing and avoiding opinion-challenging information are not equivalent. The results support the hypotheses that individuals are using control over their political information environment to increase their exposure to opinion-reinforcing information, but that they are not using this control to systematically screen out other opinions. (p. 692)

Based on what has been found with political website use, it may be that political Twitter use increases followers' exposure to opinion-reinforcing information without a comparable decrease in exposure to opinion-challenging information. That assumption would suggest that following political leaders on Twitter does not contribute to increased political polarization or harm followers' ability to understand opposing voices. One way to learn more is to examine Twitter users on both ends of the political spectrum and to compare the following habits of strong partisans with those users who are more ideologically moderate. If conservative or liberal users are more likely than moderates to say that they follow "leaders who I usually agree with politically," but are not more likely than moderates to avoid "leaders who I usually do not agree with politically," then the most harmful effects of selective exposure are being averted. Another way to prove this point would be if conservative users are not less likely than moderates to follow leaders who are Democrats or liberals, and if liberal users are not less likely than moderates to follow Republicans or conservatives.

FACTORS THAT INFLUENCE HOW MUCH A PERSON ENGAGES IN SELECTIVE EXPOSURE

A number of studies have linked selective exposure to such factors as political party affiliation, ideology, political efficacy, political interest, age, education, and communication motivations. Perhaps the most provocative of these factors are party and ideology. Some researchers have found that conservatives and Republicans are more likely than liberals and Democrats to seek opinion-reinforcing information (Iyenger, Hahn, Krosnick, and Walker, 2008) and less likely than liberals and Democrats to search for opinion-challenging information (Mutz, 2006). If these findings are indeed true, it could mean that those on the political Right are more susceptible to the harmful effects of selective exposure. However, other research indicates that being conservative increases one's likelihood of seeking diverse views (Knobloch-Westerwick and Meng, 2009). Still another perspective is provided by Wojcieszak and Mutz (2009), who found that "Democrats, Republicans, and Independents are equally likely to come across dissenting political views" in chat rooms and on message boards (p. 48). This debate is far from over, and it needs to be expanded to include the possible effects of party and ideology on selective exposure to political tweets.

High levels of political interest and *political self-efficacy* (which can be thought of as a person's political self-confidence) also have been associated with seeking opinion-challenging information (Garrett, 2009; Johnson et al., 2011; Knobloch-Westerwick and Meng, 2009). On the other hand, certain demographic factors have the opposite effect. Older people are less exposed to political disagreements on online discussion spaces than are younger people (Wojcieszak and Mutz, 2009). Those people who are highly educated are more likely to seek opinion-reinforcing information on political blogs (Johnson et al., 2009). Twitter users, who tend to be in their 30s and have a high level of education (Global Web Index, 2010), need to be queried to see how demographics influence their exposure to diverse political views. Finally, other research has looked into how social, informational, and guidance motives are related to selective exposure of offline media, such as television (Atkin, 1985), but not newer media such as Twitter.

QUANTITATIVE AND QUALITATIVE WAYS TO EXPLORE SELECTIVE EXPOSURE ON TWITTER

Most of the research into selective exposure and selective avoidance has been quantitative, with a heavy emphasis on surveys (Chaffee et al., 2001; Garrett, 2009; Johnson et al., 2011; Stroud, 2008). The quantitative nature of a survey gives a survey several advantages when it comes to examining selective exposure. Surveys can, for example, measure how much Republican Twitter users follow leaders who are conservative, moderate, and liberal. Those numbers can then be compared with Democratic users' following patterns to find out if party affiliation makes some people more likely to suffer the negative consequences of selective exposure.

Surveys also can measure the degree to which strongly partisan Twitter users differ from those users who are more moderate when it comes to following leaders with whom they agree or disagree. Those findings could confirm that political Twitter use does not cause increased polarization, which would match Garrett's (2009) conclusions regarding exposure to political websites. Closed-ended survey questions do not work well in studies exploring all the possible reasons why followers seek a diverse range of leaders and all the ways in which politically diverse tweets influence followers' views.

In comparison, the open-ended nature of an in-depth interview makes the interview technique better able to discover the various reasons why followers choose leaders who provide opinion-challenging or opinion-reinforcing information. Interviews also can reveal examples of how followers' political views are influenced by tweets from leaders who provide the other side of an argument. In-depth interviews have been used to explore whether selective exposure occurs among users of online political discussion groups (Stromer-Galley, 2003). A similar approach is needed to investigate Twitter and selective exposure.

RESEARCH QUESTIONS ANSWERED IN THIS CHAPTER

This study used surveys and in-depth interviews to extend the selective exposure debate to political Twitter use. The research questions and hypotheses of this study are based on past studies that have investigated how much people search for opinion-reinforcing and opinion-challenging information in chat rooms, blogs, message boards, political websites, and on television. Key issues addressed in the study include the degree to which following political leaders on Twitter contributes to increased polarization, and whether demographics and other factors influence how much followers engage in selective exposure. It is also important to understand why followers choose to seek or avoid diverse views, as well as how followers are affected by politically diverse tweets. The study focused on the following questions:

- Question 1: How many political leaders does the average Twitter user follow?
- Question 2: To what degree are followers choosing political leaders on Twitter with whom they agree politically or disagree politically (or is it a mix of both)?

- Question 3: Do those people who follow only current elected officials differ from all others—meaning by following those leaders they agree with politically or avoiding those leaders they disagree with politically?
- Question 4: To what degree are political variables and demographics related to Twitter users' following those people with whom they politically agree or avoiding those people with whom they politically disagree? Political variables would include an interest in politics, political efficacy, trust in government, past voting behavior, likelihood of voting, party registration, strength of ideology, and political ideology. Demographic variables would include gender, age, race, income, and education.
- Hypothesis 1: Ideological strength is positively related to selective exposure, but it is not positively related to selective avoidance.
- Hypothesis 2: Political efficacy is negatively related to selective exposure and selective avoidance.
- Hypothesis 3: Political interest is negatively related to selective exposure and selective avoidance.
- Question 5: To what degree does self-reported party identification impact the type of political leaders a user follows on Twitter?
- Question 6: To what degree does self-reported ideology impact the type of political leaders a user follows on Twitter?
- Question 7: To what degree are overall motives for following political leaders on Twitter related to users following those people with whom they politically agree or avoiding those people with whom they politically disagree?
- Question 8: To what degree is a follower's willingness to act related to following those leaders with whom they politically agree or avoiding those leaders with whom they politically disagree? Possible actions include the willingness to reply to a political leader's tweet, to retweet a political tweet, to look for information recommended in a political tweet, or to take actions that are requested in a political leader's tweet.
- Question 9: To what degree do Twitter users follow leaders with matching or directly opposing political perspectives (specifically with respect to partisanship and ideology)?
- Hypothesis 4: Republicans and conservatives are less likely than Democrats and liberals to follow at least one political leader on Twitter from the opposing political party.
- Hypothesis 5: Republicans and conservatives are less likely than Democrats and liberals to follow at least one political leader on Twitter with an opposing ideological perspective.
- Hypothesis 6: Those people with weaker ideological strength are more likely to follow at least one political leader on Twitter from the opposing political party.

- Hypothesis 7: Those people with weaker ideological strength are more likely to follow at least one political leader on Twitter with an opposing ideological perspective.
- Question 10: Why do followers seek out leaders with whom they disagree?
- Question 11: How are followers influenced by opinion-challenging tweets?

METHODS USED TO ANSWER THE RESEARCH QUESTIONS

Survey

Several of the survey questions were designed to find out the degree to which following political leaders on Twitter contributes to increased political polarization. One question asked, for example, was "How many political leaders do you currently 'follow' on Twitter?" The respondent's choices included "0" (those surveys were subsequently thrown out), "1," "2 to 4," "5 to 10," "11 to 20," and "more than 20." Respondents' answers to this question provide an initial look into how active followers are in searching for information from any political leader.

Two other types of questions examined the phenomena of selective exposure (seeking opinion-reinforcing information) and selective avoidance (avoiding opinion-challenging information). Respondents were asked this question: "What types of political leaders do you follow? Please select ALL that apply." Choices included "political leaders who I usually agree with politically" and "political leaders who I usually do not agree with politically." Respondents also were asked about their political ideology on a 10-point scale (1 = conservative; 10 = liberal) and their party registration (their options were Democratic, Republican, Independent, "other," and "not registered to vote"). In order to learn the respondents' strength of political ideology, answers were combined to form two separate measures. When looking at conservative versus liberal intensity, 1 to 2 = strong conservative; 3 to 4 = moderate conservative; 5 to 6 = moderate; 7 to 8 = moderate liberal; and 9 to 10 = strong liberal. To assess overall ideological strength regardless of left or right leanings, the scores were condensed in this manner: strong conservatives were combined with strong liberals (1 to 2 and 9 to 10); moderate conservatives were combined with moderate liberals (3 to 4 and 7 to 8); and thus moderates (5 to 6) were left to represent the weakest ideological group. This combination strategy allowed for analyses based on ideological intensity alone. Based in part on Garrett's (2009) conceptualization, strong conservatives and strong liberals were compared with moderate conservatives, moderate liberals, and moderates regarding the degree to which they followed political leaders with whom they agreed or disagreed.

Another way selective exposure and selective avoidance were measured was by comparing followers' party registration with the party of the leaders they follow. Comparisons were then made of the frequency with which followers who were Republican and Democratic, for example, followed leaders who were of like or opposing partisanship. This also was assessed for followers' ideological perspectives. Moderates and Independents were excluded from this analysis because it was impossible to determine who, exactly, would be their direct opposition.

In addition, demographic and other factors were examined to find out their influence on how much followers engaged in selective exposure and selective avoidance.

Motives for following political leaders on Twitter, as well as concepts such as political efficacy and trust in government, were examined using questions that were derived from previous research (Ancu and Cozma, 2009; Kaye and Johnson, 2004; Kaye, 2005). Those definitions are discussed in detail in the methods section of Chapter 2, which covers the uses and gratifications of political Twitter use. Chapter 2 also explains how the factors of likelihood of voting, past voting behavior, and demographics were defined and measured.

One factor to note is a person's interest in politics, which was measured on a 10-point scale (1 = very low interest; 10 = very high interest). According to Garrett (2009), political interest is a potential confounding variable that may offset results. For this reason, political interest (along with ideological strength) was controlled while examining the predictive value of respondents' motivations and willingness to take action.

Data Analysis

Data from the survey questionnaires were evaluated by analyzing frequencies and mean scores for each of the measures and conducting suitable statistical analyses. Questions 1 and 2 were addressed by analyzing frequency percentages for the total number of leaders followed on Twitter, as well as percentages for following agreeable and disagreeable political leaders. Chi-square analysis was used for Question 3 and addressed differences among those following only elected officials. Standardized residual scores were analyzed for all chi-square results to further detect significant cell influence, and these scores are reflected in the description of findings. In order to answer Question 4, logistic regression was used with demographic (first block) and political (second block) variables predicting the types of leaders who were followed. Hypotheses 1, 2, and 3 were examined by performing independent samples t-tests to reveal differences in tweet exposure for a variety of political antecedents. Chi-square analyses were used to address Questions 5 and 6. Respondents' party and ideology were scrutinized for their impact on the types of leaders who were followed. Logistic regressions were performed to answer Questions 7 and 8, to detect the predictive influence of motivations and the willingness to take action on selecting agreeable or disagreeable leaders to follow on Twitter (controlling for political interest and ideology). Question 9 was examined through frequency percentages for following leaders with matching or opposing ideology/party. For Hypotheses 4 and 5, chi-square analyses were performed to assess the impact of respondents' party and ideology on selecting to follow leaders with matching or opposing ideology/party. The final two hypotheses were analyzed by conducting independent samples t-tests to detect differences in mean scores for ideological strength among those choosing to follow at least one leader of the opposing ideology/party. All the results are depicted in Tables 4.1 through 4.6.

In-depth Interviews

The survey measured how much followers chose a diverse range of political leaders. In comparison, the interviews sought a deeper understanding of why followers chose to seek or avoid differing views, as well as how followers are influenced by opinion-challenging tweets. The interviews answer Questions 10 and 11. To discover the many reasons why followers seek out leaders with whom they disagree, participants were asked these questions: "To what degree do you follow political leaders on Twitter whose political views differ from yours? Why or why not?" To discover the influence of opinion-challenging tweets, follow-up questions included these queries: "Are you sometimes influenced by tweets from leaders whose views differ from yours? Can you give me an example of that?"

RESULTS

Survey

Survey results indicate that respondents were very active in the "Twitter-verse," with many following more than 20 political leaders' tweets. The vast majority of survey respondents follow those leaders with whom they agree; but many also follow those leaders with whom they disagree. The differences are most apparent with respect to political variables. Age is the only demographic variable with an influence—implying that younger respondents were more likely to follow agreeable political leaders. Political interest and efficacy led to selective exposure, but not necessarily avoidance. A strong political ideology emerged as the most consistent predictor of selectivity in both exposure and avoidance. Similarly, those with a stronger ideological perspective were also the least likely to follow political leaders from the opposing party or ideology. As expected, most respondents follow those with like opinions and matching party or ideological beliefs. Motives for using Twitter were relatively unrelated to the selection of types of leaders followed. Entertainment motives were the only significant indicator and predicted following more agreeable political leaders. Willingness to engage in subsequent activities in response to tweets was related to types of leaders followed. Increased action, such as retweeting, led to selectivity and often avoidance of opinion-challenging political perspectives. The paragraphs that follow offer specific findings for each of the research questions and hypotheses offered.

Number and Type of Leaders Followed on Twitter

The first two research questions assess the extent to which Twitter users follow political leaders, as well as the specific types selected to follow. Survey questions addressed following leaders of a certain ideology and party affiliation, as well as following those with whom "I usually agree with politically" and those with whom "I usually do not agree with politically." Findings show that 31 percent of respondents follow more than 20 political leaders on Twitter. Roughly 25 percent follow fewer than 5 political leaders. The majority of users fall between these figures with 43 percent following 5 to 20 leaders on Twitter.

Twitter users follow a variety of types of political leaders. More than 88 percent follow elected officials, while 71.4 percent follow political organizations. As for party, 74.2 percent follow Democratic leaders, and 56.3 percent follow Republican leaders. Just over 34 percent follow Independent political leaders, and 27 percent follow Libertarians. Ideological preferences are also apparent with 63.6 percent of the sample following liberals, 48.4 percent following conservatives, and 39.9 percent following moderates.

With respect to similar and dissimilar political exposure, the results indicate a preference for agreeable content. Eighty-three percent of those surveyed indicated that they follow leaders with whom they usually agree with politically. Only 40.8 percent noted following those they disagree with. This would indicate that 59.2 percent avoid those leaders with whom they disagree. Forty percent follow a mix of those they agree and disagree with, while 43.4 percent follow only those they agree with politically.

Differences for Those Following Solely Elected Officials

Question 3 analyzed the possible difference in types of leaders followed for those who chose to follow only elected officials versus all others. The findings indicate that nearly 84 percent of those who follow only elected officials avoid following leaders who challenge their views. These individuals are significantly more likely to avoid those they disagree with ($\chi^2(1, N = 409) = 15.12, p < 0.01$) when selecting leaders to follow on Twitter. These individuals also are less apt to follow a mix of political leaders who both challenge and reinforce their opinions ($\chi^2 (1, N = 409) = 16.78, p < 0.01$).

Influence of Demographic or Political Variables on Type of Leader Followed

Question 4 addressed the influence of various demographic and political variables on the type of leader selected to be followed on Twitter. Both demographic (first block) and political (second block) variables were assessed for their impact using logistic regression analyses. Table 4.1 provides a summary of the results. Demographic variables under scrutiny included gender, age, race, income, and education level. The findings revealed that age was the only significant predictor, with lower age predicting an increased likelihood to select political leaders on Twitter who are agreeable (B = –0.84, Exp(B) = 0.433, $p < 0.01$).

Two political antecedents emerged with a significant impact on types of leaders followed on Twitter. Higher political interest led to following a mix of opinion-reinforcing and opinion-challenging leaders (B = 0.28, Exp(B) = 1.32, $p < 0.05$). On the other hand, decreased levels of political interest predicted avoiding disagreeable political leaders on Twitter (B = –0.29, Exp(B) = 0.749, $p < 0.05$). Ideological strength also was significantly related to the types of leaders selected—but in the opposite direction. Higher levels of ideological strength (stronger liberals and stronger conservatives) predicted avoiding disagreeable content (B = 0.41, Exp(B) = 1.51, $p < 0.05$), as well as following only those with opinion-reinforcing views exclusively (B = 0.50, Exp(B) = 1.65, $p < 0.01$). Lower levels of ideological strength (moderates) were significantly more likely to follow a mix of diverse leaders (B = –0.36, Exp(B) = 0.700, $p < 0.05$).

Hypothesis 1 predicted that ideological strength specifically would lead to increased selective exposure, but that such strength would be unrelated to selective avoidance. The logistic regression analysis discussed previously indicates that ideological strength was not significantly related to selecting agreeable content, but rather that such strength was related to avoiding disagreeable content. An independent samples *t*-test further revealed differences

Table 4.1 Logistic Regression Analysis Predicting Type of Political Leaders Followed on Twitter Based on Demographics and Political Variables

Independent Variables	Type Followed							
	Follows Agreeable		Avoids Disagreeable		Follows Only Agreeable		Follows Mix of Both	
	B	Exp(B)	B	Exp(B)	B	Exp(B)	B	Exp(B)
Demographics								
Gender	0.34	1.41	0.02	1.02	0.11	1.12	0.05	1.05
Age	−0.84**	0.433	0.17	1.19	−0.23	0.797	−0.19	0.825
Caucasian	−0.01	0.986	−0.29	0.746	−0.29	0.746	0.26	1.30
African Amer.	19.8	3.82	−1.1	0.323	−0.23	0.798	1.1	3.05
Hispanic	−0.73	0.483	0.06	1.06	−0.23	0.793	−0.07	0.937
Asian	−1.7	0.176	0.76	2.13	−0.69	0.502	−0.77	0.462
HH*** income	0.11	1.12	−0.08	0.925	−0.05	0.956	0.09	1.10
Education	−0.05	0.956	−0.03	0.968	−0.03	0.967	0.03	1.04
χ^2	20.93**		4.34		6.80		4.10	
Nagelkerke R^2	0.088		0.014		0.023		0.014	
Political Antecedents								
Political Interest	0.20	1.22	−0.29*	0.749	−0.12	0.891	0.28*	1.32
Ideology	0.07	1.07	0.03	1.03	0.07	1.08	−0.03	0.973
Trust	0.14	1.15	−0.04	0.963	−0.01	0.994	0.06	1.06
Efficacy	0.55	1.74	−0.32	0.730	0.03	1.03	0.28	1.33
Ideo. strength	0.25	1.29	0.41*	1.51	0.50**	1.65	−0.36*	0.700
Vote likelihood	0.05	1.06	−0.08	0.924	−0.06	0.944	0.07	1.08
Past voter	0.75	2.11	−0.85	0.429	−0.33	0.720	0.81	2.26
Democrat	−2.8	0.063	1.8	6.09	0.57	1.77	−1.8	0.161
Republican	−2.2	0.112	2.2	8.65	1.2	3.35	−2.1	0.127
Independent	−2.5	0.085	1.1	2.99	−0.20	0.819	−0.10	0.370
χ^2	23.30*		38.26**		29.88**		36.22**	
Model χ^2	44.23**		42.60**		36.68**		40.31**	
Nagelkerke R^2	0.181		0.136		0.117		0.129	

Note: Exp(B)= exponentiated B. Female was coded higher for gender. Liberal coded higher for ideology. Other was used as the reference category for both race and party.
*$p < 0.05$; **$p < 0.01$; ***HH = Household.

for ideological strength mean scores. Results confirmed that mean scores were not significantly different for those people selecting to follow agreeable leaders. Means for ideological strength were, however, significantly higher for those people avoiding disagreeable leaders ($t(422)= -2.90$, $p < 0.01$). These findings do not support the hypothesis because followers did not have significantly increased selective exposure, but they did practice selective avoidance (see Table 4.2).

Hypothesis 2 predicted that political efficacy would be negatively related to selective exposure and avoidance. Logistic regression analysis did not reveal any significant findings, so an independent samples t-test was used to detect differences in efficacy mean scores for those people who follow and avoid political leaders with similar and dissimilar views. Results showed that those people with higher efficacy are significantly more likely to follow agreeable content ($t(423) = 3.76$, $p < 0.01$), but that they are less likely to avoid those with disagreeable views ($t(423) = -2.96$, $p < 0.01$). For this reason, Hypothesis 2 is partially supported (refer to Table 4.2).

Hypothesis 3 predicted that political interest would be negatively related to both selective exposure and avoidance. Logistic regression revealed a negative relationship with selective avoidance and an increased likelihood to follow a mix of leaders with various views. An independent samples t-test was performed to further investigate these trends and the results indicated that those people with higher political interest indeed do not avoid those with whom they disagree ($t(422) = 3.73$, $p < 0.01$), but they also are significantly likely to follow those with similar views ($t(422) = 3.55$, $p < 0.01$). This result lends partial support for Hypothesis 3 (see Table 4.2).

Impact of Party Registration and Ideology on Type of Leader Followed

Question 5 examined the relationship between the self-reported party registration for respondents and their selection of political leaders to follow on Twitter. Table 4.3 details the findings. Not surprisingly, Democrats were more likely to follow Democrats ($\chi^2(4, N = 423) = 131.88$, $p < 0.01$), and Republicans were more apt to follow Republicans ($\chi^2(4, N = 423) = 94.78$, $p < 0.01$). Similarly, conservatives were more likely to follow conservatives ($\chi^2(4, N = 423) = 87.48$, $p < 0.01$), and liberals were more likely to follow liberals ($\chi^2(4, N = 423) = 92.05$, $p < 0.01$). Independents were more likely to follow independents ($\chi^2(4, N = 423) = 23.29$, $p < 0.01$), as well as Libertarians ($\chi^2(4, N = 423) = 53.43$, $p < 0.01$) and moderates ($\chi^2(4, N = 423) = 16.05$, $p < 0.01$). Independents also were more apt to follow a mix of diverse leaders ($\chi^2(4, N = 423) = 12.87$, $p < 0.05$) and less likely to avoid those leaders with disagreeable views ($\chi^2(4, N = 423) = 11.66$, $p < 0.05$).

Table 4.2   *T*-tests Comparing Mean Scores for Political
Variables for Those Following Agreeable and Disagreeable
Leaders on Twitter

	Mean (SD)	t
Agreeable		
Ideological Strength		
Follows	2.5(0.65)	t = 1.15
Does not follow	2.4(0.73)	
Political Efficacy		
Follows	4.6(0.55)	t = 3.76**
Does not follow	4.3(0.76)	
Political Interest		
Follows	9.2(1.3)	t = 3.55**
Does not follow	8.6(2.0)	
Disagreeable		
Ideological Strength		
Follows	2.3(.67)	t = −2.90**
Does not follow	2.5(.65)	
Political Efficacy		
Follows	4.7(0.50)	t = −2.96**
Does not follow	4.5(0.65)	
Political Interest		
Follows	9.5(1.0)	t = 3.73**
Does not follow	8.9(1.7)	

Note: **$p < .01$, *$p < .05$.

Question 6 addressed the impact of self-reported ideology and type of leaders selected to be followed on Twitter. Table 4.4 offers a summary of the findings. As expected, moderate-to-strong liberals are more likely to follow Democrats ($\chi^2(4, N = 422) = 137.73$, $p < 0.01$) and liberals ($\chi^2(4, N = 422) = 106.80$, $p < 0.01$). Moderate-to-strong conservatives are more prone to follow Republicans ($\chi^2(4, N = 422) = 103.80$, $p < 0.01$) and conservatives ($\chi^2(4, N = 422) = 120.05$, $p < 0.01$). Those people with a more conservative ideology also are more likely to follow Libertarians ($\chi^2(4, N = 422) = 43.59$, $p < 0.01$), and moderate liberals are more likely to follow moderates ($\chi^2(4, N = 422) = 22.55$, $p < 0.01$). Strong liberals are the most likely to select only agreeable leaders to follow on Twitter ($\chi^2(4, N = 422) = 14.04$, $p < 0.01$).

Table 4.3 Chi-square Analysis of Types of Political Leaders Followed on Twitter, by Party Registration

Follows...	Party Registration			
	Democratic	*Republican*	*Independent*	
	Number (%)	*Number (%)*	*Number (%)*	χ^2
Democrats	**201 (93.5)**	**31 (32.3)**	46 (69.7)	131.88**
Republicans	**78 (36.3)**	**91 (94.8)**	41 (62.1)	94.78**
Independents	**59 (27.4)**	30 (31.3)	**39 (59.1)**	23.29**
Libertarians	**27 (12.6)**	**36 (37.5)**	**31 (47.0)**	53.43**
Conservatives	**62 (28.8)**	**82 (85.4)**	35 (53.0)	87.48**
Liberals	**174 (80.9)**	**24 (25.0)**	38 (57.6)	92.05**
Moderates	86 (40.0)	**25 (26.0)**	**37 (56.1)**	16.05**
Agreeable	183 (85.1)	82 (85.4)	54 (81.8)	7.50
Disagreeable	82 (38.1)	35 (36.5)	**39 (59.1)**	11.66*
Only agreeable	104 (48.4)	48 (50.0)	**15 (22.7)**	16.16**
Mix of both	79 (36.7)	34 (35.4)	**39 (59.1)**	12.87*

Note: Percentages exceed 100% because respondents could select more than one answer. Standardized residuals were examined for each cell, and figures in bold represent those significantly different from expected.
$N = 423$; $df = 4$; $*p < 0.05$; $**p < 0.01$.

Influence of Motives and Willingness to Take Action on Type of Leader Followed

Previous chapters assessed the influence of motivations and actions on respondent behavior in the political context. Questions 7 and 8 specifically inquire about the influence of motivations and willingness to take action based on the types of political leaders selected to be followed on Twitter. A series of logistic regressions were performed to answer these questions (see Table 4.5). Political interest and ideological strength were entered as controls to accurately reflect the influence of motives and actions. While many of the combined models for motivation variables indicated predictive influence, only entertainment motives emerged as a significant contributor to following agreeable leaders (B = 0.30, Exp(B) = 1.35, $p < 0.05$).

Several significant variables can be noted with respect to the actions that followers expressed a willingness to do. Willingness to retweet predicted following agreeable political leaders (B = 0.53, Exp(B) = 1.69, $p < 0.01$). Willingness to reply to a political tweet was inversely related to following agreeable leaders exclusively (B = –0.27, Exp(B) = 0.762, $p < 0.05$). Taking

Table 4.4   Chi-square Analysis of Types of Political Leaders Followed on Twitter, by Political Ideology

Follows...	Ideology					
	Strong Conserv.	Moderate Conserv.	Moderate	Moderate Liberal	Strong Liberal	
	Number (%)	Number (%)	Number (%)	Number (%)	Number (%)	χ^2
Democrats	**22 (29.7)**	**25 (48.1)**	33 (80.5)	**88 (90.7)**	**146 (92.4)**	137.73**
Republicans	**69 (93.2)**	**44 (84.6)**	25 (61.0)	53 (54.6)	**47 (29.7)**	103.80**
Independents	27 (36.5)	21 (40.4)	20 (48.8)	30 (30.9)	47 (29.7)	6.76
Libertarians	**35 (47.3)**	20 (38.5)	**18 (43.9)**	20 (20.6)	**20 (12.7)**	43.59**
Conservatives	**70 (94.6)**	**37 (71.2)**	22 (53.7)	40 (41.2)	**35 (22.2)**	120.05**
Liberals	**17 (23.0)**	**20 (38.5)**	24 (58.5)	72 (74.2)	**136 (86.1)**	106.80**
Moderates	**18 (24.3)**	24 (46.2)	23 (56.1)	**51 (52.6)**	52 (32.9)	22.55**
Agreeable	63 (85.1)	42 (80.8)	31 (75.6)	84 (86.6)	134 (84.8)	3.16
Disagreeable	25 (33.8)	27 (51.9)	20 (48.8)	47 (48.5)	54 (34.2)	10.45*
Only agreeable	38 (51.4)	**15 (28.8)**	**12 (29.3)**	39 (40.2)	**81 (51.3)**	14.04**
Mix of both	25 (33.8)	27 (51.9)	19 (46.3)	45 (46.4)	53 (33.5)	9.35

Note: Percentages exceed 100% because respondents could select more than one answer. Standardized residuals were examined for each cell, and figures in bold represent those significantly different from expected.
$N = 422$; *df* = 4; *p* < 0.05; **p* < 0.01.

specified actions, such as signing a petition or contributing to a candidate, predicted selective avoidance (B = 0.44, Exp(B) = 1.55, *p* < 0.01) and choosing to follow only agreeable political leaders (B = –56, Exp(B) = 1.75, *p* < 0.01).

Following Leaders with Matching or Opposing Political Perspectives

Question 9 evaluated the extent to which Twitter users follow leaders with matching or directly opposing political perspectives. Frequency data were assessed for those followers of matching/opposing party identification, as well as ideological perspectives. The findings indicate that 93.9 percent of Democrats and Republicans in the sample followed at least one leader with a matching viewpoint. Only 35 percent followed at least one leader with an opposing view. This result implies that 65 percent avoided those leaders with opinion-challenging beliefs. More than 82 percent of those people espousing strong conservative or liberal ideology specified following leaders with

Table 4.5   Two Logistic Regression Analyses Predicting Type of Political Leaders Followed on Twitter Based on Motivations and Actions Taken

Independent Variables	Type Followed							
	Follows Agreeable		Avoids Disagreeable		Follows Only Agreeable		Follows Mix of Both	
	B	Exp(B)	B	Exp(B)	B	Exp(B)	B	Exp(B)
Motivations								
Social utility	0.17	1.19	–0.08	0.919	–0.00	.999	0.09	1.10
Self-expression	0.15	1.16	0.00	1.00	0.07	1.07	0.00	1.00
Info/Guidance	0.07	1.07	0.05	1.04	0.06	1.06	–0.04	.966
Convenience	0.26	1.29	0.07	1.08	0.20	1.23	–0.04	.957
Entertainment	0.30*	1.35	–0.16	0.851	0.05	1.05	0.14	1.14
Model χ^2	28.57**		28.72**		23.26**		25.33**	
Nagelkerke R^2	0.118		0.091		0.074		0.081	
Actions								
Reply to tweet	–0.22	0.804	–0.15	0.860	–0.27*	0.762	0.15	1.16
Retweet	0.53**	1.69	–0.19	0.827	0.06	1.06	0.24	1.27
Look for info.	0.02	1.02	0.03	1.03	0.02	1.02	–0.03	0.975
Take suggested action	0.19	1.21	0.44**	1.55	0.56**	1.75	–0.44**	0.641
Model χ^2	22.02**		39.99**		39.33**		38.23**	
Nagelkerke R^2	.090		.125		.123		.120	

Note: Exp(B) = exponentiated B. Controls for political interest and ideological strength were included in the analysis, but they are omitted here for clarity.
*$p < 0.05$; **$p < 0.01$.

matching ideological perspectives. Only 29.4 percent followed at least one leader with the opposing ideological view. This result means that 70.6 percent avoided those of the opposite ideology.

Hypothesis 4 contended that Republicans and conservatives would be less likely than Democrats and liberals to follow at least one political leader on Twitter from the opposing political party. Results showed that more Democrats followed Republicans than vice versa, but not with statistical significance. However, moderate liberals were significantly more likely to follow Republicans ($\chi^2(4, N = 311) = 22.09$, $p < 0.01$). This finding offers partial support for Hypothesis 4.

Hypothesis 5 makes the assertion that Republicans and conservatives are less likely than Democrats and liberals to follow at least one political leader on Twitter who has an opposing ideological perspective. The number of Democrats following more conservative leaders exceeds the number of Republicans following more liberal leaders, but not with statistical significance. The results do indicate that those followers with a moderately liberal ideology are significantly more likely to follow at least one political leader with directly opposing ideological viewpoints ($\chi^2(3, N = 381) = 14.08, p < 0.01$). This result lends partial support for Hypothesis 5.

Hypothesis 6 maintains that Twitter users with weaker ideological strength are more likely to follow at least one political leader on Twitter from the opposing political party. An independent samples t-test revealed lower strength scores for those people who followed leaders from the opposing party ($t(311) = -3.73, p < 0.01$). This finding supports Hypothesis 6 (refer to Table 4.6).

The final hypothesis under analysis predicted that those people with weaker ideological strength are also more likely to follow at least one political leader on Twitter with an opposing ideological perspective. T-test results indicated that those people with lower ideological strength were indeed more likely to follow leaders with opposing ideologies ($t(381) = -3.79, p < 0.01$). Hypothesis 7 is thus supported (see Table 4.6).

In-depth Interviews

Participants' comments were helpful in clarifying and adding to several of the survey findings. While 40.8 percent of those in the survey follow "political leaders with whom I usually do not politically agree," it is not clear whether such participants followed just a few opinion-challenging leaders or many. In-depth interview comments reveal that those who followed leaders whose political views differ from their own seek out many such leaders. Between 30 percent and 50 percent of the leaders being followed provide opinion-challenging information, according to participants. The interviews also give a better understanding of which leaders qualify as opinion-challenging and opinion-reinforcing leaders. For many participants, it is not as simple as saying that Republican leaders challenge Democratic followers and vice versa.

In answering Question 10, participants cited two reasons why they seek out leaders whose views differ from theirs. Such leaders help participants to be more politically educated, and following opinion-challenging leaders is part of the intelligence-gathering process for participants who are political insiders. The final section of the in-depth interview results deals with Question 11: the reasons why participants do (or do not) have their views influenced by opinion-challenging tweets. Only a handful of participants could think of examples of their political views changing as a result of leaders' tweets.

Table 4.6 *T*-tests Comparing Mean Scores for Ideological Strength for Those Following Leaders from the Opposing Party or Ideological Perspective

	Mean (SD)	t
Ideological Strength		
Follows opposing party	2.4(0.61)	$t = -3.73$**
Does not follow	2.6(0.58)	
Follows opposing ideology	2.5(0.50)	$t = -3.79$**
Does not follow	2.7(0.47)	

Note: *p* < 0.05; **p < 0.01,

Those followers who did remember examples mentioned the value of the detailed information being linked-to in the tweets. (More on this idea will subsequently be discussed.) Additionally, participants' political party affiliations are mentioned with their quotes to give some context to the points they are making. When party registration was not available, participants were asked to rank their ideology on a scale of 1 to 10, with "1" being very conservative and "10" being very liberal.

How Ideologically Diverse Are the Leaders Being Followed?

All but one of the participants said that they follow political leaders on Twitter whose political views differ from theirs. That one participant (Ed, a Republican) said, "I don't follow any Democrats. I feel people in both parties are too partisan in what they transmit. But I do follow Republicans to help keep track of changes within the party's culture, leadership, and structure." For everyone else, the number of opinion-challenging leaders participants cited was quite high. Steve, a Republican, said, "I try to balance it out and follow Republicans and Democrats."

Many participants talked about the diversity of the views that they seek on Twitter as a ratio of opinion-challenging leaders to opinion-reinforcing leaders. For some, such as Michael, a Republican, the ratio is pretty even: "I would say as many as 50/50. Following the opponents is just as important as following supporters. If they use the vehicle to communicate serious information, you know, that's important." The same is true for Esta, who ranked herself as an 8 out of 10, with 10 being very liberal:

> I pretty much try to make it 50/50, even though some of them I cringe when I have to read what they said, you know? If I'm going to say that I follow politics, then I have to follow all of it.

For other participants, the ratio was not quite 50/50. Nancy, a Democrat, said, "If I had to quantify, I would say a good 70–80 percent of the tweets are from people with whom I share an ideology. That leaves 30 percent for those with whom I don't." Amanda, a Republican, said, "I would say 60 percent are conservative or libertarian, and about 40 percent could be considered liberal. I follow almost all of the leadership in Congress, so I'm indiscriminate of party affiliation on that issue." Jim, who ranked himself as a 1 out of 10, with "1" being very conservative, said about one-third of the leaders he follows are opinion-challengers. However, he makes a distinction between opinion-challengers who provide useful political updates and others, such as one former Florida congressman, who are known more for making controversial statements. Jim said, "Depends more on who they are and what value you can get out of them. If it's just Alan Grayson spouting off, no. But the White House press secretary? Sure. Nancy Pelosi is on there probably."

Time constraints prevent other participants from following a high number of opinion-challengers. Jeff, an Independent, said it comes down to how many hours in the day he can devote to gathering political information on Twitter:

> I definitely follow fewer opposing views/candidates than like-minded ones. This is more due to the exposure I get in other venues and my own personal use of Twitter. Had I unlimited time and energy, I would follow more dissenting/opposing viewpoints, but I do not lack for them.

What Constitutes Opinion-Challenging Leaders?

It is not always easy to guess which political leaders provide opinion-challenging information for any given follower. Many people, whether or not they are on Twitter, lean conservative on some matters but are more liberal or libertarian in other areas. Participants such as James, a Republican, reflected the diversity of views that people often have:

> I'm not so easily definable to nail down on so many issues. I'm a conservative on some issues, I'm a libertarian on others, so I kind of grab from all over the place. Most of mine are from a conservative, center-right perspective, but at least a third are left of center. I'd say at least a third of the people I follow are people who I would not probably agree with on every issue or I adamantly disagree on a few issues, and I use that as a counterbalance.

Based on James' comments, a libertarian leader's tweets could supply opinion-reinforcing information a large part of the time to him, despite James being a Republican. For Brett, a member of his state's Progressive Party, leaders from almost any party constitute opinion-challengers. "I follow people with a very wide spectrum of views, in order to keep a broad perspective. There are few people in positions of power who have similar views to mine, anyway," he said. On the other hand, Nathalie, a Democrat, screens out opinion-challenging leaders if their views are too dissimilar to hers or if their tweets are not newsworthy. One example of an opinion-challenger who meets her criteria is David Frum, a blogger and former speechwriter for George W. Bush:

> I don't carry it far enough to follow [Rush] Limbaugh or any of those nonsense people. There's no point. There's nothing to learn because you know what that person's position is going to be on just about everything. But there's a point in following someone whose interests are at least similar to mine in some ways, to see what they have to say. I've got David Frum on this list because every now and then (like a clock), he says something useful. But they're rare. It's just the same with liberal people. I don't follow [MSNBC commentator] Ed Schultz because I know what he's going to say. I like practically everything he says, but it's not news.

Other participants brought up an often-overlooked point: Opinion-challenging information can be gleaned from leaders who are in the same political party as their followers. Noel, a Democrat, said a tweet from the Obama White House regarding the bipartisan National Commission on Fiscal Responsibility and Reform challenged her beliefs, causing her to change her actions:

> When the debt commission first came out, it sounded like a good idea. But then the more I read about it, I was feeling a little bit nervous about it. It sounded like they were going to do a lot of slashing and burning. So I was beginning to think I was going to be against the debt commission. And then there was a tweet referencing Obama's comments on the debt commission. It said basically he can't comment until they finish their report, and we should do the same. I think it was a White House tweet. And that did give me pause, because after reading some of the comments so far coming from [commission co-chair] Alan Simpson and everything like that, I was like, "This is a bad idea. I'd better get on my Twitter horse and get on out there and start saying we should knock this down." But it did give me pause. So, actually, I haven't even tweeted on the debt commission.

Conversely, opinion-reinforcing information can sometimes be sent to followers from leaders who are not in their political party. Amanda mentioned then-House Speaker Nancy Pelosi as a leader she usually disagrees with, but whose tweets can occasionally include like-minded information (such as tweets regarding gay marriage). She said, "I consider myself a libertarian Republican, and that's one issue where I tell my followers, 'Yes, I'm a Republican, but the Speaker happens to be right on this issue.'"

Reasons to Seek Out Opinion-Challenging Tweets

While almost every participant said that they followed a large number of leaders whose views differed from theirs, each had a slightly different reason for doing so. The reasons can be grouped into two categories: to be more well-rounded and educated on the key issues of the day, and to conduct opposition research on leaders that can later be helpful when battling those leaders.

In terms of being more politically educated, participants said that they were politically curious and wanted to learn about the various sides of important issues. Nancy said, "It's fun and gratifying to read things that support one's own positions, but you really learn more from trying to read and understand the opposing position." Steve said, "I generally don't discriminate by political party, and I tend to follow political leaders on Twitter based on how informative their tweets will be." Carole, who ranks herself a 7 out of 10, with "10" being very liberal, said, "How do you know both sides of an issue if you only look at 'your side because it is the right side'?" Dana, a Democrat, wants to see what her opponents are thinking so that she can form a rebuttal:

> I'm trying to understand their thinking, and I'm somebody who enjoys actual debate, not the screaming and yelling kind of debate. But I think it makes people's arguments better, makes your thinking better, so it's just trying to understand the thinking process of, you know, "Well, you and I disagree. How are we disagreeing?" I don't want to just say, "You're wrong." So it's a way to find some civil discourse.

Like Dana, Esta wants insight into the thinking of the "other" side. Esta then uses that information to better understand the prevailing views in her community:

> I'm following people I think other people are listening to. Now I also follow people that I'm interested in, but I live in South Carolina and, obviously, I'm on a different political planet than most of the people in South Carolina, so it's important for me to not only listen to my neighbors but listen to the people they're listening to.

Other participants seek out opinion-challenging tweets to test their allegiance to various political positions. James said such tweets can alter his position on key issues or confirm that his position is able to withstand scrutiny:

> You get different perspectives. I'm double-checking my assumptions of why I believe in an issue or what I think about an issue. So I think that making the Bush tax cuts permanent is a great idea, then I'll read something from the left of

center that says, "Look, here's a consideration or perspective I think you should consider." So maybe I need to change my perspective on that issue, or I need to take that into account; or you know what, that argument is a red herring; I don't need to pay any attention to that at all.

Opinion-challenging leaders also are selected when they are in some way relevant to followers' personal interests. Amanda said that she follows leaders she disagrees with if they speak about issues that have particular significance to her:

> Even though I'm a Republican, I follow Democrats and Republicans. I follow the RNC and the DNC and the DCCC [Democratic Congressional Campaign Committee]. So, I'm objective on that issue. When it comes to more, like, individual politicians, it depends on what issues they're discussing that interest me. So with the health care debate, I obviously started following President Obama and the White House to see what they were saying.

Amanda also follows a number of opinion-challengers to discover the differences between leaders in the same political party. Two leaders she mentioned were Obama and Organizing for America, an organization started by Obama to help him pass his legislative agenda. One might assume these two leaders send tweets with a similar political perspective, but Amanda has found otherwise:

> I follow the president because he is the president. I follow Organizing for America because I want to see what the campaign side of President Obama has to say. I've found through experience that there are some differences in the message. Organizing for America wants to reach their base and give them some red meat to really chew on, whereas Barack Obama the president has to be more objective and a little bit more toned down to reach the entire public.

While these followers regularly seek out leaders with whom they disagree, participants noted one concern about following opinion-challengers: It makes those leaders seem more popular than they are. However, that concern does not stop participants, such as Noel, from following leaders who are at the opposite end of their political spectrum:

> Sometimes it makes it a little tough because you don't want to necessarily be a follower of them because then you know you're pumping up their numbers. For example, I'm not a fan of Sarah Palin. I'm not a fan of Michele Bachmann. I'm not a fan of Newt Gingrich, but I do follow a lot of the GOP, you know, and the Green Party and other people like that, and Tea Party members as well, because

I want to see what they're thinking. I'm a registered Democrat (a cranky one); but, you know, I still want to hear opposing viewpoints.

The second main reason for following opinion-challengers, to gather political intelligence on the opposing party, was mentioned by the political insiders in the group of participants. Several of the participants who work as lobbyists or political consultants, such as John, a Democrat, said that Twitter is ideal for doing opposition research:

> Oh, absolutely. I mean you have to. You know, "Keep your friends close and your enemies closer." It really helps. A lot of times people don't really understand what these tweets can really do. We follow some of these governors. I'm in the Democratic Party, so I follow some of the Republicans, and it helps us looking into the mindset of where they're going. That's how we do our analysis. For example—not to name the candidates—but our firm is working with a candidate in Georgia, very high profile, and we're following their opposition on Twitter and checking the facts. You know, when he says, "We got endorsements by XYZ groups and I'm really thankful," we take that tweet and print it out for evidence and then we go back and look at his legislative record and see specifically how much money that group has spent on this candidate, this elected official. That's how we do our analysis.

Likewise, Jim said it helps his business to follow leaders who have different political views than himself and his clients. The information he collects on Twitter allows him to "find out what they're doing, what they consider important. It's a primary source of news. If you can get it immediately from a source rather than someone else forwarding it to you, why not?" Information from opposition leaders can then be used to formulate a strategy when battling those leaders. Michael said tweets from leaders in the opposing party give him a heads-up to political points being made on issues that he works on, so that he can then devise a response. "If an opponent says something, it may mean I need to get out a letter dealing with issues or dealing with this argument that's being made, or something along those lines."

Reasons Why Followers Are (or Are Not) Influenced by Opinion-Challenging Tweets

Only a few participants could recall examples of opinion-challenging tweets that altered their political views. The rest said that tweets from leaders in the opposing ideological camp are useful to look at, but that these tweets do not make convincing arguments. When asked to give examples of whether she had changed her beliefs after seeing opinion-challenging tweets, Dana said, "I can't think of anything. It might just be that I'm very hard-headed or it might be that they haven't used the medium well enough." Jim said, "Honestly, I hate to say it, but I can't recall anything like that. Maybe I'm just jaded." For Jon, a Democrat, his entertainment motive for following opinion-challenging leaders partially explains why he is not swayed by opposition tweets:

> The perfect example of this is Sarah Palin. I follow her on Twitter and Facebook despite disagreeing with virtually everything she has ever said. In a way, I do this to keep tabs on the opposition; but the real reason I do so is just to have a good laugh from time to time. I also click through to most of her links and read what she has to say for herself, but I've never once become more sympathetic to her point of view because of a tweet or Facebook post.

Other participants, however, did provide examples of having their political views changed by tweets from leaders with whom they disagree. Nansen, a Republican, said that her opinion has been altered by tweets that concerned issues that matter where she lives: "There have been multiple times I've listened and changed my mind. It goes both ways. It usually has to do with some local issue." James said one tweet from Washington Post blogger Ezra Klein was influential because it showed how political compromise was possible:

> Ezra Klein had a thing about Social Security reform talking about all we need to do is just kind of raise the retirement age a little more, and that made me consider that maybe we can just ride this thing out. We can fix things at the margin rather than go wholesale change. I understand that perspective better now.

Klein also was referenced by Nathalie when she was asked if she had ever been influenced by a tweet that contained a message she disagreed with:

> Ezra Klein had a tweet today that pointed out that it may not be that important if we extend the Bush tax cuts, and he explained why. And I was so convinced that I sent it off to my e-mail list in addition to retweeting it. He had a very, very good point.

CONCLUSION AND DISCUSSION

In terms of Twitter's contribution to democracy, the findings presented here represent both good and bad news. On the positive side, quite a large number of those people in the survey, 41 percent, choose to follow political leaders with whom they usually disagree. To put that percentage into context, only 22 percent of blog users seek out blogs that challenge their views, according to one study (Johnson et al., 2009). Another hopeful sign: The percentage of respondents in the Twitter survey who choose to follow leaders with whom they usually disagree (41 percent) is about the same as the percentage of those who choose to follow only leaders with whom they agree (43 percent). Based on this evidence, it is hard to say that Twitter is making most users shut themselves off from diverse views. After all, the percentage of those who are walling themselves off politically is similar in size to the percentage of those followers who are going out of their way to seek leaders with whom they usually disagree.

However, there were some disturbing findings, the most troubling of which concerns ideological strength. Results suggest that those followers who are strong conservatives or strong liberals are more likely than the less-ideologically strong to avoid leaders with whom they disagree, and to follow only leaders with whom they agree. Ideological strength consistently emerged as a key factor in determining which followers would practice selective exposure and avoidance. Strong ideological perspectives led to more dramatic selectivity and more avoidance of opinion-challenging political tweets. Based on Garrett's (2009) conceptualization, the findings indicate that political Twitter use among ideologically strong followers does contribute to increased political polarization and potentially harms those followers' ability to understand opposing voices. The current study also confirms Garrett's assertion that seeking opinion-reinforcing and avoiding opinion-challenging content are not equivalent.

Finding that political Twitter users prefer to follow leaders with whom they share a similar ideology makes sense, given the results from the study's findings on word-of-mouth communication (see Chapter 3). Tweets from leaders with whom survey respondents usually politically agreed (a homophilous tie) were as influential as family members when it came to shaping respondents' political beliefs.

Other noteworthy findings from the survey include the role of age, political interest, and political efficacy with regard to selective exposure and selective avoidance. The young were the most likely to seek opinion-reinforcing leaders. This result conflicts with past research indicating that older individuals have less exposure to disagreeable content online (Wojcieszak and Mutz, 2009). Those people with a high political interest were more likely than those people with lower interest to follow a mix of leaders with whom they agreed and disagreed. Those people with high political self-confidence were more likely than the less confident to follow a politically diverse mix of leaders. In addition, selective avoidance was practiced less among those followers who had high levels of political interest and efficacy.

The in-depth interviews clarified and expanded upon several of the survey findings, especially with regard to how much opinion-challenging information is being sought by followers, and the reasons for doing so. According to the in-depth interview comments, most participants follow a mix of leaders with whom they agreed and disagreed, and between 30 percent and 50 percent of the leaders they follow provide opinion-challenging information. The interviews also show that opinion-challenging information sometimes can come from leaders with whom followers usually agreed, and leaders with whom followers usually disagreed do occasionally provide opinion-reinforcing information.

Participants in the interviews cited several reasons why they seek out leaders whose views differ from theirs. Participants said that following leaders they disagree with allows them to do three things: test their allegiance to a particular position, learn as much as possible about the "other side," and see what their opponents are thinking so that they could devise a response. The reasons mentioned match past research showing that those people who are politically curious, who are politically knowledgeable, or who enjoy discussing politics are likely to search for diverse views (Chaffee et al., 2001). The final section of the in-depth interview results explained the reasons why opinion-challenging tweets can sometimes change followers' views. The handful of participants who could remember opinion-changing tweets cited the detailed nature of the information as being important.

The findings also can be compared with previous research on Twitter, blogs, and other forms of communication. For example, one survey finding (that 40 percent of people follow a mix of leaders with whom they agreed and disagreed) is slightly higher than what Golbeck and Hansen (2010) found in their survey of those people who follow congressional leaders. In their study, just 33 percent of surveyed people followed a mix of agreeable and disagreeable members of Congress. Also of note, political Twitter use seems to encourage more selective exposure than blog use. While 53 percent of those people who visit blogs for political information go to blogs that have agreeable information (Johnson et al., 2009), 83 percent of those people on Twitter follow leaders with whom they usually agree.

Another comparison of this present study to prior research deals with how many Twitter accounts followers track. While one survey on general Twitter use found that the vast majority of users follow 10 accounts or fewer (Saleem, 2010), results presented in this book show that 43 percent of respondents follow 5 to 20 political leaders and 31 percent follow more than 20 leaders. (These numbers do not include anyone being followed who is not a political leader.) As a result, either the respondents are following a larger number of accounts than the average Twitter user, or the respondents are mostly following political leaders and little else.

In terms of the survey findings, several specific political variables emerged as predictors of selective exposure and avoidance. Increased political interest aligned with selecting a variety of leaders to follow. This result is similar to results in past analyses noting that those people with higher interest do not avoid opposing viewpoints (Johnson et al., 2011) and that these people actually seek out opinion-challenging information (Knobloch-Westerwick and Meng, 2009). This same study (Knobloch-Westerwick and Meng, 2009) also noted those people with a strong party preference as less likely to avoid challenging information, whereas the current study found the opposite. In the study in this book, those people with stronger ideological perspectives were actually more likely to avoid leaders on Twitter with whom they disagree. Twitter users with higher political efficacy were more likely to follow agreeable leaders, but they did not appear to avoid those leaders with opinion-challenging views. These findings are similar to past analyses that assert higher levels of political interest and efficacy reflect political self-confidence and often lead to seeking opinion-challenging information (Garrett, 2009; Johnson et al., 2011; Knobloch-Westerwick and Meng, 2009). Future study is needed to explore this difference between those who exhibit political confidence versus intensity of ideological preference.

Self-reported party and ideological identification had an impact on the types of leaders followed on Twitter. As expected, many users follow those leaders of the same party or ideology. This result has been common in past research addressing Twitter users (Golbeck and Hansen, 2010), as well as for online news searches and website viewing patterns (Iyengar and Hahn, 2009; Tancer, 2008). It seems only natural to follow those leaders with matching political perspectives to keep up-to-date with the current political climate. The problem arises when such selectivity leads to an avoidance of additional points of view. Research has indicated that such avoidance is not always the case (DiMaggio and Sata, 2003), as many online users seek out diverse opinions. Interestingly, for the current study, Independents were the most likely to seek out a wide range of viewpoints.

Motivations for using Twitter were again explored for their influence on the types of leaders followed. Results indicate minimal influence. The only impact noted was for those users with entertainment motivations. These individuals were more prone to select agreeable leaders to follow on Twitter. Perhaps those followers interested in entertainment are less interested in being aware of opposing viewpoints for the sake of being informed (because information is not their primary reason for using Twitter in the first place).

Willingness to engage in activities related to Twitter were analyzed for potential influence. Selective exposure was practiced by those users who were willing to retweet. In comparison, those followers willing to reply were less likely to selectively expose and avoid challenger content. A user's willingness to take subsequent actions, such as signing a petition or donating money, predicted both selectivity and avoidance of opinion-challenging information. Possibly, more active users select like-minded tweet interactions so that they may demonstrate support for the leaders with whom they agree (by making donations or retweeting, for example). Those followers who use the "reply" feature may be more interested in voicing their disapproval or rebuttal arguments and would, therefore, be less likely to avoid challengers.

Selective exposure and avoidance were assessed in the survey by analyzing the number of Twitter users who said that they specifically followed at least one political leader from the directly opposite party or ideological perspective. These findings revealed that while the majority follows like-minded leaders, many followers also avoid those leaders with different views. Some differences are noted with respect to party and ideology. Republicans and conservatives were less likely to follow the opposition in several cases. This result aligns with past analyses that suggest that those people on the political Right are more susceptible to political polarization (Iyenger, Hahn, Krosnick, and Walker, 2008; Mutz, 2006). However, other data from the survey suggest the opposite. In terms of ideological strength, strong liberals were the most likely to select only agreeable leaders to follow on Twitter. As a result, the debate will continue over which political persuasion is the least open to diverse viewpoints.

The Twitter users under analysis selected a variety of political leaders to follow on Twitter with opinion-reinforcing and challenging viewpoints. This chapter has revealed trends in those followers seeking agreeable information and avoiding dissimilar content. The implications are important, as increased political polarization can be detrimental to the political process. Similar to past research, the number of people on Twitter following agreeable leaders greatly exceeded those seeking out opinion-challenging leaders on Twitter (Johnson et al., 2009). In-depth interviews further revealed why followers gravitate toward agreeable information and often consume disagreeable content as well. It would appear that Twitter provides unique access to a diversity of viewpoints that many find appealing.

Chapter 5

In Their Own Words

Exploring the Role and Value of Political Twitter Use in Followers' Lives

Twitter's sudden rise to prominence is impressive, yet the microblog is not currently an essential resource for most people in terms of information gathering and communication. Twitter's ability to attract 175 million users worldwide pales in comparison with Facebook's 600 million monthly visitors and to the billions of people who watch television (Carlson, 2011; Penner, 2010; Weeks, 2010). In addition, Twitter users make up just 13 percent of U.S. Internet users (Smith, 2011), and no state has more than 2 percent of its population on Twitter. By contrast, 30 percent to 50 percent of the people in most states are on Facebook (DCI Group, 2011). To become more widely adopted by people for politics, Twitter will have to prove that it has distinct advantages over other types of media, that it is compatible with people's needs, and that it is easy to use. To find out if Twitter is up to the challenge, the study discussed in this book used in-depth interviews with followers of political tweets. The results showed what they like and dislike about Twitter as a source of political information. The study also revealed how Twitter compares with blogs, social networking sites, and other forms of new media for politics. This chapter will explore the findings.

In-depth interviews are frequently used to delve into people's behaviors. The open-ended nature of the questions can reveal how and why people make the choices they do. For example, past studies using this method have discovered several things: the process by which advertising strategies are created (Ashley and Oliver, 2010) and interpreted by viewers (Millard, 2009); the role media use plays in people's lives (Shumow, 2010); and which social and personal experiences influence people's attitudes toward buying certain products (Blair and Hyatt, 1995). In-depth interviews are especially useful in understanding the many ways in which people adapt to changes in their media environment, such as when new technology (Dupagne and Garrison, 2006) or political and economic forces (Parmelee, 2009a) influence the news-gathering process.

Several in-depth-interview studies dealing with Internet use and political communication are particularly helpful in guiding this chapter's exploration of political Twitter use. Interviews of Internet users have revealed social and psychological reasons that drive people online for both cultural information (Kayahara and Wellman, 2007) and political information (Parmelee and Perkins, 2012). Several of the reasons had not been found previously using other methods, such as surveys. One reason for this lack of findings is that in-depth interviews encourage participants to talk as long as they feel is necessary to fully explain their feelings and actions. In terms of Twitter, interviews with followers can uncover the reasons why they feel that the microblog is useful for their political information gathering and political engagement.

Other in-depth interview research has looked at how users of online discussion groups describe the types of political information they are getting and the value of this information to them (Stromer-Galley, 2003). Similarly, research into political Twitter use must find out how followers judge the value of the information that they receive from political leaders via Twitter.

One aspect to take into consideration is that those who follow political leaders are often political activists or leaders themselves. As a result, questions for followers must explore what they feel are the major advantages and disadvantages of using Twitter as a tool for influencing the political process. Past in-depth interviews have shed light on how political leaders and producers of political advertising craft media messages (Driessens, Raeymaeckers, Verstraeten, and Vandenbussche, 2010; Parmelee, 2003). However, there are still other questions that must be asked to make any predictions regarding Twitter's future success in the political arena.

UNDERSTANDING WHY SOME INNOVATIONS BECOME POPULAR AND OTHERS DO NOT

A number of factors can indicate whether a new technology, such as Twitter, is likely to become widely adopted for politics or other activities. Questions for political Twitter users need to take these factors into account. Rogers (2003, pp. 229–264) identifies five characteristics that show the potential of an innovation: relative advantage, compatibility, observability, trialability, and complexity. Relative advantage refers to whether a new product or technology has identifiable advantages over existing products and technologies. In addition, a new technology must be compatible with the values and needs of users. Observability and trialability are achieved if a technology is easy to find and sample before a long-term commitment is made. Finally, those technologies that are considered to have low complexity are more likely to be adopted than those technologies that seem difficult to use.

According to a review of 75 academic studies that investigated the adoption of various innovations, the most important factors in determining success are compatibility, relative advantage, and complexity (Tornatzky and Klein, 1982). Consequently, in-depth interviews with political Twitter users should investigate these factors. Followers of political leaders can shed light on Twitter's potential by sharing their perceptions of how compatible the microblog is with their political and informational needs, its advantages over other political information sources, and its level of complexity.

Another way to assess the impact of a new technology is by using Robertson's (1971) continuity–discontinuity framework. According to this model, a new product or technology that causes minimal impact on people's behavior is called a *continuous innovation*, while technology that sparks a major shift in people's behavior is a *discontinuous innovation*. In the middle of these polar opposites are *dynamically continuous innovations*, which cause more moderate alterations in behavior.

Understanding Twitter's place within the continuity–discontinuity framework can show where the microblog fits within the larger context of past communication innovations. For example, if political Twitter use has drastically changed how users gather information and engage politically, then Twitter should be considered a discontinuous technology, on par with the introduction of the home computer (Anderson and Ortinau, 1988) and the digital video recorder (Smith and Krugman, 2010). On the other hand, political Twitter use may be less revolutionary. Twitter may be merely a continuous innovation (as when touch-tone phones replaced rotary-dial phones), or a dynamically continuous innovation (similar to how pay cable TV opened up new options for TV viewers; Krugman, 1985).

RESEARCH QUESTIONS ANSWERED BY THIS CHAPTER

Two broad research questions helped to guide the creation of the in-depth interview questionnaire:

- Question 1: What role does political Twitter use play in followers' lives?
- Question 2: How do followers interpret the value of political Twitter use?

These research questions are meant to explore the relationship that followers form with Twitter and how that use fits into the political process. Also addressed in the questions are Robertson's (1971) continuity–discontinuity framework and Rogers's (2003) innovation characteristics.

METHOD USED TO ANSWER THE RESEARCH QUESTIONS

The recruiting of participants, the procedures used during the interviews, and the data analysis were conducted based on traditional in-depth interview guidelines (McCracken, 1988).

PARTICIPANTS

The participants for these questions were the same respondents mentioned in previous chapters. There were 18 people who consented to be interviewed via e-mail or on the phone for 30 minutes. All of them said that they followed at least one political leader on Twitter. The demographic form they filled out indicates that the sample included six Democrats, seven Republicans, one Independent, and four people who listed themselves as "other" or "not registered to vote." The average age was 42, and most participants (78 percent) were white. There were nine men and nine women. The average annual income was between $65,001 and $100,000, and 78 percent of participants had a bachelor's degree or a graduate degree.

PROCEDURE

The participants used a one-name pseudonym while answering the questions so that they would feel free to speak their mind about the political leaders they follow and the political activities in which they engage. Several main questions and follow-up questions (called *probes*) were designed to draw-out responses that would answer the two research questions. To find out how followers interpret the value of political Twitter use, participants were asked: "What are the best and worst parts about getting tweets from political leaders? What would you change about them? Why?" Participants who used the microblog for political activism also were asked about the best and worst parts of using Twitter for that activity. Another probe asked how happy participants were with the level of engagement they have with political leaders on Twitter. Participants were asked: "To what degree is political Twitter use compatible—or not compatible—with your political needs, and do you find Twitter easy to use?" These questions were useful in addressing some of Rogers's (2003) innovation characteristics, such as whether political Twitter use is compatible with followers' needs and lifestyle, as well as whether using the microblog is complex.

Another way for participants to interpret the value of political Twitter use is for them to compare it with other forms of political information gathering and engagement. Such a comparison also can reveal whether political Twitter use plays a unique role in followers' lives. Thus participants were asked: "How does using Twitter for politics compare to using other sources for politics, such as social networking sites (Facebook, MySpace) and blogs?" Probes included questions such as: "What can Twitter give you that you can't get from these other sources? What can these other sources give you that you can't get from political tweets?" These questions touch on Rogers's (2003) innovation characteristic of relative advantage by showing what advantages Twitter has over its competitors. In addition, the questions place Twitter use within Robertson's (1971) continuity–discontinuity framework by finding out whether political behavior on Twitter is unique (or similar) to what is found on other forms of new media. Other questions that focused on the continuity–discontinuity framework include the following: "To what degree has your political Twitter use changed the way you gather political information, or engage politically, or do your job (whichever of these apply to you)? Please give an example that demonstrates how large—or how small—these changes have been."

Another interview question compared the various types of political information sources that are found on Twitter. The question was: "Aside from political leaders such as politicians and political organizations, who else do you follow on Twitter for political information? News organizations? Friends and family? Why?" These questions look at the relative advantage that political leaders' tweets have over politically oriented tweets from social ties and news media. In taking this inquiry tact, it becomes easier for the researcher to make distinctions between the relationship that followers form with politicians and political organizations—versus other sources of political information. Finally, participants were asked: "Is there anything that I've not asked about how you use Twitter for politics that I should have asked?" This question helps to avoid missing key information from participants and allows them to talk further about the value of Twitter and the role it plays in their political life.

ANALYSIS STRATEGY

As is true with most other in-depth interview studies, the data from the participants was analyzed using a grounded theory framework (Glaser and

Strauss, 1967). The data that were analyzed included transcripts of the phone interviews and printouts of the e-mail interviews. The analysis that was done was similar to Smith and Krugman's (2010) in-depth interview study (regarding the role that DVR use plays in viewers' lives). Those researchers analyzed their transcripts to re-examine and shed new light on concepts such as Rogers's (2003) innovation characteristics and Robertson's (1971) continuity–discontinuity framework. The data analysis done for this chapter re-examines old concepts, as well as seeks to discover new themes regarding the role that political Twitter use plays in people's lives and the value of Twitter to them.

Results

Interviews with participants indicate that they feel that their political Twitter use is quite valuable and serves a number of functions in their lives. The participants were self-described "political junkies" either for personal reasons or because their job requires a deep understanding of the political scene. In terms of answering Question 1, there are several roles that the microblog plays in their lives. The advantages of Twitter are that it is:

- The quickest way to get unfiltered information and insight from political leaders.
- A soapbox that allows anyone to reach and influence a wide spectrum of politicians and politically interested individuals.
- An important resource for political consultants, lobbyists, journalists, and anyone else whose business relies on political information.

Research Question 2 was answered when participants said that they interpret Twitter as a highly valuable political tool on a personal and professional level. They feel Twitter gives them unique advantages when it comes to receiving and spreading political information. Participants' comments show that Twitter possesses the characteristics of successful innovations, such as compatibility, relative advantage, and low complexity (Rogers, 2003; Tornatzky and Klein, 1982). Twitter's interactive features and its requirement that messages be short and to-the-point are compatible with participants' need for political information and activism. Participants said Twitter's interactivity and brevity give it advantages politically over social networking sites, such as Facebook; traditional news outlets; friends and family; and, in some ways, blogs. Twitter also is considered easy to use.

There was one improvement that participants said would make political Twitter use more valuable and compatible with their needs. Participants indicated that political leaders should do more two-way communication, such as replying and retweeting, which would make the leaders seem more engaged with their followers. Right now, leaders usually limit themselves to one-way communication, such as tweeting followers a steady stream of information about what the leader is doing politically and personally.

Participants said their political Twitter use has caused a major shift in their personal and professional behavior. This finding suggests Twitter is a discontinuous innovation (Robertson, 1971), which places the microblog in the same category as the digital video recorder (DVR) and the home computer. Similar to how DVR technology "introduces meaningful changes to how viewers use television" (Smith and Krugman, 2010, p. 258), Twitter's features have caused major changes to how participants use their computer or mobile phone to gather political information and to engage politically. A more complete review of the participants' comments can be found on the pages that follow.

THE ROLE OF TWITTER IN POLITICS

Twitter plays many roles for the participants. The people in this study included highly connected political insiders, as well as outsiders who had no link to government but had a keen interest in all things political. Some roles of Twitter are more important to insiders, but some roles overlap both groups.

Quick, Unfiltered Political Information

Participants said speed is what gives Twitter an edge over other sources of political information. Comments include the following: "The best part about political tweets is how fast the information moves," from Ed; and "The best part of getting these tweets is the real-time information," from Jeff. *Speed* refers not only to how quickly political information shows up on Twitter, but also how quickly one can read over tweets to find the ones that are valuable. Jim said, "It's faster. It's easier to just take a bunch of information and aggregate it in a very simple format and just scan through it. I mean I can go through a hundred people in less than a minute." From the perspective of speed, Twitter's 140-character format is a real strength.

Quick access to political information is especially helpful to political insiders. One such operative said speedy tweets straight from Congress help him serve his clients:

> John: I am very much satisfied because you can get updated information, how they have voted. For example, on Twitter, there's an account called @HouseFloor and @SenateFloor, where there's certain staffers of the Ways and Means

Committee or Homeland Security Committee, they just tweet right off the bat what's going on and how people have voted, and that general information is very helpful for especially political analysts, and like myself, to get that information as soon as possible.

Interviewer: How does that help you exactly?

John: Because we have clients, and we have to update them. I work with the Democratic Party very closely, so we have to update our constituencies to make sure that we have the information of how they voted. The breaking news and the analysis, it's kind of like on your fingertips. The whole race is all about who gets the information first and who puts out the information first. So when I get my tweets every single day from Congress or local from some of the newspapers, it's about who gets the most information and how quickly you can get the information.

In addition to the speed at which information travels on Twitter, participants said they enjoy the unfiltered information and insight they get from politicians' tweets. Nancy said she prefers information straight from politicians rather than media coverage of politicians:

> I like getting the tweets because (1) they're "real time" and (2) they are not filtered by the media or a pundit, so I know it's their true thoughts and intentions as opposed to spinning about things being taken out of context…. Twitter lets me hear directly from people as opposed to others talking about these people.

Unfiltered information from members of Congress can be useful not only to political operatives, but to those people who have never been political insiders. Esta is one of many participants whose interest in political tweets is personal, not professional:

> I just truly enjoy seeing their point of view, although I do realize to a very strong degree I'm being manipulated on both sides, on all sides. But I find it real interesting where something may occur and I read from one end of the spectrum to the other, and the twists and turns that everybody wants you to go through. I find that very interesting. It's a maze.

Tweets from politicians also are valued because the messages may spur action on the part of participants. Carole said this possibility is especially true during a campaign:

> What I do like to see when they are running is where they are going to speak in advance, as I might go, and what they thought at a debate or event. For politicians not currently campaigning, I like them to tweet about bills or things they are working on. What they like, what they don't. Any article they read that might give them some insight.

Of course, politicians are not the only source of political tweets. Participants said they also rely on tweets from political journalists for many of the same reasons that they follow politicians: the latest news and insight. In terms of speed, Nathalie said, "The best thing is when they let me know about some exciting thing that has happened, like, 'Our poll shows this,' or updates to things happening." Jon said Twitter is "the first place a news story breaks—or at least the first time I hear about it. I keep updated on tweets in order to seek out the latest political news before it hits other forms of media." In addition, he said that the insight he gets from journalists' tweets can be more helpful to him than the stories they write:

> I follow many news organizations and political journalists on Twitter for their quick responses to the latest breaking news and interesting takes, which are often more interesting to read in quick 140-character clips than they are in full-length reporting. I think this is because the short takes are just their first thoughts on the matter rather than an in-depth look, which can sometimes obscure the interesting bits as they get lost among paragraphs of background information that I already know.

Nancy's comments are similar to Jon's point (that journalists' tweets can be more revealing, and therefore more useful, than journalists' stories): "It allows me to get more insight from reporters who are more objective on the air or in print than they are in their tweets."

Twitter as a Soapbox

Participants said Twitter is not just about receiving information from politicians and journalists. Participants also desire to send information to these people and to others. In this role, Twitter helps participants be more politically engaged and influential. Amanda said the microblog lets her engage with people she otherwise would not have access to:

> Twitter is one of the places where you actually have your own soapbox to stand up and give the world your views, and people can choose to ignore you or comment. And a lot of times people that I don't know, that I've had absolutely no connection with, reply to me, message me, ask me a question, and we build discourse, and I would say that at least half of the people who follow me on Twitter I've never met, but they happen to agree with me or disagree with me and we have that discourse—and through traditional means like news media that doesn't really happen. It's essentially the public's own place to have that forum.

Like Amanda, Nathalie is eager to share her opinions. Nathalie, who used to write political op-eds for her local newspaper, now prefers Twitter as a way to influence people: "I have what is obviously a fantasy that there are people out there who don't know what it is I'm about to send them and they really should."

Hashtags are an important aspect of Twitter's ability to be used as a soapbox.

A hashtag, which is designated in a tweet by the "#" sign, can be a word or abbreviation, and it can be searched on Twitter's website. The tweets of anyone who includes that hashtag are grouped together on the site. The information sharing that occurs on hashtags allows anyone to inject their opinion and influence others. Nansen, who was involved in the early days of the Tea Party movement and the #tcot hashtag, said that hashtags helped her organize conservatives during the first years of the Obama administration. "Hashtags are what mobilized and allowed people with common interests to find each other," she said. "And so instead of coming home and turning on the news, you'd just go to your Twitter stream and look up what was being said on #tcot."

The discourse Twitter facilitates is not limited to any one country, according to Dana:

> Things will pop up and you immediately want to respond to that, which is amazing for me to be sitting there looking at folks from Afghanistan and Kenya and be able to bounce things back and forth, and say, "We've never met, we don't know each other; but, hey, I wanted to respond to what you just put out."

Politicians are often the intended audience of participants' tweets. The hope, they said, is that they can influence the officials' thinking. On some occasions, participants have succeeded in sparking dialog (however brief) with political figures. Cecily, who said her political Twitter use gives her "self-satisfaction in that my voice and opinion is being heard," had one such encounter with Newt Gingrich, a former college professor and Speaker of the House in the 1990s. In 2009 she tweeted: "I admire him as historian, and teacher. I would love to take his class. But I would never vote for @NewtGingrich." Gingrich tweeted her back and asked: "Why not?" Cecily then tweeted him a link to a blog that included disparaging comments about a commercial he did in 2008 with then House Speaker Nancy Pelosi on the topic of climate change. Even if there is no reply, tweeting politicians can have an effect, according to Cecily:

> The good thing about Twitter is that you don't have to follow someone to contact them and tell them how you feel. You can tweet it to the world, hashtag it, and somebody in the social media department in their office/party will read it.

Jon also said he finds value in tweeting politicians regardless of whether they reply back:

> The best part is when you know that your response to someone's tweet is going to be seen by that person. Even if they don't reply, you know they got the message. That is very satisfying and provides access to politicians we previously have not had.

A Resource for Businesses Involved with Politics

Many participants said Twitter helps them do their jobs. Some participants advise political clients. Other participants do not have inherently political jobs, but they work in industries that require up-to-date political information. Jim, whose company does lobbying and marketing for political clients, said that the microblog increases his access to information that can assist his customers:

> I use it as a news service, as a news aggregating service. I can follow things in real time. If there's a news story or something that applies to one of our clients, I can get it and send it to them faster than one of their staff members will find it. It's a lot like the old-fashioned neighborhood bar that all the politicos would hang out at. You don't have to do that anymore. Yeah, you can do that; but you can have people from all over the country. If you know who you want to follow, you can follow and you can kind of see how a news story will move or one reporter can get something going, how individual reporters or activists or bloggers or whomever and members of Congress interact.

John, who provides policy analysis to his clients, also finds Twitter an effective way to transmit information to his customers:

> My audience, because I'm in politics, is obviously elected officials, candidates who are running for political office, political magazines from Washington, D.C., some of these lobbying firms, trade associations. The information we send out is very helpful to those folks whether we're presenting a policy analysis or we're trying to push more information. So our tweets are very specific.... We will put studies from the State Department; we will put studies from Homeland Security, the new laws, specifically when it comes to politics, when it comes to polling, when it comes to what's going on in local politics. That's what we do.

Those participants who are not lobbyists or political consultants also find political tweets to be an important resource. James, who works in the health care industry, said political tweets were especially helpful to him as Congress hammered out healthcare legislation in 2009–2010:

> My background is in policy, and I work for a hospital. So for the healthcare debate, and even now, you're following different policy organizations, policy wonks, and of course the political leaders, and getting information that there's some new report out or here's an article about a particular aspect of healthcare reform. So, yeah, I use it as a way of crowd-sourcing information and data.

In addition, journalists look to Twitter when they are trying to generate story ideas or to gather information for stories that they are already working on. Steve, who writes for a newspaper, said political tweets are often newsworthy:

> The best part is any inside information that comes out or when a politician like Sarah Palin or someone else makes news with their comments. Because it's on Twitter, it's fair game to use for the news media.... As a journalist, that's what I look for in tweets: nuggets of interesting, new, and exclusive information.

THE VALUE OF POLITICAL TWITTER USE

In many ways, all of the participants' views thus far presented are a testament to Twitter's worth. But while all the participants find Twitter valuable, they had several interpretations of its value to them and society. Many, such as John, said they consider Twitter to be revolutionary: "I think that Twitter has changed politics—in what we do in the United States—in fact, all over the world." Others, such as Brett, see Twitter as connected to a larger revolution: "It's part of a general transformation of society that the Internet culture is driving."

On a personal level, participants said that Twitter is valuable because it gives them access to information and insight that they never had before. Steve said, "It's a great way to have access to statements of politicians that otherwise I wouldn't have access to. In some situations, it also provides a strong glimpse into what life is like for a politician."

Others, such as Jeff, said Twitter's emphasis on speed and mobility is what makes the microblog valuable: "Twitter's become indispensable very quickly—most notably in a way Facebook has *not* for me. It's easier to use, viable on the go, and much faster paced." Still others, such as Nancy, said Twitter's high value comes mostly from the feeling of empowerment the microblog gives them:

I have the opportunity to share my thoughts with journalists and politicians who would never cross my path otherwise. It's a powerful feeling to be able to read, comment and maybe even have a short dialogue. For something with such a small number of characters with which to communicate, it's a very powerful tool.

Those people who did not talk about Twitter in terms of empowerment, speed, or insight, still found Twitter valuable because they said it is now simply a necessity. Ed said, "My wife and I resisted Facebook, Twitter, etc., until we decided it was impossible to ignore in our nonprofit work, business work, and political work."

However, almost all participants added that their political Twitter use would be even more valuable to them if the political leaders they follow would interact with them more. Amanda is one of many participants to be disappointed by the inconsistent level of engagement they have with leaders:

Amanda: The worst thing I would say is that a lot of politicians don't take advantage of the fact that they can interact with voters on Twitter. I find a great deal of them really just post what they have to say, but don't @reply any of them, and I think it's actually a really great tool for them to get what I want without having to be in a sort of forced conversation, so they can correspond with voters quickly and efficiently.

Interviewer: Are there times you've tried to interact with leaders on Twitter? And how has that gone?

Amanda: I've had positive and negative experiences with it. I think one of the best people on Twitter who actually responds to people is [former Bush adviser] Karl Rove. Karl Rove to me is one of the most involved. I think he's the one who most effectively uses Twitter, and he interacts with everyone, and his tweets are both political and personal, so you get both sides of it. The big disappointment for me has been [Congressman] Jason Chavitz. I follow him, and I happen to really enjoy him. I picked up on him freshman year, and I was really intrigued by him, and every time I would @reply him, I never got a response. But he doesn't seem to @reply anyone.

Brett is likewise interested in more interaction with the leaders he follows. One solution he proposes is for leaders to enlist members of their staff to help them be more engaged on Twitter:

The best is when someone is actually on Twitter and actually engaged, and the worst is when they're distant and obviously not really there. A lot of politicians' tweets are painfully empty, with no responses to all the people trying to talk to them, no living organic commentary on the Twitter zeitgeist, no presence. This is what I would change: If a politician doesn't want to personally engage with

Twitter, and they just want to have staffers come stand in for them, that's fine; but what the staffers should do is start their own accounts, identify who they are and what their role is, and truthfully engage from their own perspective.

Brett's proposal sounds similar to how Twitter is already being used by many corporations, such as Pepsi, Dell, and JetBlue. Dell, for example, has more than 100 Twitter accounts where employees reply to tweets and solve customers' problems (Milstein, 2010b). Using this model for members of Congress, for example, key legislative and communication staff members would have congressional Twitter accounts dedicated to answering questions, getting advice from followers, and engaging in constituent services.

Nansen built a large Twitter following by being known as someone who engages. Nansen said politicians are not using the microblog effectively if they do what she calls "celebrity tweets" most of the time. She added: "What I mean by that is one-way pontificating. There's no conversation. A celebrity tweet is somebody who says, 'I'm driving by 7-Eleven. I think I'll have a Slurpee.' There's no invitation to dialog, no call to action." Politicians should look at what their followers are saying and regularly act on those comments, she said. Nansen gave one personal example of when she acted on a follower's comments to illustrate the reach that Twitter can have if used in this way:

> I'm sitting at my computer, it's Saturday morning, and I see a tweet that a guy outside of Orlando, a retired elderly priest, his car has broken down and he is asking by way of Twitter for some help.... So I retweeted it, my friends retweeted it, they retweeted it, they retweeted it. Within half an hour, a pastor from a local church in the same area had arrived with a can of gas and a sandwich, and they were happily on their way, and they tweeted it. Politics works the same way in that I may not, you know, live in Texas; but it might be that my neighbor's family is in Texas. It's that communication on six degrees of separation. Good leadership on Twitter (and I think the politicians, especially the Republican side) are really learning about how you can't just talk to your own people. You have to talk to everybody because you never know the connections.

Some participants are somewhat forgiving of leaders' lack of engagement. Jim is one of several participants who figure it is nearly impossible for leaders to interact with the thousands of followers who try to interact with them every day:

> Interviewer: How do you feel about the level of interaction you get to have with leaders on Twitter?
>
> Jim: There's none, unless you personally know a person. The problem, which is a benefit but also a disadvantage, is that anyone can pile in there, and it's a

huge amount of information just flying around. The way to use the darn thing is to be selective and only be following folks that you actually care about.... You can find some prominent people and follow their discussions and kind-of spy on them. But unless you know them, you can't interject yourself into it.

Interviewer: Do you sometimes try to reply to or direct message leaders? Do they engage you or ignore it?

Jim: Oh, they ignore it. I don't know if it's even necessary. I mean, sure, I've done it before, but I don't know they're necessarily ignoring it. It's just not possible for them to respond. They respond by blind luck. They just happened to see your message in their massive stream of thousands and reply.

Despite their concerns about the level of interaction between followers and political leaders, the participants still find their political Twitter use quite valuable because it plays several roles in their personal and professional lives.

It is important in the upcoming section to answer two other questions about Twitter: Is it an innovation that can have widespread, long-term success? How dramatically does it change users' political behavior?

TWITTER AS AN INNOVATION

Participants' comments suggest that Twitter has greatly altered their behavior, which places the microblog on the discontinuity end of Robertson's (1971) continuity–discontinuity framework. Twitter has the major characteristics of other successful innovations (Rogers, 2003; Tornatzky and Klein, 1982). While the participants' comments about Twitter as an innovation were overwhelmingly positive, a few participants said there were several aspects of the microblog that did not pass the test of compatibility, relative advantage, and low complexity.

Compatibility

"Twitter is very compatible with my political needs. There is not a single thing that I would change about it," said Amanda. Other comments focused more specifically on the variety of needs that political Twitter use satisfies. Some political insiders, such as Jim, need information from Twitter that can help them in their business: "For what I use it for (namely gathering information so my clients can remain on top of issues important to them), it is perfectly compatible." Other insiders said Twitter is most compatible when it helps them to transmit information. John said, "Twitter is highly compatible with my political needs because we communicate through Twitter. In fact, we recommend any political candidate or elected official to get on Twitter because constituencies like nontraditional access."

Twitter also can be a teacher. Dana said she learns things that help her in her professional life: "Being in the international development field, I am interested to see how many people in other countries use Twitter as an organizing tool for protests, movements, etc."

Participants said that their political Twitter use fits other aspects of their lifestyle, which is increasingly fast-paced, social, media-saturated, and politicized. Nancy said that she uses Twitter for many of these reasons:

> It gives me a "heads up" on issues to delve into often much earlier than I would have heard about them via news media. Also, it gives a broader perspective of media slant, which isn't as evident if you consistently only watch or read one or two providers.

Cecily said Twitter is compatible with her need to influence others:

> I find it extremely important to be able to have the knowledge and ability to stay in touch with my network of friends and politicians. Politicians can ignore faxes, e-mails, letters because only their office receives it. If you tweet it, the whole world knows what you're telling politicians and they have to respond.

Some comments, however, reveal that there are certain aspects of Twitter and how it is used politically that are not compatible with participants' needs. Chief among their complaints: the feeling that political leaders' tweets do not come from the leaders themselves. Jon said, "The worst part about getting tweets from actual politicians is when it's clear the tweets are coming from a ghostwriter or a campaign staffer rather than the politicians themselves." Participants said ghostwritten tweets do not satisfy their need for direct, unfiltered information from political leaders.

Even when tweets are composed by a leader's own hands, some content can fail to be compatible with participants' needs and expectations. Tweets that are overly personal or self-centered can be a problem. Michael called some tweets useless because they involve discussions such as "someone saying they're frustrated because the bartender hasn't gotten to them soon enough. The self-absorbed type of ones that don't transfer any real information." John also said that his need for useful political information is not met by tweets that focus on personal details:

> I can understand in politics you have to get at the personal level. But as a professional, I would be more interested in how they have voted and where do they

stand on issues, rather than wanting to know if their granddaughter is having a baby.

One of the more important features of Twitter, retweeting, also can be disruptive. Jeff said that his need for quick, easily accessible political information is sometimes not met because of how much retweeting goes on:

> The worst part is how busy the talk can be. For instance, I follow [GOP candidate] Charlie Baker and many of his operatives regarding the 2010 Massachusetts gubernatorial race. If one person tweets information, it almost immediately gets retweeted a half-dozen times. The next thing you know, my timeline is flooded with identical material.

Relative Advantage

In talking about Twitter's advantages and disadvantages, participants said that the microblog was more useful to them for political information and engagement than many other sources. Participants such as Brett appreciate the access that Twitter gives them: "One reason I like Twitter (compared with other media) is that it seems like there's a much better chance there of getting a message through to someone famous or powerful."

Of all the social networking sites, Facebook was overwhelmingly mentioned as Twitter's key competitor, partly because almost all of the participants have Facebook accounts. Because of this familiarity, participants' comparisons of Facebook and Twitter are especially valuable. Only one participant said Facebook served them better politically than Twitter. The rest considered Twitter faster, more professional, and more secure than Facebook. In terms of speed, it is again important to note that Twitter's weakness is also its strength: 140-character messages limit discussion but make information gathering and interaction easy. Twitter is just quicker and simpler than Facebook when it comes to finding useful political information, according to Amanda:

> In Facebook your news feed is clogged with personal updates. It's clogged with people who play those games, and I find that their pages for news organization and politicians, it actually is counterproductive to the cause because you get a person out there who disagrees and it gets ugly, and you just end up in a fight, whereas on Twitter, simpler format, you don't have anything clogging your feed. You can make lists, so if you look at my Twitter home page, I have about 20 lists that I made, and it breaks down into different categories, so I can just click between the lists depending on the topic I want to see at the time. It's essentially the fact that you can pick and choose in ways that you can't on Facebook. You can discriminate on Twitter much more easily.

Jeff also appreciates the ease with which he can engage politically on Twitter: "Facebook feels useless to me politically—a lot less interactive, a lot more noise with limited value. Twitter, being completely opt-in, means I cut through the noise." John said that Facebook's many features make it too cluttered and not in tune with peoples' hectic lifestyle:

> Facebook is very interesting, but it's highly unprofessional. When it comes to being professional, I think there's too much going on on Facebook.... I see Twitter as more influential than Facebook because the information is in snippets. Nowadays, it's a 24/7 media cycle or circus. Because of too much information, we have to weed out what we're looking at. Sometimes what you want to do or what you want to follow, you can't follow on CNN or Fox News or MSNBC because you're looking for specific information. So with selecting tweets, that information comes to you directly. And you don't even have to read the whole article, because people are busy.

John added that he feared that changes Twitter introduced during summer 2010 would make it more like Facebook and, therefore, less useful to him: "Twitter has come out with a new strategy where you can put, like, videos and pictures and more stuff. I hope that Twitter doesn't go to that Facebook level."

A theme repeated by participants was that they use Facebook for their personal life but Twitter for their political life. As Esta put it: "Facebook is where I put pictures of my grandchildren." Jim said, "The truth is, I only use Facebook for basically personal stuff. You know, pictures of family and a way to hunt down one of my relatives. I use Twitter more for business and politics than Facebook." Noel said, "I don't use Facebook for politics at all. I use Facebook for my own personal use to interact with my friends and family." James made an especially stark comparison of the types of people he engages with on the two sites:

> Facebook is worthless because the people I interact with on Facebook are more my social friends and family and people who aren't at the level of sophistication or expertise on political issues. So, if someone posts something on Facebook, it's a friend of mine, a fraternity brother from college who is talking about Obama being a Muslim. If I interact with somebody on Twitter, it's my friend who worked in the House Ways and Means Committee who's linking to an important report or article. I draw a very clear, bright line between the two.

Carole is another participant who compartmentalizes her relationships on Facebook and Twitter, which suggests that the two sites serve different functions:

Someone said Facebook is full of people you used to be friends with and Twitter is for people you should be friends with. I believe that. I have people on Facebook that I haven't had a real friendship since high school. I am not going to talk to them about politics, especially in the partisan climate of the last couple of years.

Facebook also does not seem to be as helpful as Twitter for political organizing, according to participants. Dana said Facebook was disappointing when she used it for activism:

I have not found Facebook to be as useful in a professional, political sense. I kind of discovered Twitter and found that was just a cleaner way to get information. ... I haven't found Facebook very useful. It's very useful for exchanging baby photos, but I've not found it very helpful for really gathering people. I worked on a grassroots student campaign against legislation that would have allowed concealed weapons in schools here in Texas at universities, and we did the whole, you know, "Please attend," and we had all these hundreds of people say, "Yes, we'll attend the training to do lobbying," and then you're making follow-up calls, and people are saying, "Oh, did I click on that? Oh, I didn't know what it was. I just clicked on the button."

Participants also found Twitter to be more secure and private than Facebook. Nathalie said, "I tried Facebook briefly and then I saw they had so many issues with privacy, I canceled and cleansed and purged all connections, so I never really used it." Cecily said, "I trust Twitter more for security and anonymity."

The one participant who ranked Facebook ahead of Twitter did so because of all the features Facebook has to offer. Ed said, "Twitter isn't comprehensive enough. Facebook has been more useful and clearer." Interestingly, Twitter's minimalist approach is a major reason why the other participants favor the microblog over Facebook. As a result, any attempt by Twitter to satisfy Ed's concerns could drive away more users than it would attract.

Twitter also compares favorably with blogs, though the comments show that political blogging and microblogging are considered quite different and valuable in their own ways. Once again, the speed with which a user can look over a wide variety of political information is a big advantage of Twitter. James said that kind of speed causes him to choose tweets over blogs:

Twitter is more useful than blogs. I don't have time to sit down and go through a blog roll. Twitter is my de facto blog roll. And also, I don't want to have to scroll through somebody's blog and read the headlines and read the first paragraph, I can just look at the tweet and decide. And, yeah, maybe that's not the best way of doing things, but if you write it well, that tweet can help me decide whether I'm going to read it now or just delete it and ignore it.

Other participants, such as Dana, said Twitter is better than blogs for political engagement:

> The problem with a blog is, I've had a blog for six years, and people read it, but people don't leave a lot of comments, and so it's a bit isolating, I think, unless you're really, really focused in developing your audience, so I think that's a much harder path to developing conversation and exchange.

Some participants also said they have reduced their blog usage because Twitter is better able to meet their needs. Nathalie said, "Some blogs I really like to follow, but I have to say that with the information I get from Twitter, I've cut back somewhat on blog shopping."

However, most participants use blogs and consider them to be valuable, just in a way that is distinct from Twitter. As Jim put it: "Of blogs and so forth, they're different. Depending on the quality of them, blogs are basically columnists, with added comments, sometimes from the public. It's more in-depth. It's different." Participants noted that Twitter is better than blogs when they want a quick scan of the political headlines, but that blogs offer more when participants want additional detail. The ability to get in-depth information on blogs was the sole advantage over Twitter that participants mentioned. According to Noel, Twitter and blogs are important political resources, but blogs provide a deeper look at issues:

> Noel: If I had to rank them, I'd probably go blogs No. 1, Twitter No. 2, and then Facebook, and MySpace isn't really on the radar.
>
> Interviewer: What makes blogs better for your political consumption than Twitter?
>
> Noel: More information. Even though you get a lot of information, it's still 140 characters. For a blog, you get the subject, you get the body, you get the conclusion. It's all there in one space. It's not like with Twitter where you read something and then, because it's only 140 characters, people can't even provide a link to it. People are trying to cram it into 140 characters, and sometimes it isn't very coherent. But on a blog, everything is there.

Like Noel, Jeff ranked Twitter ahead of Facebook but not blogs. He said blogs better satisfy his need to thoroughly explore political topics: "I do prefer blogs to Twitter for the information, though, because I'm a data collector at heart and desire more information than 140 characters can generally provide."

While blogs and Facebook were mentioned the most in comparison to Twitter, other sources also were discussed. Friends and family often came up as sources of political information, but participants said Twitter has clear advantages. Twitter offers more valuable and more easily accessible information, according to John:

> I would rather have my information from Twitter because it is coming from the sources that I want or I want to do opposition research on. I can get to Twitter faster through my Blackberry than calling my friends in Pakistan or calling my friends in India or the UK and asking for information.

Low Complexity

Participants consider Twitter easy to use. As Nancy put it: "I find it so easy; it's downright addictive." Amanda said, "It is a simple interface that makes it easy for anyone to use it." In addition, Twitter's simple format does not prevent it from meeting participants' varied political needs. John said, "Twitter is extremely easy to use, convey your message, develop new friendships, promote/market business opportunities and allow me to develop a stronger relationship with the media and elected officials all across the world."

On the other hand, no innovation is free from problems. Twitter can sometimes crash when too many people are using it. Such glitches led Jim to say, "It's always easy to use, when it is working." In addition, one participant, Esta, mentioned an aspect of Twitter that she does not consider easy: "I am not clear on how to personally, without being published, respond to a twitter."

Also, some participants found Twitter to have low complexity for what it was designed for, but they wished that the microblog could take on other tasks. Brett said, "Sure, Twitter's easy to use. That's how it blazed into popularity so quickly." Yet he added: "There's a lot of things that are especially difficult on Twitter, like having a structured, deep conversation." That said, within the limits of 140-character conversations, Twitter has a simplicity that participants appreciate.

Twitter: A Discontinuous Innovation

Innovative products and services can cause three types of changes to consumers' behavior: "major," which is called *discontinuous*; "moderate," called *dynamically continuous*; and "minor," meaning *continuous*. Robertson (1971) noted that it is often difficult to judge whether an innovation causes major or minor changes in people's lives. As a result, he argued that researchers should "rely on consumer perception and, as suggested, accept majority consumer opinion" regarding which products they feel are innovations and how much those innovations change their behavior (p. 7). Using consumer perceptions as the criteria, Twitter can be labeled "discontinuous." Participants said Twitter has caused major changes in how they engage politically and gather information.

Twitter opens new opportunities for participants to interact with political leaders and fellow political junkies, according to Brett:

> There's something special about how Twitter changes the way people relate to the famous, well-connected, powerful.... Twitter has definitely changed how likely I am to engage directly with political leaders. It's a lot easier to tweet at someone powerful than to write them a letter, and it feels less pointless since I can address my tweet to my own followers as well. There's a sense of everyone collectively engaging with powerful people, working together to create a stream of information for them.

As with Brett, Nancy's political involvement has been altered since using Twitter. She said Twitter has "increased my activism and allowed me to 'recruit' others." She added that she has "engaged on a much more intense level," contacting elected officials more than twice as much as she used to. Esta provided a more specific example of how Twitter has increased participants' engagement:

> I have been much more likely to respond to politicians and/or political causes because of the influences of information received on Twitter. My example would be the lack of [congressional] funding for those heroes injured or killed on 9/11. I contacted a dozen politicians about that subject.

Ed said that the 140-character limit on Twitter has altered the way he communicates politically, forcing him to get to the point:

> Politically inclined people love sending links on news stories. Twitter bridles our impulse to write too extensively on the link. It gives us a chance to go straight to the link and read a story or news piece for ourselves. It has, by default, generated a certain discipline in the way we share things with each other, politically, that has made access to information more concise and clear.

Twitter also has altered the campaign process. Amanda said that Twitter has changed the way she helps elect candidates:

I can teach others about my viewpoints or those of the candidate whom I am working for. I can engage elected officials and others to create a dialogue for an issue that is of concern to me and even engage other people who might not be traditionally engaged in politics. By way of an example, I was able to double my candidate's Twitter presence because I was able to communicate with people who might not otherwise call the campaign office or send the campaign an e-mail. This generated interest in my candidate and raised the community's awareness of him. It even resulted in several campaign donations from people who might not otherwise have donated.

Another example of Twitter's impact on campaigning comes from Jeff. He said hashtags are a vital feature that allows those in campaigns to better receive and transmit information: "Engaging politically, it has revolutionized it for certain. I was involved with a local campaign here, and a lot of information got passed along using the hashtag for our race: #ma02 [Massachusetts second district]."

The political information mentioned in tweets often creates a domino effect that impacts other media. Trends can be started on Twitter that then move to blogs, social networking sites, and traditional news sites. As Nansen put it: "Twitter has the ability to drive traffic across all platforms."

Twitter can change how political businesses interact with clients and the general public. John said he has now integrated Twitter into how he markets his firm. "After writing a political press alert on our firm's page," he said, "I post it on Twitter. Since I have started using Twitter, views/clicks on our website increased significantly."

Participants' information gathering behavior is the other aspect of their political lives that they feel Twitter has changed. The speed and diversity of the information has shifted the way that participants learn about issues and candidates. Jim said, "I can gather information more quickly and in near real-time simply by following a good selection of people much faster and comprehensively than following even a set of different 'news' sites. That's a profound change." Twitter also has altered some participants' behavior toward other information sources. Dana said her Twitter use "has replaced traditional media, at least when I want more consistent updates from people on the ground."

Twitter's vast pool of political information has enticed participants to become more inquisitive and knowledgeable. Nancy said, "I find myself pointed to publications I didn't know existed, so I'm reading political material to a far greater extent.... I have a better overall understanding of issues and viewpoints." Jeff, too, has learned things he never would have using other sources:

It gives me a different way of gathering information in a faster way. Instead of having a ton of blogs in my Google Reader, for instance, I can follow certain hashtags, like #tcot (Top Conservatives On Twitter), or certain twitterers to get links that may be of interest to me and may be overlooked by my own reading.

CONCLUSION AND DISCUSSION

Twitter, like any innovation, will not last long unless it plays roles that are compatible with users' lives and has advantages that make it more valued than the competition. The interviews presented in this chapter were designed to discover the roles and value of political Twitter use. Participants' comments point to three main roles, and all of these roles are high in value to the participants: Twitter is the best way to get quick and unfiltered political information; it is a soapbox to engage politically; and it is a helpful tool for businesses that participate in and cover politics. In addition, comments indicate that Twitter does have the key characteristics of most successful innovations, and that the microblog has caused major changes in participants' political behavior. Taken together, these findings suggest that Twitter is a significant innovation for politics that is up to the challenge of competing in a crowded field of social networking sites, blogs, traditional media, and other venues.

The roles and value of political Twitter use include one-way and two-way types of communication. In terms of one-way communication, participants find value in receiving political information and in transmitting their views to their followers. In addition, participants enjoy two-way communication in the form of engaging in discourse with politicians, political activists, journalists, and fellow political junkies. The value that participants place on two-way communication helps explain their disappointment at the lack of interaction by many political leaders on Twitter. As a result, political leaders would do well to make more of an effort to reply to followers' questions and ask for their advice. Doing so could make those leaders seem more valuable to followers and more compatible with their political needs.

The findings also expand Rogers's (2003) concept of innovation characteristics, which have been used to better understand innovations in fields such as energy conservation, transportation, and mass communication (Tornatzky and Klein, 1982). Updating the concept to include Twitter further shows what a wide range of innovations can be studied in this way. Participants have said that Twitter is compatible with their political needs, has advantages over competing sources, and is easy to use. These comments indicate that the microblog has the characteristics of a widely adopted innovation. Two other characteristics on Rogers's list, observability and trialability, were not examined during the interviews. This exclusion is partly because Tornatzky and Klein found that observability and trialability are not related to adoption in the way that compatibility, relative advantage, and low complexity are. Also, Twitter has observability and trialability because Twitter is free and easy to find online, and many of its features can be sampled before making the commitment of signing up for a Twitter account.

Twitter's advantage over social networks such as Facebook is worth further discussion. Participants said that they use Facebook and like it, but not for politics. They said that Twitter is faster for receiving and distributing political information, has a more professional look, and is more secure. This finding has implications for political leaders, many of whom devote more resources to Facebook than to Twitter. One survey found that congressional staffers view Facebook as more important than Twitter for communicating the views of those in Congress (Congressional Management Foundation, 2011, p. 7). In-depth interview participants' comments suggest that members of Congress and other political leaders may be overestimating Facebook's political value relative to Twitter's.

Twitter can now be compared in importance with other communication innovations. The major shift in personal and professional behavior that participants said Twitter has caused suggests that the microblog is as discontinuous an innovation as the home computer and the DVR. It might be difficult at first to think of Twitter as *this* revolutionary. After all, many of Twitter's features, such as tweeting, retweeting, replying, and hashtags, have existed in somewhat different versions for years in the form of bulletin boards, electronic mailing lists, chat rooms, and social networking sites. However, as Robertson (1971) notes, discontinuous innovations do not need to be completely new. Discontinuous innovations tend to "perform either a previously unfulfilled function or an existing function in a new way" (p. 8). In the case of Twitter, the microblog's features perform several existing informational and discussion functions in a way that is faster and easier than before, and all on one site.

This chapter broadly explores participants' general political use of Twitter. The point of this is breadth of coverage is to provide a wide perspective of the political impact that Twitter makes in people's lives. It should be noted, however, that the themes reported here regarding the roles and value of political Twitter use come from a small, nonrandom sample of Twitter users in 2010. Different themes may occur later as the demographics of who uses Twitter for politics changes over time. For example, participants' comments suggest that those who use Twitter now for political information and engagement are political junkies either personally or professionally. As the average political Twitter user becomes more mainstream in terms of their interest and involvement in politics, the microblog may play roles in users' lives that differ from the ones presented here. Furthermore, the roles and value of Twitter could change considerably if another microblog emerges that is perceived to be better than Twitter at political information gathering and engagement.

Chapter 6

Tweets on the Campaign Trail

An Analysis of Frames Used in 2010 Campaign Tweets

While tweets are made up of messages that are no more than 140 characters in length, much can be conveyed in that limited space. Political leaders' tweets can contain such information as policy proposals, explanations of votes, personal information, quotes, statistics, reactions to other tweets, links to websites, and hashtags. Because political tweets include such a wide variety of information, it is important to understand how political leaders portray their policies and personality on Twitter. Specifically, does the information in tweets connect to a single theme or many themes? Also, do those themes differ depending on the political experience, ideology, age, or gender of the leaders? Answering these questions can explain how the messages in political tweets are packaged, as well as reveal a bit about the leaders who send them. For example, research into other forms of political communication, such as political advertising and speeches, has found that successful politicians craft messages that stick to a few main themes, such as change, values, and freedom (Devlin, 1994; Parmelee, 2002; Sing, 2010; Sloan, 1996).

In addition, candidates often emphasize issues relating to the campaign race itself, promoting a strategy frame (Bichard, 2006; Capella and Jamieson, 1997; Druckman, 2005). When looking specifically at online platforms, studies indicate the frequent use of message content that attacks the policy or character of opposing candidates (Bichard, 2006; Wicks and Souley, 2003). Some research also asserts that candidates display a more personal and interactive tone in online communications, such as blogs (Trammell, Williams, Postelnicu, and Landreville, 2006). If political tweets reveal the use of frames such as those found by other researchers, then Twitter is being used to package political leaders in a way that is similar to what is found in other forms of political communication.

To understand how political leaders package themselves on Twitter, this chapter includes a *frame analysis* and *content analysis* of campaign tweets from 2010 gubernatorial and senatorial candidates. Frame analysis finds themes that are embedded in messages. Frame analysis looks for a message's frame, which is the "central organizing idea or story line that provides meaning to an unfolding strip of events" (Gamson and Modigliani, 1987, p. 143). Content analysis allows for an additional and more quantitative assessment of frame intensity. By using both methods, a complete examination of the framing used in the 2010 election can be conducted. For this book, campaign tweets from political candidates were studied so that comparisons could be made with more traditional forms of campaign communication (such as press releases and political advertising).

HOW FRAMING THEORY CAN SHOW THE POWER OF TWEETS

Past analyses have found that the visual and verbal information in political advertising often unites around a central theme or story line to influence viewers' opinions of candidates (Morreale, 1991; Parmelee, 2003). Frame analysis is based on framing theory. This theory posits that communicators (such as journalists and political advertisers) create story lines, or frames, to organize large amounts of information into an efficient package for audiences to interpret (Gamson and Modigliani, 1987; Gitlin, 1980). Seen from this perspective, the wide array of information in a candidate's tweets may connect to a few themes that paint a portrait of who the candidate is or who the candidate wants to be.

Several other aspects of framing theory apply to the examination of political tweets. Entman (1993) says that frames are powerful because they focus an audience's attention on certain issues and away from other issues:

> To frame is to select some aspects of a perceived reality and make them more salient in a communicating text, in such a way as to promote a particular problem definition, causal interpretation, moral evaluation, and/or treatment recommendation for the item described. (p. 52)

Tankard puts it another way, "the power of framing comes from its ability to define the terms of a debate without the audience realizing it is taking place" (2001, p. 97). Thus framing can be an effective tool in a political campaign. Because there are an infinite number of frames that the writers of campaign tweets can choose from, examining in this study why certain frames were picked provides insight into how candidates tried to define the terms of their campaign.

Experiments have shown that how an issue is framed can affect how people think about that issue (de Vreese, 2004) and can affect the choices people make regarding that issue. In one of the most well-known framing experiments, Kahneman and Tversky (1984) demonstrated that framing manipulates people's decisions by increasing awareness of certain issues, while directing attention away from other issues. Experiment participants were told to choose between two options to fight an impending health crisis. While both choices were the same, each was framed differently. Findings indicated that participants based their choice depending on how each option was framed. Strategically framed tweets also may have this kind of influence over followers' voting decisions.

Each location of a frame can impact the meaning of a message (Scheufele, 2000). Frames (Entman, 1993) exist in four locations of the communication process:

1. *Within the writer of a message.* A writer's cognitive frame is the mental story line that writers use to make sense of political issues and the world generally. The writer thus determines what information will be included or excluded in a message. Consciously or unconsciously, a writer's perception of the world shapes content.
2. *Within the message.* Frames within a message are reflected in the words, phrases, images, and sources of information that provide "thematically reinforcing clusters of facts or judgments" (Entman, 1993, p. 52).
3. *Within the receiver.* Receivers of the messages have cognitive frames that shape how they comprehend the messages. The receivers' cognitive frames, which help receivers make sense of their world, often shape meaning in ways that the writer did not intend (Iyengar and Simon, 2000; Shen, 2004).
4. *Within the culture.* This location includes the common perceptions that the larger culture has about politics and society.

The following material will examine each of these locations in respect to Twitter. For example, the first location (within the writer) refers to the people who compose campaign tweets. The writer may be the candidate. The writer may be a staff person. But either way, writers' cognitive frames about politics shape what they put in their tweets. Some researchers use the terms *schemata* or *schemas* to describe cognitive frames (Entman, 1993; Fiske and Taylor, 1991). These terms mean someone's preconceived view on life.

The belief system of writers affects their actions. One study of political magazine coverage of President Ronald Reagan found that journalists tended to select those frames that fit their already-established perceptions, or *schemas*, of the president and politics in general. In contrast, the journalists ignored frames that clashed with their schemas (Parmelee, 2006a). This finding confirms Smith's (1997) point that "the individual frames issues within his or her established schemata" (p. 7). Consequently, analyzing the frames in campaign tweets can provide a window into how the writers (candidates and their staff) perceive key issues and the political process.

The second location is the message. The message is the most important location in this chapter's exploration of campaign tweets. Frames in messages can trigger positive or negative feelings through the process of *priming*, a technique in which a receiver's perceptions and memories are activated through visual or verbal stimulation (Price and Tewksbury, 1997; Richardson, 2002). In one study of this concept, college students reacted negatively to political ads because they said that the themes predominately addressed older voters. Such framing triggered their established perception that politicians ignore their age group (Parmelee, Perkins, and Sayre, 2007).

In addition, the meaning encapsulated in a message's frame can be highly symbolic. Symbols can be displayed visually or verbally and are important to research because they represent many layers of subtext. In a study of Reagan's press coverage, for example, some journalists used cowboy symbolism to frame the president, which could cause pleasant or unpleasant feelings about his personality and policies based on the shared cultural subtext of that symbol (Parmelee, 2006a). Tweets, too, may be framed with words or phrases that trigger positive or negative emotions in followers based on symbolism or other factors.

Past researchers have identified specific framing categories that have emerged with respect to message content. Iyengar and Simon (1993) used *episodic* and *thematic* framing categories to evaluate news media coverage of the Persian Gulf crisis. *Episodic framing* refers to a context of specific events or concrete instances, whereas *thematic framing* refers to the placement of news issues in a more broad or general context. McCombs and Ghanem (2001) explored the convergence of agenda setting and framing by depicting frames as the transfer of attribute salience. Ghanem (1997) uses the description of a metaphorical "picture frame" to outline the following four framing categories: (1) topic (what is included in the frame), (2) presentation (size and placement of frame), (3) cognitive attributes (details of what is included in the frame), and (4) affective attributes (the tone of the picture). Chyi and McCombs (2004) take a similar approach and present a two-dimensional structure for assessing media frames with categories including both a time and space dimension. This focus on time (past, present, and future) and space (individual, community, regional, societal, and international) provides a more objective framing analysis tool that can be applied to a variety of content. Most analyses have focused on more traditional media, so it is unclear if such categories are relevant to new emerging media platforms such as Twitter.

POLITICAL CANDIDATE FRAMES IDENTIFIED IN PREVIOUS STUDIES

To put the framing of candidate tweets into a larger context, it is useful to review what other framing studies have found. Framing theory has been used in a variety of research studies with a focus on political candidates and frames used during elections. Content analysis and frame analysis have yielded some intriguing findings that pave the way for the Twitter analysis in this chapter.

Content Analysis Framing Categories

Political elections serve a distinct purpose in providing information on potential political leaders. Many studies have examined how such information is provided and digested by the general public. McCombs, Llamas, Lopez-Escobar, and Rey (1997) identified substantive and affective dimensions for evaluating framing in the 1995 Spanish election. *Substantive content* focused on specific issue positions, qualifications, and personality, whereas the *affective dimension* revealed the tone of frames (positive, negative, or neutral). Their content analysis and survey findings indicate a significant match between frames offered and the public perception of candidates. The strongest correspondence was on the affective dimension.

Capella and Jamieson (1997) looked specifically at issue and strategy frames used to describe the political election process. They assert that *strategy frames* primarily emphasize the political game of winning and losing, while *issue frames* stress specific content related to policy. Druckman (2005) further explored the use of *issue, personal*, and *strategy* frames for an assessment of the 2000 Minnesota Senate campaign. That study's content analysis of newspapers and television campaign media coverage revealed that the media primarily emphasized the use of strategy frames.

Cho and Benoit (2005) examined press releases by Democratic presidential primary candidates in the 2004 election according to Functional Theory. The *Functional Theory* of political campaign discourse proposes that candidates use a combination of acclaim, attack, and defense actions in order to increase their favorability. Cho and Benoit discovered that the majority of candidates focused on the acclaim function in order to demonstrate their desirable character, policy stances, and accomplishments. Candidates also emphasized policy issues with more intensity (compared to character or campaigning topics).

Content categories have been asserted and studied with frequency, but it is uncertain if such groupings will apply to new platforms such as Twitter. It may be useful to draw from past analyses and examine a selection of categories to detect their applicability in an online context (albeit one containing only 140 characters of text).

Themes Revealed in Frame Analysis

Studies have examined framing for a variety of candidate types: challenger, incumbent, Democrat, Republican, female, male, African American, and Caucasian. Morreale (1991) used a textual frame analysis to explore verbal and visual elements in Reagan's 1984 re-election campaign film, "A New Beginning." She found that the Republican "used framing to create a 'reality'" (p. 96) through the use of ideological, mythic, and rebirth frames in the film.

A frame analysis (Parmelee, 2003) reviewed the 2000 presidential primaries of "meet the candidate" videos, which are ten-minute political ads that include a candidate's biography and issue positions. This analysis indicated that *change* and *values* frames are common. George W. Bush's video, for example, exemplifies the change frame by mentioning a barrage of changes that Bush made as Texas governor, and by Bush speaking about the country's need for "a fresh start after a season of cynicism" (p. 38). The values frame is seen in Al Gore's video, which visually and verbally framed Gore as a rural man with small-town values and avoided almost any reference to the then vice president's decades of Washington experience. Friends and neighbors from Gore's boyhood home in Carthage, Tennessee, described his upbringing and early career with phrases such as: "He got his values out of the hills of Tennessee" (p. 31).

One frame that was seen with every 2000 candidate was the *media validation* frame. In other words, much of the personal and policy information that the candidates provided was supported with quotes or clips from the news media. For example, while Bush talked about his education agenda, his video showed a quote from *BusinessWeek* magazine: "Is Bush's record on education really that good? In short, yes." Other candidates included positive quotes from *Newsweek, National Journal*, CNN's *Crossfire*, PBS's *The NewsHour*, and NBC's *Meet the Press* (pp. 45–48).

The values frame also has been found in meet the candidate videos from candidates seeking other offices. Former U.S. Attorney General Janet Reno and lawyer Bill McBride, candidates in Florida's 2002 governor's race, spent almost no time in their videos discussing their careers. Instead, they tried to prove, as McBride said in his video, that their "Florida roots run deep" (Parmelee, 2006b, p. 90).

In the 2008 presidential campaign, Barack Obama's primary video focused on the *unity* frame, which suggested that Obama could unite America in terms of ideology, class, and race. The video addressed many issues (such as healthcare, arms control, and ethics legislation) by mentioning how he built bi-partisan coalitions to solve many problems during his time as a legislator in Illinois and the U.S. Senate. The video notes, "In all these efforts, he's brought Democrats and Republicans together for the common good" (Parmelee and Perkins, in press).

Framing Candidates Online

As candidates become increasingly advanced technologically, the need for online campaigning platforms has become a necessity. The type of content used to frame messages appears to vary with respect to online platforms. Wicks and Souley (2003) examined topics and thematic frames in news releases found on candidate websites during the 2000 presidential campaign. Frames using an opponent attack were the most prominent.

Candidate blogs provide a unique environment for analysis by offering message content in a more conversational tone. Such blogs sometimes even allow users to post their own content. The 2004 election cycle showcased the use of campaign blogs with great intensity and thus began the push toward a more interactive election campaign climate. Trammell, Williams, Postelnicu, and Landreville (2006) analyzed the 2004 Democratic presidential primary and identified candidate blog content with a majority focused on supporter testimonials and statements of thanks. Many candidates encouraged fundraising and other campaign interactivity by using hyperlinks. Hyperlinks also were used frequently to connect users to favorable media excerpts. A conversational tone was prominent in the posts, with roughly half of the sample employing a more personal address such as "you" or "you all" to appeal directly to readers.

Bichard (2006) conducted a content analysis of blogs in the 2004 presidential election campaign and identified several dimensions of framing in the blog entries of George W. Bush and John Kerry. Drawing from categories identified by Chyi and McCombs (2004) as well as Ghanem (1997), a multidimensional approach was used that identified time, space, tone, and topics used to frame the messages posted on each candidate's campaign blog. The findings indicate that a majority of messages focused on the present, addressed the individual, and had a tendency to attack opponents. The challenger was more likely to feature a negative tone, whereas incumbent content was more positive. Interestingly, when candidates posted negative content, they often used media excerpts to soften the blow and to thus avoid backlash.

YouTube provides yet another interactive venue for candidates. Public feedback on it is prominent, as YouTube allows viewers of video content to rate and post comments. A content analysis of online-message framing was conducted with respect to Sarah Palin's 2008 vice presidential nomination acceptance speech—as viewed on the Cable-Satellite Public Affairs Network (C-SPAN) channel on YouTube—as well as subsequent user postings on YouTube (Chambers and Bichard, in press). Benoit's Functional Theory of political discourse (2005) was used to provide context; and as the theory posits, the speech primarily emphasized the acclaim function. User comments used a variety of frames, but comments were primarily negative in tone and focused on the issue of character. This finding coincides with Papacharissi, who noted that online communication often provides a more anonymous venue for heated debate (2004).

An investigation of frames in the campaign tweets from 2010 may find themes and message content similar to those revealed in past research, or ones that are unique to Twitter. As interactive tools become more popular to engage the electorate, Twitter messages may provide an easy outlet for increased two-way communication and interactivity. An assessment of the strategies used in messages on Twitter provides a unique context for examining how candidates frame their candidacy in a new media environment.

RESEARCH QUESTIONS ANSWERED IN THIS CHAPTER

This chapter employs both frame analysis and content analysis to investigate how candidates frame their messages on Twitter. Past analyses have revealed a variety of frames in the political arena, but there has been no substantial focus primarily on Twitter. Therefore, the following research questions were developed to offer a broad exploration into the framing practices used by candidates in their tweets.

- Question 1: What frames were used in candidate tweets during the 2010 campaign?

- Question 2: What differences in framing can be found with those tweets, in terms of the candidates' political experience (such as incumbents, challengers, first-time candidates, and political veterans), gender, age, and party?

METHODS USED TO ANSWER THE RESEARCH QUESTIONS

Candidate tweets were collected in 12 races from October 1st to November 2nd. During the 33 days selected for inquiry, every tweet was captured for each candidate in the 12 races analyzed. This large sample yielded more than 40,000 words and a total of 4,174 tweets. The races included those for the U.S. Senate in Alaska, California, Connecticut, Florida, Kentucky, Missouri, Nevada, and Pennsylvania; and for governor in California, Florida, Ohio, and South Carolina. In addition to these elections being competitive, the races were selected because the candidates represented variety in terms of party, gender, and political experience. The age of candidates in the sample ranged from 38 to 72, with the average age being roughly 54. For the 33 days analyzed, the tweet frequency varied by candidate, ranging from a single tweet (Marco Rubio) up to 456 total tweets (Harry Reid). A list of candidate information, including their Twitter accounts as well as their total number of tweets, can be found in Table 6.1.

Content Analysis

A content analysis was conducted as one avenue to explore answers to the research questions. This form of analysis is frequently used in communication research and offers a systematic quantitative technique for studying messages and developing inferences concerning the relationship between messages and their context (Krippendorff, 1980). The current content analysis followed an a priori design, where all decisions for variable coding and measurement were formed prior to the gathering of data.

A variety of variables were coded for each of the tweets in the sample. The unit of analysis was the individual tweet (each did not exceed 140 characters). For the content analysis, assessments were made of each tweet alone (without following hyperlinks or watching video content). Each tweet was identified by candidate, their party registration, seat, gender, and age, as well as the date and subsequent outcome of the election. When looking specifically at differences among candidate frames by party affiliation, the two candidates who ran as independents (Charlie Crist and Lisa Murkowski) were recoded to reflect their dominant prior party affiliation (both were coded Republican) in order to have sufficient cell sizes for comparison. The number of Twitter

Table 6.1 12 Twitter Accounts Analyzed in the 2010 Campaign

Twitter Accounts Studied	Total Tweets	Party/Seat
AK Senate		
Lisa Murkowski (@Lisa4Senate)	261	Independent/Incumbent*
Joe Miller (@JoeWMiller)	68	Republican/Challenger
Scott McAdams (@McAdamsforAK)	217	Democrat/Challenger
CA Governor		
Jerry Brown (@JerryBrown2010)	197	Democrat/Open*
Meg Whitman (@Whitman2010)	153	Republican/Open
CA Senate		
Barbara Boxer (@Boxer_2010)	66	Democrat/Incumbent*
Carly Fiorina (@CarlyforCA)	343	Republican/Challenger
CT Senate		
Dick Blumenthal (@DickBlumenthal)	81	Democrat/Open*
Linda McMahon (@LindaForSenate)	230	Republican/Open
FL Governor		
Rick Scott (@ScottForFlorida)	126	Republican/Open*
Alex Sink (@AlexSinkFlorida)	199	Democrat/Open
FL Senate		
Marco Rubio (@marcorubio)	1	Republican/Open*
Charlie Crist (@charliecristfl)	71	Independent/Open
Kendrick Meek (@KendrickMeek)	119	Democrat/Open
KY Senate		
Rand Paul (@DrRandPaul)	39	Republican/Open*
Jack Conway (@ConwayforKy)	153	Democrat/Open
MO Senate		
Roy Blunt (@RoyBlunt)	243	Republican/Open*
Robin Carnahan (@RobinCarnahan)	229	Democrat/Open

OH Governor

John Kasich (@JohnKasich)	147	Republican/Challenger*
Ted Strickland (@Ted_Strickland)	86	Democrat/Incumbent

PA Senate

Pat Toomey (@ToomeyForSenate)	132	Republican/Open*
Joe Sestak (@Sestak2010)	220	Democrat/Open

SC Governor

Nikki Haley (@nikkihaley)	145	Republican/Open*
Vincent Sheheen (@vincentsheheen)	61	Democrat/Open

NV Senate

Harry Reid (@HarryReid)	456	Democrat/Incumbent*
Sharron Angle (@SharronAngle)	131	Republican/Challenger

Note: * asterisk denotes the winner of the election.

followers and the number of accounts followed by each candidate were also recorded.

The data collected also allow for an assessment of how interactive the tweets were. One definition of *interactivity* focuses on how candidates encourage supporters to take actions (actions such as posting comments or clicking on URL links) on behalf of the campaign (Trammell, Williams, Postelnicu, and Landreville, 2006). Perhaps more importantly, another definition of *interactivity* measures the degree to which candidates engage in two-way conversations with their supporters or critics, such as when candidates reply to supporters' questions. The present analysis includes both definitions. Coded-for in the research was the absence or presence of replies/mentions, hashtags, retweets, direct quotes, URL links, photos, and video content. Replies and mentions were included in the same coding category partly because Twitter considers replies to also be mentions (Twitter Help Center, 2011). Also, both replies and mentions can help a leader seem interactive. A reply also can be called an "@reply." An "@mention" is Twitter-shorthand for mentions. A reply looks similar to a mention, except that the "@username" appears at the beginning of the tweet. Another difference between the two functions is that a candidate's mentions are sent to all the candidate's followers, while a reply is sent only to those people who follow both the candidate and the user getting the reply.

As mentioned, photo and video content were not accessed through click-through, so these contents were coded as present only when mentioned explicitly. The multidimensional analysis of framing (as featured in past study; Chyi and McCombs, 2004; Bichard, 2006) included both the topic and tone featured in each tweet. Several representations of topic frames, as well as affective tone and formality, were used from prior research (Bichard, 2006; Chambers and Bichard, in press; Ghanem, 1997; McCombs, Llamas, Lopez-Escobar, and Rey, 1997; Trammell, Williams, Postelnicu, and Landreville, 2006; Wicks and Souley, 2003).

The topic dimension included seven levels. If a variety of topics were apparent in the tweet, coders were trained to select only the single most dominant frame featured. Frames were identified as dominantly focused on one of the following seven levels:

1. *Campaign Trail.* Tweets about specific events and the candidate's daily activities, as well as polls and advertising.
2. *Personal.* Tweets covering family or personal life, primarily nonpolitical in nature.
3. *Candidate Ideology.* Tweets offering policy/issue positions.
4. *Opponent-Focused.* Tweets focusing on the opponent, including ideology/character.
5. *Call to Action.* Tweets directly calling for specific supportive action, such as volunteering, voting, retweeting.
6. *Endorsements.* Tweets offering information regarding an official endorsement, or offering supporter testimonials.
7. *Unsure/Other.* Coders were also offered this option just in case an additional topic emerged worthy of analysis (less than 2 percent fell into this category).

The tone dimension included a focus on both the affective and formality of tweets. Coders were instructed to code only the dominant tone in each tweet, both affectively and with regard to formality.

Coders selected the dominant affective tone from the following three choices: (1) *Negative.* The tweet contained negative, aggressive, sarcastic, or hostile language. (2) *Neutral.* The information was void of judgment. The tweet stated only the facts. It gave a nonevaluative description of events. (3) *Positive.* The tweet was enthusiastic and offered evaluations in noninflammatory language, stressing fairness/sensitivity.

The formal tone of each tweet was assessed in three ways: (1) *Formal.* The tweet was delivered in an impersonal tone, in neutral press-release style or mass-journalistic-delivery style. (2) *Conversational.* The tweet was casual in nature, with a personal quality, as if spoken face-to-face. (3) *Other.* This option was offered for coders if the tweet tone seemed neither formal nor conversational (less than 1 percent fell into this category).

Two coders were given the coding definitions to review and discuss. Once they demonstrated a satisfactory understanding of the coding scheme, a random sample of 10 percent of the total tweets was analyzed to establish reliability. Cohen's kappa was used to calculate reliability coefficients in order to account for agreement by chance (Lombard, Snyder-Duch, and Bracken, 2002). The inter-coder reliability check produced Cohen's kappa coefficients of 0.85 for the *topic* variable, 0.92 for the *affective tone*, and 0.83 for the *formality tone.*

The data obtained were analyzed using a variety of statistical techniques. To address the research's Question 1, frequencies and mean scores were used to provide a descriptive assessment of the different frames used by candidates. Figures also were constructed to offer an overall depiction of the framing categories used over time (see Figures 6.1 through 6.4). Chi-square analyses investigated differences among the framing dimensions to answer Question 2. Standardized residual scores were analyzed for all chi-square results to further detect significant cell influence; this analysis is reflected in the description of findings. ANOVA analyses and independent samples *t*-tests were used to detect differences in age among the framing dimensions. Finally, logistic regression analyses revealed the influence of framing variables on the outcome of the 2010 election. Age, gender, seat, and party registration were entered in the first block to control for influence. The results can be viewed in Tables 6.2 to 6.4.

Frame Analysis

While a single, precise definition of what to look for in a frame analysis has historically been hard to come by (Matthes, 2009), many frame analysis studies (Parmelee, 2003; Wall, 2006) have used Entman's (1993) definition. Using this approach, the researchers in this study examined the candidate tweets for "Keywords, stock phrases, stereotyped images, sources of information, and sentences that provide thematically reinforcing clusters of facts or judgments." In addition, close attention was paid to how the tweets chose to: "Promote a particular problem definition, causal interpretation, moral evaluation, and/or treatment recommendation for the item described" (p. 52). The researchers took extensive notes while they examined the keywords, images, and moral evaluations that were found in the tweets. The themes that emerged from viewing the tweets were agreed upon by both researchers.

RESULTS

Content Analysis

A variety of frames were used to offer campaign information. It is clear that even when candidates were limited by Twitter to 140 characters, they were able to express themselves in numerous ways. During the time frame under scrutiny, candidates tweeted over 4,000 times. Approximately 63 percent of the overall tweets occurred during the last 17 days leading up to the election (illustrated in Figure 6.1). Candidates likely intensified their communication efforts in order to encourage voters to get engaged as the election drew near. Most tweets gravitated toward topics relating to the campaign trail or events surrounding the race itself. The second most frequent topic focused on opponents. Most tweets were positive in tone and did not feature a conversational style, but instead they used a more formal rhetoric. Republican candidates were more apt to use a positive tone than Democratic candidates, and Republican candidates also were more likely than their Democratic rivals to engage in replying/mentioning. In addition, hashtags and URL links were a very popular way for candidates to encourage interactivity and further actions on behalf of the candidates. The following paragraphs detail

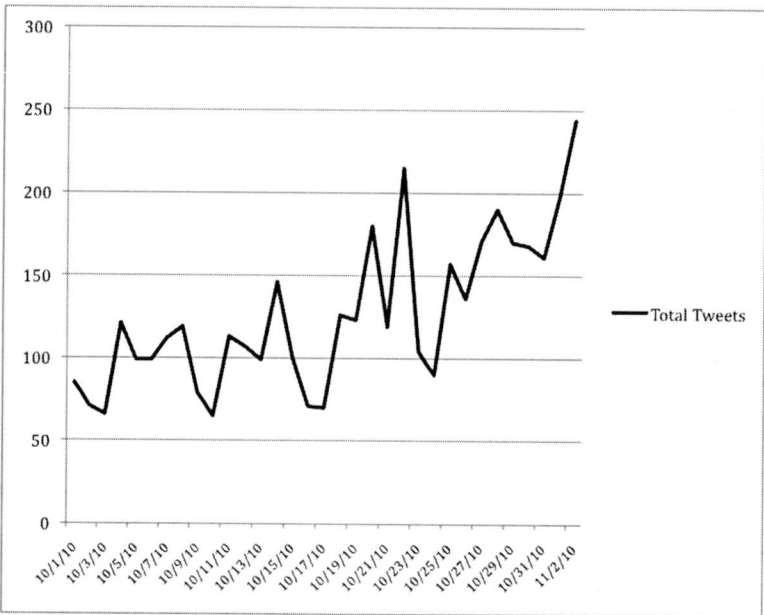

Figure 6.1   Total Number of Tweets for 12 Races in the 2010 Campaign

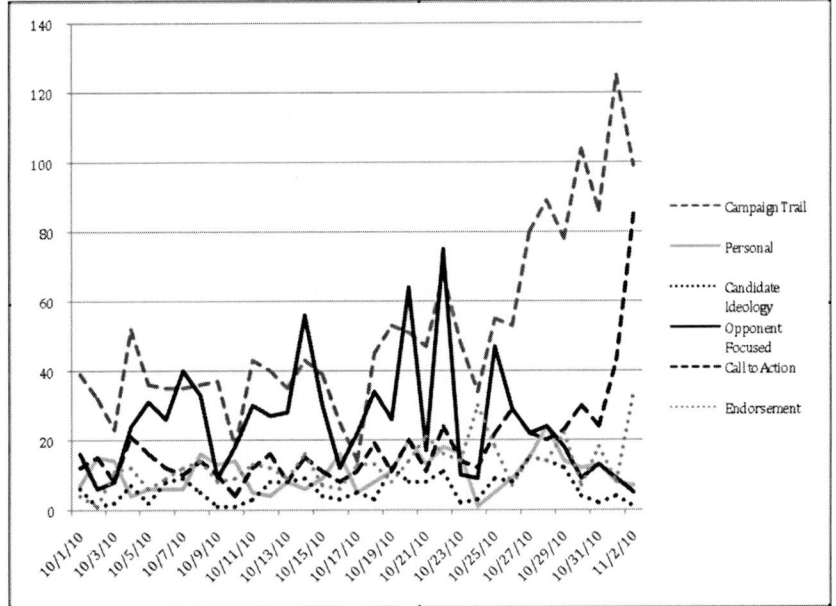

Figure 6.2 *Topics* Used to Frame Campaign Tweets

some of the differences noted with respect to the topics, tone, formality, and interactivity of the 2010 campaign tweets. In the section after the discussion of differences, an assessment is provided of tweet characteristics and their predictive influence on the election outcome.

Topics Used to Frame Campaign Tweets

The overall sample of tweets revealed that the campaign trail topic was the most popular, as it was the dominant frame in 40.7 percent of the tweets analyzed (Figure 6.2). Candidates also focused intensely on opponents (19.8 percent) as well as messages featuring a call to action (14.7 percent). Endorsements were a focus for roughly 10 percent of the tweets, while the least used topics were personal (8.3 percent) and candidate ideology (4.7 percent).

Some differences were detected when looking at the topics used to frame content and the political experience of the candidate. Incumbents were significantly more likely to emphasize topics related to opponents as well as endorsements. Challengers, on the other hand, emphasized the campaign trail topic most frequently. Tweets from races with open seats were more focused on personal topics and call to action content ($\chi^2(12, N = 4{,}174) = 306.98$, $p < 0.01$).

The candidate's party affiliation also appeared to influence the topic used to frame campaign tweets. Chi-square analysis indicated that Republicans were significantly more likely to feature personal topics in their tweets, while Democratic candidates focused more on offering content about their opponents ($\chi^2(6, N = 4,174) = 171.15, p < 0.01$).

The gender and age of the candidate tweeting was influential in determining the topics featured. Male candidates were significantly more likely to use an opponent focus, while female candidates were more apt to concentrate on personal issues or endorsements ($\chi^2(6, N = 4,174) = 84.82, p < 0.01$). ANOVA analysis revealed that the mean age for candidates tweeting was significantly higher for those candidates selecting to focus on their opponent as the dominant tweet topic ($F(6, 4173) = 19.07, p < 0.01$).

Interestingly, some differences emerged with respect to topics featured in tweets and the tone emphasized. Messages with a dominantly positive tone were most likely focused on the campaign trail, personal topics, candidate ideology, or endorsements. Those messages with a more negative tone overwhelmingly focused on opponents (90.9 percent). Tweets with a neutral tone stressed the campaign trail as well as call to action information ($\chi^2(12, N = 4,174) = 3,830.15, p < 0.01$). Tweets with a more conversational tone were more likely to concentrate on personal topics or the campaign trail. A more formal style was used for content regarding candidate ideology, opponents, and call to action ($\chi^2(12, N = 4,174) = 1,361.57, p < 0.01$).

Tone Used in Campaign Tweets

The affective tone used by candidates in campaign tweets varied throughout the 33 days preceding the election (as illustrated in Figure 6.3). A positive tone was the most frequent overall (used 56.8 percent of the time). The final week of the election showed a pronounced increase in positivity and a decrease in negative tone. Candidate experience, party, and demographics did appear to impact the tone featured in tweets.

Tweets from incumbent candidates were significantly more likely to feature a negative tone; whereas in contrast, challenger tweets emphasized a positive tone ($\chi^2(4, N = 4,174) = 215.46, p < 0.01$). Interestingly, candidates in open-seat races were the most prone to use a neutral tone (26.6 percent). Republican candidates used significantly more positive tones, while Democrats used negative tones more often ($\chi^2(2, N = 4,174) = 87.32, p < 0.01$).

Demographic variables influenced the tone accentuated in campaign tweet content. Male candidates were more likely to tweet with a negative tone, and female candidates were more likely to feature a positive tone ($\chi^2(2, N =$

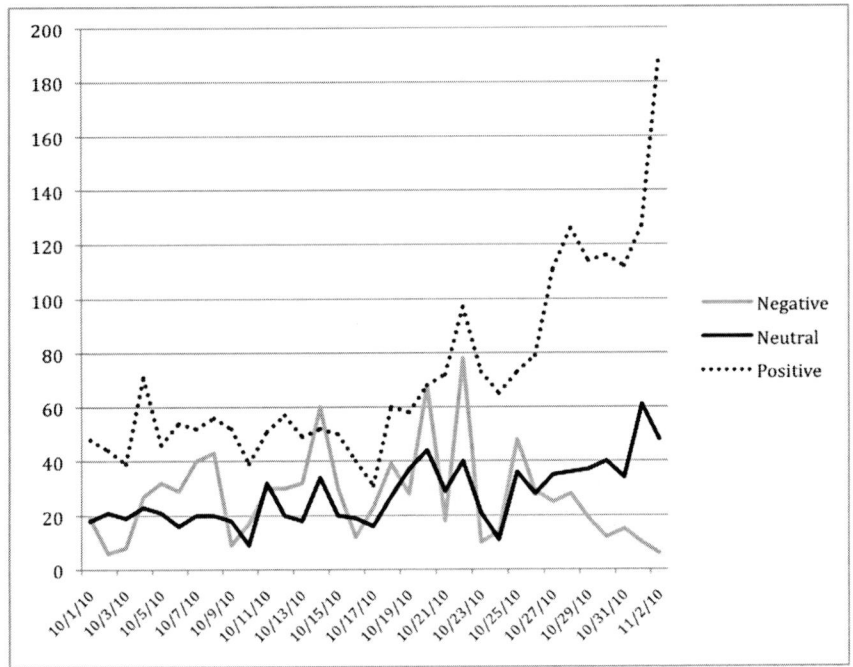

Figure 6.3   *Tone* Used in Campaign Tweets

4,174) = 49.80, $p < 0.01$). ANOVA analysis indicated that the mean age for candidates tweeting was significantly higher for those candidates choosing to use a more negative tone ($F(2, 4173) = 62.60$, p < 0.01).

The tone often varied based on the topic emphasized in the tweets. The tone used in tweets was also different when analyzing the formal versus the conversational style of tweet content. Chi-square analysis specified that conversational tweets were significantly more likely to be positive in tone, while tweets with a formal style were more apt to have a negative tone ($\chi^2(4, N = 4,174) = 382.03$, $p < 0.01$).

The Formality of Campaign Tweets

The tweets examined were much more likely to feature a formal tone or style of rhetoric when compared to a conversational tact. For example, over 71 percent of the tweets in the sample were formal in nature. The formality of tweet content remained fairly constant during the final month of the election, although the use of informal/conversational messages did increase in the final days of the election (Figure 6.4 illustrates this difference). The

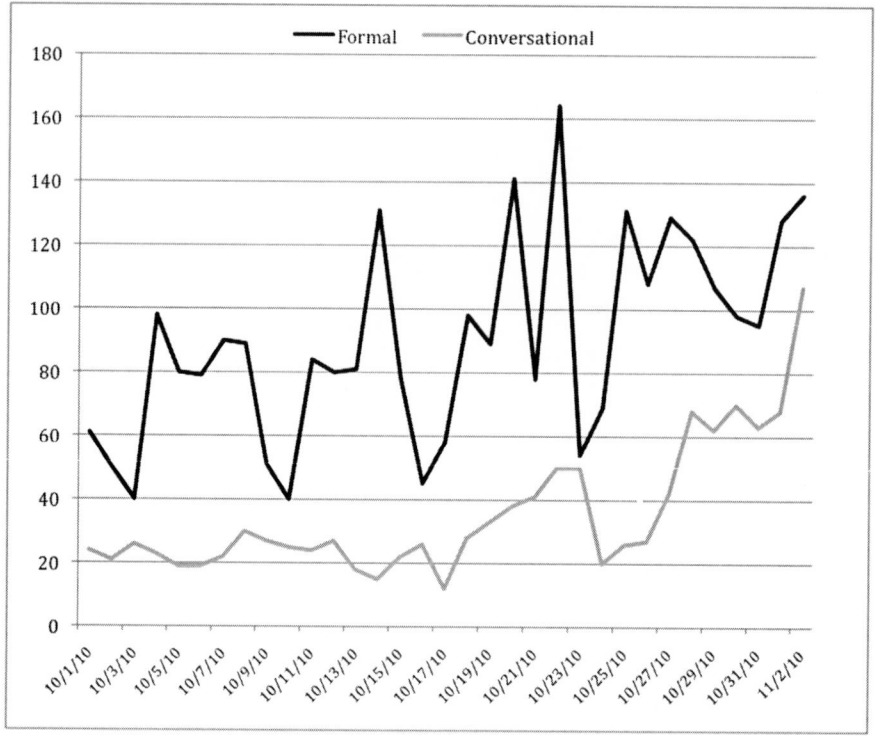

Figure 6.4 *Formality* **of Campaign Tweets**

disparity in formal tone appeared when evaluating differences based on candidate seat, party, and demographics.

Political party identification as well as experience influenced how conversational candidates were willing to be. Incumbent candidates as well as challengers were significantly more likely to feature a formal tweet style. Candidates for open-seat races were the most likely to try a more conversational tone ($\chi^2(4, N = 4,174) = 132.60, p < 0.01$). Republicans were also more likely than Democrats to tweet with a conversational style ($\chi^2(2, N = 4,174) = 43.61, p < 0.01$).

The candidate's gender had an impact on his or her chosen style of formality. Tweets from female candidates were significantly more likely to feature a conversational tone when compared with male candidate tweets, which were more formal ($\chi^2(2, N = 4,174) = 46.98, p < 0.01$). The mean age for candidates did not vary significantly when examining formal versus conversational style.

The formality used by candidates in their tweet content did vary as noted previously with respect to topics and affective tone. Overall, tweets with a more conversational tone were more likely to be positive and feature personal or campaign trail information. Tweets that featured a more formal style were more likely to have a negative tone. Tweets with an emphasis on topics regarding candidate ideology, opponents, or a call to action also were more apt to use a formal style.

The Interactivity of Campaign Tweets

One of the most unique features of Twitter is the user's ability to increase engagement and voter interactivity with candidates. This ability is evident in the current sample, as each candidate followed anywhere from 117 up to 8,928 other Twitter accounts, and each garnered anywhere from 786 to over 1,000,000 followers themselves. Candidates in the sample also used a variety of interactive features in their tweets. Some features encouraged supporters to take further actions, such as clicking recommended links, while other features facilitated two-way communication between candidates and their supporters or critics. The most popular technique used involved posting a URL link to additional information. Over 72 percent of the tweets featured such a link. Approximately 60 percent of the tweets featured a hashtag, allowing tweet content to be accessible in other popular Twitter forums. This interaction allows for increased connectivity with Twitter users, even beyond a candidate's followers. Roughly 25 percent of the tweets used the @reply/@mention features, while 12.4 percent were retweets and 12.8 percent showcased a photo or visual to further engage users. The least popular interactive element used by candidates involved tweets with direct quotes (2.7 percent) and video content (6.7 percent).

Some significant differences were detected in the assessment of interactive elements used by candidates with varying experience and party affiliation. Replies/mentions were used significantly more in challengers' tweets (33 percent) when compared to incumbent or open-seat candidate tweets ($\chi^2(2, N = 4,174) = 56.91, p < 0.01$). Retweets were used more often by challengers as well ($\chi^2(2, N = 4,174) = 24.57, p < 0.01$), while hashtags were a more likely feature in tweets from incumbents ($\chi^2(2, N = 4,174) = 85.03, p < 0.01$). Approximately 75 percent of the tweets from incumbents featured a hashtag. Incumbents were also significantly more likely to use direct quotes ($\chi^2(2, N = 4,174) = 15.52, p < 0.01$) and URL links when compared with other types of candidates ($\chi^2(2, N = 4,174) = 60.71, p < 0.01$). Tweets from candidates in open-seat races were the most likely to use photos or visual content ($\chi^2(2, N = 4,174) = 33.89, p < 0.01$). Republican candidate tweets were significantly more likely to have a reply/mention ($\chi^2(1, N = 4,174) = 17.81, p < 0.01$) or photo ($\chi^2(1, N = 4,174) = 209.68, p < 0.01$), while tweets from Democratic candidates were more likely to offer a direct quote ($\chi^2(1, N = 4,174) = 32.39$, $p < 0.01$).

Demographic differences were also apparent in the candidates' use of interactive elements. Female candidate tweets were significantly more likely to feature retweets ($\chi^2(1, N = 4,174) = 15.17$, $p < 0.01$) or photo content ($\chi^2(1, N = 4,174) = 79.03$, $p < 0.01$). Male candidates featured hashtags ($\chi^2(1, N = 4,174) = 49.15$, $p < 0.01$) and video content with more intensity ($\chi^2(1, N = 4,174) = 5.96$, $p < 0.05$). Roughly 65 percent of tweets from male candidates offered a hashtag to increase tweet dispersion. A series of independent samples t-tests assessed differences linking the age of candidates with the interactive elements they featured in tweets. The mean age was significantly higher for those tweets featuring direct quotes ($t(4,172) = -4.16$, $p < 0.01$), retweets ($t(4,172) = -2.60$, $p < 0.05$), URL links ($t(4,172) = -7.27$, $p < 0.01$), as well as photos ($t(4172) = -2.63$, $p < 0.01$) and video content ($t(4,172) = -4.43$, $p < 0.01$).

Interactivity also was examined with respect to topic choices and the tone used in tweets. A variety of differences were detected using chi-square analyses. Tweets with an emphasis on the campaign trail and endorsements were the most likely to feature replies/mentions ($\chi^2(6, N = 4,174) = 104.39$, $p < 0.01$). Replies/mentions also were used with increased frequency in tweets with a conversational style ($\chi^2(2, N = 4,174) = 73.71$, $p < 0.01$) and a more positive affective tone ($\chi^2(2, N = 4,174) = 19.17$, $p < 0.01$).

Tweets featuring a hashtag were significantly more likely to focus on opponents ($\chi^2(6, N = 4,174) = 152.77$, $p < 0.01$). A large majority of the candidate tweets focused on opponents had a hashtag present (77.4 percent). Hashtags were also more likely present in tweets that were formal ($\chi^2(2, N = 4,174) = 58.31$, $p < 0.01$) and negative in tone ($\chi^2(2, N = 4,174) = 150.55$, $p < 0.01$). Just over 75 percent of all negative tweets in the sample analyzed featured a hashtag.

Retweets were significantly more likely to be present in tweets emphasizing the campaign trail or specific endorsements ($\chi^2(6, N = 4,174) = 91.85$, $p < 0.01$). They were also more likely to be used in tweets displaying a more conversational style of rhetoric ($\chi^2(2, N = 4,174) = 18.22$, $p < 0.01$).

Candidates using direct quotes in their tweets most often focused on topics related to their opponent or endorsements ($\chi^2(6, N = 4,174) = 72.00$, $p < 0.01$). Surprisingly, the tweets featuring direct quotes were also significantly more likely to be negative in tone ($\chi^2(2, N = 4,174) = 25.40$, $p < 0.01$) and display a formal language style ($\chi^2(2, N = 4,174) = 15.95$, $p < 0.01$).

URL links were prevalent in the campaign tweets. The links were used with increased intensity for topics related to opponents and call to action ($\chi^2(6,$

N = 4,174) = 140.93, $p < 0.01$). Roughly 82 percent of tweets focused on opponents and 81 percent of those featuring a specific call to action also displayed a URL link. These tweets were also more prone to feature a formal style ($\chi^2(2, N$ = 4,174) = 19.17, $p < 0.01$) and were most often negative or neutral in tone ($\chi^2(2, N$ = 4,174) = 106.69, $p < 0.01$).

Candidates showcased photos in their tweets most often when the message posted dealt with the campaign trail or personal topics ($\chi^2(6, N$ = 4,174) = 385.21, $p < 0.01$). Personal tweets contained photos more than any other topic analyzed (36.8 percent). Tweets with photos were also significantly more likely to be positive ($\chi^2(2, N$ = 4,174) = 137.21, $p < 0.01$) and conversational in tone ($\chi^2(2, N$ = 4,174) = 159.01, $p < 0.01$). Videos, on the other hand, were used in candidate tweets most often as an interactive tool when the topic focused primarily on opponents ($\chi^2(6, N$ = 4,174) = 54.26, $p < 0.01$). Tweets of this nature were also more likely to have a negative or neutral tone ($\chi^2(2, N$ = 4,174) = 46.92, $p < 0.01$).

Tweet Influence on the Election Outcome

Logistic regression analyses were performed in order to detect the predictive influence of several tweet characteristics on the likelihood that the tweet was posted by a winning candidate. Candidate age, gender, party, and seat were the first variables examined because of their previously discussed impact. The results indicate that these factors do, indeed, have an influence on the election outcome for the sample examined (see Table 6.2). Gender is inversely related to a campaign win, with males being significantly more likely to secure a win (B = −3.0, Exp(B) = .052, $p < 0.01$). Age is a significant factor, with higher ages predicting a win (B = 0.06, Exp(B) = 1.06, $p < 0.01$). Political variables were significant predictors, with an increased likelihood to win by Republicans (B = −3.2, Exp(B) = 0.039, $p < 0.01$) and incumbents (B = 3.1, Exp(B) = 22.7, $p < 0.01$). Each of these variables was entered in the first block for subsequent logistic regressions in order to control for their influence.

When looking at the multiple dimensions used to frame tweet content, additional predictive variables emerged. The topic selected to feature in campaign tweets influenced the likelihood that a tweet was from a campaign winner or loser. An inverse relationship revealed that a focus on the campaign trail (B = −.89, Exp(B) = 0.413, $p < 0.01$), personal topics (B = −1.4, Exp(B) = 0.252, $p < 0.01$), candidate ideology (B = −1.4, Exp(B) = 0.247, $p < 0.01$), or opponents (B = −0.66, Exp(B) = 0.517, $p < 0.05$) predicted a campaign loss (refer to Table 6.3).

Table 6.2 Logistic Regression Analysis Predicting Campaign Outcome by Demographic and Political Characteristics

Independent Variable	Campaign Win	
	B	Exp(B)
Demographic/Political Characteristics of Sender		
Gender (female coded higher)	–3.0**	0.052
Age	0.06**	1.06
Party (Democrat coded higher)	–3.2**	0.039
Incumbent	3.1**	22.7
Challenger	–2.0**	0.130
Model χ^2	2,693.22**	
Nagelkerke R^2	0.636	

Note: Exp(B) = exponentiated B. Seat was represented as two dummy variables with "Open Seat" serving as the reference group for both incumbent and challenger.
N = 4,174; *$p < 0.05$; **$p < 0.01$.

Table 6.3 Logistic Regression Analysis Predicting Campaign Outcome by Topics Emphasized in Tweets

Independent Variable	Campaign Win	
	B	Exp(B)
Topic Emphasized		
Campaign trail	–0.89**	0.413
Personal	–1.4**	0.252
Candidate ideology	–1.4**	0.247
Opponent focus	–0.66*	0.517
Call to action	–0.45	0.641
Endorsement	–0.02	0.984
Model χ^2	2,762.99**	
Nagelkerke R^2	0.647	

Note: Exp(B) = exponentiated B. Topic was represented as six dummy variables with "Other/Unsure" serving as the reference group. Controls for gender, age, party, and seat were included in the analysis, but they are omitted here for clarity.
N = 4,174; *$p < 0.05$; **$p < 0.01$.

Interactivity features were entered into a logistic regression analysis to determine their influence on the election outcome. Several significant findings emerged (see Table 6.4). Tweets that offered a reply/mention (B = 0.33, Exp(B) = 1.39, $p < 0.01$) or URL link (B = 0.92, Exp(B) = 2.52, $p < 0.01$)

Table 6.4 Logistic Regression Analysis Predicting Campaign Outcome by Interactivity Featured in Tweets

Independent Variable	Campaign Win	
	B	Exp(B)
Interactive Elements		
@reply/@mention	0.33**	1.39
Hashtag	−1.5**	0.224
Retweet	0.08	1.08
Direct quote	-0.38	0.683
URL link	0.92**	2.52
Photo	−0.92**	0.400
Video	−0.02	0.984
Model χ^2	2,986.57**	
Nagelkerke R^2	.683	

Note: Exp(B) = exponentiated B. Controls for gender, age, party, and seat were included in the analysis, but they are omitted here for clarity.
N = 4174; *$p < 0.05$; **$p < 0.01$.

were more likely to be from campaign winners. Whereas, tweets with a hashtag (B = −1.5, Exp(B) = 0.224, $p < 0.01$) or photo (B = −0.92, Exp(B) = 0.400, $p < 0.01$) were significantly predictive of a campaign loss. The affective tone and formality of the study's tweets were entered as variables in a logistic regression, but these factors did not have any significant impact on the election outcome.

Frame Analysis

Tweets from the 2010 races revealed two overall framing themes that were consistent across the many campaigns. One of these, the media validation frame, matches how politicians often frame their political advertising (Parmelee, 2003). In the media validation frame, tweets link to (and/or mention) news media outlets that say positive things about a candidate or negative things about their opponent. Such a frame relies on followers' trust of journalism to persuade them to like or dislike the candidate being discussed. The other frame that was found can be called the *source frame*, meaning the "I am a purveyor of important political information" frame. In the source frame, tweets link to (and/or mention) timely political information, such as voter registration forms, position papers, ways to contribute, how to find polling places, polls, and news about the campaign. This frame helps to establish a candidate's Twitter account as a vital resource for campaign information. The source frame matches the study's content analysis findings regarding the prevalence of tweet topics such as campaign trail and call to action.

In addition, there were several noteworthy themes about the content of the tweets, some of which confirm findings from other methods used in this study. In-depth interviews with followers of political leaders found that political tweets tend to be limited to one-way communication rather than engaging in two-way communication. Frame analysis of the 2010 campaign tweets found the same thing. Campaign tweets were telling followers what to do, not answering followers' questions or soliciting their advice. Even attempts by the campaign tweets to seem interactive (such as retweeting, replying, and mentioning) were done in a way that simply broadcast a one-way message to followers.

In terms of the style of this one-way communication, most campaign tweets were written to sound as if they came exclusively from the candidate's hand, while a few candidates had some tweets labeled as coming from their staff. The tweets also included a mix of personal and political information.

The candidates spoke with a single linguistic voice. So although the tweets often were crafted with a personal touch, the words in the tweets did not exhibit the kind of regional differences in dialects that research has found with nonpolitical tweets (Eisenstein, O'Connor, Smith, and Xing, 2010; in other words, regional slang was not present in the campaign tweets).

Many opposing candidates included the same hashtags in their tweets. For example, the Democratic and Republican candidates for Florida Governor often used the #flgov hashtag when tweeting information about their record and that of their opponents. This result is an important finding because such a practice may increase the amount of politically diverse views to which Twitter users are exposed. The tweets of anyone on Twitter who includes a common hashtag are grouped together (and then can be searched for). As a result, those people who regularly viewed hashtags such as #flgov during the campaign were able to see a wide range of political information about the candidates. The pages that follow include a sampling of campaign tweets that demonstrate the themes that were found.

Frames Present in the 2010 Campaign Tweets

The media validation frame and the source frame were present in candidate tweets from all of the races studied. Only one candidate, Florida Senate candidate Marco Rubio, did not exhibit these frames. However, this exception can be discounted because of how little he tweeted. (While most candidates tweeted hundreds of times during the final month of the 2010 race, Rubio had just one tweet in October and two tweets in September.) The other campaigns used Twitter to display their candidates as vital political information sources, backed by the news media.

Media Validation Frame

The heavy use of media validation spanned various types of tweets. It did not matter whether tweets included positive or negative information. Mentions of news media outlets and links to their stories were used to promote or attack candidates. One of the most common examples of media validation was found with candidate tweets that talked about the newspaper endorsements they received:

- JerryBrown2010: In Case You Missed It: SJ Mercury News, Oakland Tribune and Merced Sun-Star Endorse Jerry Brown for Governor http://t.co/smzxZIe
- CarlyforCA: Did you hear? The LA Daily News endorsed Carly! http://www.dailynews.com/opinions/ci_16238068 #casen
- Boxer_2010: STAFF: LA Times endorsed Barbara Boxer for Senate. Saying: "Issues matter, especially in the United States" http://ow.ly/2O3HX
- JohnKasich: I am humbled by the Cleveland @PlainDealer's endorsement of our campaign - http://blog.kasichforohio.com/?p=2615
- AlexSinkFlorida: It's officially a sweep: 16-0! Every major newspaper has endorsed me from Pensacola to Miami. http://bit.ly/bWAJvo
- Nikkihaley: "Haley's views on govt spending, accountability and reform should encourage support from SC's voters." The Post and Courier http://bit.ly/bvqxlA
- Sestak2010: PSU's @dailycollegian picks #Sestak for "true ability to enact change in Senate" http://bit.ly/cS8iSm #Thats12 #p2 Toomey

The inclusion of media endorsements spans all types of candidates and gender. Media validation was used by Democrats such as Joe Sestak; Republicans such as Nikki Haley; challengers such as John Kasich; incumbents such as Barbara Boxer; first-time candidates such as Carly Fiorina; political veterans such as Jerry Brown; both men and women.

Media endorsement tweets included links to the news media websites that gave the endorsements. This tactic provided proof of the candidate's claim of support, as well as a way to learn more about what the media outlet considered to be the candidate's positive attributes. Even in this new media age, candidates relied on linking to traditional newspaper endorsements, which indicates that traditional news media still wield a great deal of influence.

Candidate tweets that attacked an opponent also included media validation, usually by providing a link to an article or video from a news outlet that was critical of something the opponent had said or done:

- HarryReid: The most unbelievable clip of Sharron Angle and the media this entire cycle, from KLAS-TV in Vegas: http://bit.ly/dv5zlE #nvsen #p2 #unfit
- SharronAngle: Washington Post: "Angle to Reid: Man up, man up, man up" http://ow.ly/2XV6G #nvsen #tcot #dumpreid
- Boxer_2010: STAFF: Los Angeles Times article, "HP benefited from state tax breaks while Fiorina was CEO" http://lat.ms/d8LPf0
- DickBlumenthal: STAFF: #McMahon spent $1 million on lobbyists and tried to deny it. Rachel @Maddow of MSNBC reports at 4:25 mark http://bit.ly/Lobby425 #CTSEN

Some tweets used media validation to defend themselves against attacks:

- LindaForSenate: Claim-checked! In case you missed it, the Hartford Courant refutes Blumenthal's minimum wage attack: http://bit.ly/b2otEf #Linda2010 #CTSEN

In other cases, tweets used media validation to be positive *and* negative, in kind of a one–two punch. In the following tweet, Sestak, a Pennsylvania Democrat, starts out positive by mentioning one of his newspaper endorsements. However, the only part of the endorsement shown (in the tweet) attacks his opponent, Pat Toomey:

- Sestak2010: Erie Times-News Endorsement of #Sestak: #Toomey "represents the most extreme views on the political spectrum" http://bit.ly/cR3mY9

Another form of media validation can be found in tweets that directed followers to watch a candidate's appearance on a news show:

- Lisa4Senate: In case you missed it, catch my interview with CNN from today: http://bit.ly/9TDPsY #AKsen #writeinlisa #AK

In addition to helping followers learn more about the candidates, tweets such as these subtly imply that candidates should be taken seriously because major news outlets consider them important enough to interview.

Source Frame

Candidate tweets did not include frames such as change, unity, or values. Some candidates would occasionally describe themselves as *job creators* or *political outsiders*, or they would call their opponents *extremists*. However, these descriptions were few and far between and, therefore, cannot be considered frames. It is the *source* frame that stands out consistently in all the races studied. The candidates framed themselves as purveyors of important, timely political information. One type of information dealt with how people could get involved in helping a candidate, whether by volunteering, voting, or fundraising:

- Whitman2010: Find your nearest volunteer field office using our map - walk-ins welcome. Over 90 locations across CA! http://meg4.me/veuy #cagov #gomeg
- LindaForSenate: Do you know where your polling location is? Click the link below to find it: http://bit.ly/VOTETUES #Linda2010 #CTSEN #GOTV
- Boxer_2010: STAFF: Fight Back Fund is over $900k - goal is $1M - deadline is midnight tonight! http://ow.ly/32krP
- ScottForFlorida: It's the final day of the Scott Surge to 25K! There are 12 hours left, and we need your help to reach our goal. Give: http://ow.ly/2QF8d

Some campaign tweets were more creative than others in providing information on how to assist candidates. Jerry Brown included a link in one of his tweets to a YouTube video that humorously looked and sounded like a training film from the 1950s. The video offered several suggestions for how viewers could use Twitter to help Brown in the California governor's race:

- JerryBrown2010: Use Twitter to help the campaign (video): http://youtu.be/DRvlo0sgrao

Many candidate tweets included videos with how-to campaign advice. Lisa Murkowski, the first candidate in a half-century to win a Senate seat as a write-in, linked to a music video that helped remind viewers how to correctly spell her name on the ballot:

- Lisa4Senate: Check out another great supporter video – "Write it in the line" http://bit.ly/azN0Iq #AKsen #writeinlisa

Another type of information in the campaign tweets provides details about the candidates' policy positions:

- DickBlumenthal: STAFF: Small business is the engine of our economy. To read more about how I would help small businesses: http://bit.ly/cgeXGS #CTSEN #CTBLU

The link connects to information on the campaign website of the Connecticut Senate candidate about his position on small-business development. Policy position tweets also often attacked one's opponent:

- SharronAngle: FACT CHECK: Reid said English is official language. Reid voted against making English official language in 2006. http://bit.ly/aR2r8e #nvsen

The Nevada Senate candidate's tweet links to a U.S. Senate website that shows Senator Reid's May 18, 2006, vote against an amendment to "declare English as the national language of the United States and to promote the patriotic integration of prospective U.S. citizens." Using a nonpartisan website such as this one helps add credibility to the claim. One of Reid's tweets provides another example of information sharing from a nonpartisan site.

- HarryReid: Factcheck.org calls yet another Angle TV spot "false" http://bit.ly/chicw4 #nvsen #p2

Clicking the link shows an October 22, 2010, article from FactCheck. org, a project of the Annenberg Public Policy Center of the University of Pennsylvania. The article rebuts several charges made by Reid's opponent. However, other candidates' tweets linked to partisan sites when attacking their opponents' record:

- AlexSinkFlorida: I just unveiled a tough and true TV ad on Rick Scott's record of unethical business practices: http://bit.ly/ci8tKp

This tweet from the Florida gubernatorial candidate links to a website titled "What is Rick Scott Hiding?" The site, run by the Florida Democratic Party, served as a clearinghouse for various attacks (in written and video form) on her opponent. Links to attacks in other candidate tweets came from supporters, rather than from a campaign or party, and these attack links have a home-grown quality:

- CarlyforCA: Check out this great video made by Students for Carly! We love you! http://bit.ly/apRavA #casen #weloveourvolunteers

The two-minute YouTube video being linked-to in the tweet features several California college Republicans. They criticize Carly Fiorina's Senate opponent for votes that they say had hurt local agriculture.

The source frame includes tweets that provide the latest polling data:

- Boxer_2010: STAFF: New Field Poll has Sen. Boxer up 49 percent-41 percent! But the only poll that matters is the one on Election Day! http://bit.ly/bQNOPP
- DickBlumenthal: 5 new polls. All great news for @dickblumenthal. For the poll roundup, click here: http://bit.ly/ct28OT #CTSEN #CTBlu Pls RT

The One-Way Nature of Campaign Tweets

The two frames found in campaign tweets (media validation and source) point to another important aspect of how Twitter is used in politics. Politicians are using Twitter for one-way communication rather than for two-way discourse. In other words, the campaign tweets that were studied regularly transmitted favorable media information about themselves and unfavorable news about their opponents, and the tweets provided timely information about issues, polls, and how to help the campaigns. However, there was little effort by the leaders to engage the millions of people who saw their tweets. As a result, campaign tweets focused on telling people what to do, rather than asking for their advice:

- CarlyforCA: Good morning! 29 days until Election Day- what are you doing to help Carly?
- AlexSinkFlorida: Monday is the deadline to register to vote. Can you commit to getting one more person registered by then? http://bit.ly/bvTUIe
- Sestak2010: "The hour is late, but the agenda is long" -JFK. 30 minutes til polls close. VOTE.
- Lisa4Senate: Want to show your support? Change your Facebook or twitter profile picture - click here: http://bit.ly/d71YeG #AKsen #writeinlisa
- JoeWMiller: I will be in Fairbanks tonight at 411 4th Ave, Suite 300 6:30 to 8:30. Bring an undecided friend so we can convert 'em.

Alaska Senate candidate Joe Miller did provide one rare moment in the campaign tweets where a politician asked his followers for their opinion:

- JoeWMiller: Loads of new ads on T.V. and radio. Let me know what you think. Your thoughts are appreciated. joemiller.us

Even when candidates were replying, mentioning, and retweeting (which could have been used to facilitate more dialog between candidates and their followers), it was done in a manner that merely broadcast a one-way message. That message was usually one of self-promotion:

- CarlyforCA: gotubsgo: My uncle has been a union member for 30 yrs and never voted for a Republican, but he is voting for @CarlyforCA because things need to change (Retweeted by CarlyforCA and 6 others)
- JerryBrown2010: @ladykayaker Glad to have your vote! (via web in reply to ladykayaker)
- charliecristfl: Schwarzenegger: I endorse Gov @charliecristfl for Senate. Great leader, works with both parties, and our country needs someone like him in DC right now. (Retweeted by charliecristfl and 76 others)
- HarryReid: iambajingo: Also, today my 6 year old told me she's voting for @HarryReid. That's so sweet, but she's still got 12 more years! But I'm voting for him! (Retweeted by HarryReid and 7 others)
- JohnKasich: karr_pe: Nevermind the awesome polls... WE MUST GOTV for @JohnKasich this weekend. Don't let up for the next 19 days. #ohio #gop #OHGov (Retweeted by JohnKasich and 3 others)

The Personality of the Tweets

In addition to transmitting politically oriented information, campaign tweets often included the candidates' personal side. In these tweets, candidates talked about everything from the weather to their taste in music:

- Lisa4Senate: Brrrrrr it's cold in Bethel today, good thing I have my copper river fleece!
- Charliecristfl: In the car listening to Stealers Wheel "Stuck in The Middle With You" Great tune! - Right down the middle! #fb
- LindaForSenate: http://twitpic.com/31cx9p Eagle's Nest Restaurant in Plymouth; had some tasty beef barley soup and great conversation. #LINDA2010 #CTSEN

Personal tweets are not meant to be overtly political, though Florida Senate candidate Charlie Crist's "right down the middle" comment references his position as a self-proclaimed political moderate. Tweets that include a candidate's nonpolitical side are able to show a well-rounded candidate and, perhaps, appeal to voters on a more personal level. In this regard, sports references were regularly made in nonpolitical campaign tweets:

- Whitman2010: Good luck to the @SFGiants tonight!
- RoyBlunt: It's official! ESPN College GameDay is coming to #Mizzou. http://bit.ly/9FlFMu #MizzouGameDay
- JohnKasich: Browns vs. Bengals today. On this date in 1920, another intra-state game. Dayton Triangles beat Columbus Panhandles in 1st NFL game.

Whether transmitting political or nonpolitical information, campaign tweets often used words such as "I" and "my" to give the impression that the messages came from the candidate's hand:

- Boxer_2010: I wish Carly Fiorina a speedy recovery. Her staff has said she will be released from the hospital today and that's good news.

However, some candidate tweets either implied they were written by staff, or the tweets were actually labeled as coming from staff. Campaign tweets that referred to a candidate in the third-person suggest that a campaign staff member was the true author:

- DrRandPaul: Rand Paul makes stop in Northern Kentucky to rally supporters prior to election - http://bit.ly/9td58s
- HarryReid: Nevada needs Harry Reid. Harry Reid needs your vote. VOTE NOW. Polls close at 7pm! 1-888-525-VOTE http://bit.ly/9RObpg
- Sestak2010: Mrs. Sestak talks about Joe here: http://youtu.be/4fCpDnrfp30 #p2
- ToomeyForSenate: Pat Toomey has been endorsed by the FOP and the PA State Troopers: http://bit.ly/9FMrDQ #sestak

A much smaller number of campaign tweets let it be known that messages coming from a candidate's Twitter account were written by staff:

- Boxer_2010: STAFF: Voter turnout is key this year. Find out how you can help get out the vote! http://ow.ly/30ndc

The Political Value of Using Common Hashtags

Many gubernatorial and senatorial candidates used the same state-specific hashtag when tweeting information regarding their policies, record, endorsements, and attacks on opponents. Usually, the hashtags were an abbreviation of the state that the candidates were from, followed by "sen" for Senate or "gov" for Governor, such as #nvsen for the Nevada Senate race or #cagov for the California Governor's campaign. The use of common hashtags came from candidates who represent a wide political and demographic spectrum: Democrats, Republicans, conservatives, liberals, incumbents, challenges, first-time candidates, political veterans, men, and women. Those twitterers looking at such hashtags were able to receive diverse perspectives about the opposing candidates. In the Nevada Senate campaign, for example, viewers of #nvsen learned about several economic considerations to take into account before voting for Republican Sharron Angle or Democrat Harry Reid:

• SharronAngle: Natl Taxpayers Union endorsement: "Angle a true champion for taxpayers" http://ow.ly/2Xklv Thanks, @NTU! #nvsen #tcot #dumpreid
• HarryReid LV Sun LTE: "Voting for Reid will make Nevada better off" http://ow.ly/2ZGbR #nvsen

Angle's tweet links to a press release on the website PR Newswire from the National Taxpayers Union, a nonprofit advocacy group. The press release said that Angle would work to keep taxes low and limit the growth of the federal government. Reid's tweet links to a Las Vegas Sun letter-to-the-editor by a businessman who said Reid's status as Senate Majority Leader makes him most able to protect Nevada's economic interests.

In Connecticut, Democrat Dick Blumenthal and Republican Linda McMahon used the #ctsen hashtag to provide information about the campaign, which also focused heavily on the economy. Blumenthal's tweet links to video testimonials on YouTube, and McMahon includes an op-ed from *The Hour,* a Norwalk, Connecticut, online newspaper site:

• DickBlumenthal: STAFF: ICYMI @DickBlumenthal has helped so many CT families. They're sharing their stories with you VIDEO: http://bit.ly/9VaHNT #CTSEN PlsRT
• LindaForSenate: Job Creators Can't Afford Tax Hikes http://bit.ly/op-ed #Linda2010 #CTSEN

Candidates in the Kentucky Senate race used a common hashtag, #kysen, when tweeting links to videos and news sites:

• DrRandPaul: Video: Jack Conway's Stamp of Approval of Obama - http://bit.ly/d1RsAg #tcot #kysen #efca #RNC #NRSC #capandtrade

- ConwayforKy: Washington Post's Greg Sargent on our new ad about Rand Paul's support for a 23 percent national sales tax: http://wapo.st/bWCUJc #KYSen

Republican Rand Paul's tweet links to one of his ads on YouTube that questions opponent Jack Conway's political independence. The Democratic candidate's tweet links to a news story about a Conway advertisement that attacked Paul's ideas about taxes.

Those twitterers who visited common hashtags during the 2010 campaign could easily find positive and negative information about the same candidate. In the following example, viewers of #cagov could learn differing opinions of Republican Meg Whitman's ability to create jobs from links to the U.S. Chamber of Commerce and the *Los Angeles Times*:

- Whitman2010: Thank you to the US Chamber of Commerce for their endorsement. Creating jobs is my top priority. http://meg4.me/ks6a #cagov #gomeg
- JerryBrown2010: CATeachersAssoc Whitman's economic plan will do little to bring jobs to #California, experts say (via @LATimes) http://lat.ms/d8XLy9 #cagov #caelection (Retweeted by JerryBrown2010 and 23 others)

In addition to using state-specific common hashtags, some candidates used other hashtags to reach groups who might not otherwise be exposed to their messages:

- AlexSinkFlorida: danrichman I'm begging. If you are even THINKING about voting for Rick Scott, watch this. http://youtu.be/EYgTjVULTbk #FLGov #tcot (Retweeted by AlexSinkFlorida and 6 others)
- ScottForFlorida: New post on www.SinkScandals.com detailing @ CFOAlexSink's state office licensing of ex-cons in the insurance business. ~Staff #flgov #sayfie

While both gubernatorial candidates used #flgov, the Democratic candidate, Sink, also included a hashtag used mostly by conservative Republicans: #tcot, known as Top Conservatives on Twitter. As a result, the attacks in Sink's tweet could be seen by those who were likely some of Scott's strongest supporters. Scott's attack tweet used the #sayfie hashtag, which is connected to the *Sayfie Review*, an influential news website on Florida politics.

Another way candidates reached out beyond those who agreed with them politically was to tweet with a hashtag that included the name of their opponent:

- ToomeyForSenate: Video: Why are Democrats supporting Pat Toomey?: http://bit.ly/bzp8Rf #sestak #tcot #pasen
- Sestak2010: Just spoke about creating jobs in Pennsylvania and standing up for American workers http://yfrog.com/izrwqvj #p2 #setak #toomey

As can be seen, Republican candidate Toomey wanted to win-over Democrats who were still undecided about their party's nominee, Sestak. For his part, the Pennsylvania Democrat was trying to poach some votes from Toomey. By both candidates tweeting with the #sestak and #toomey hashtags, both could appeal directly to their opponent's supporters.

CONCLUSION AND DISCUSSION

The framing of political content is a powerful tool in the election process. This chapter addresses the use of a relatively new media platform, Twitter, to frame campaign issues. A quantitative content analysis and frame analysis revealed several themes of interest. Campaign tweets from 2010 show that Twitter is used by politicians in ways that are both similar and different when compared to how politicians use other forms of political communication, such as websites and traditional advertising.

Several topics emerged as popular in the campaign tweets analyzed. The emphasis on campaigning in general (campaign trail) was a dominant focus. This result aligns positively with past research identifying that the strategy frame often is stressed in elections (Bichard, 2006; Capella and Jamieson, 1997; Druckman, 2005). This emphasis is likely chosen by candidates as a way for them to keep voters aware and involved with campaign activities and progress. Tweets also were likely to contain information (mostly negative) regarding opponents. This informative quality about opponents is also a common characteristic noted by researchers of elections in online media discourse (Bichard, 2006; Wicks and Souley, 2003). Endorsements of support were only a moderately popular feature in tweets when compared to other topics. This result contrasts with past research on blogs indicating a dominant focus on supporter testimonials (Trammell, Williams, Postelnicu, and Landreville, 2006). It would appear that Twitter provides a context in which candidates feel more comfortable discussing the negative qualities of their competitors. Future research may be useful to further examine these differences in strategy.

The use of specific topics to frame Twitter content did vary according to several factors. Incumbents, Democrats, males, and older candidates were more likely to discuss their opponents in tweets (which were most often negative in tone). Endorsements were more likely tweeted from female candidates and incumbents. Personal information was offered with more intensity from female candidates and Republicans, and these missives were most often in a positive or enthusiastic tone. Twitter can cater to a variety of candidate preferences, and the 2010 campaign showcases how different candidates were able to use Twitter to personally appeal to voters, as well as provide more formal campaign information.

The dominant affective tone for the campaign tweets was very positive, especially in the final days leading up to the election. This result aligns positively with other studies that assert candidates use media platforms primarily to acclaim their desirable qualities (Chambers and Bichard, in press; Cho and Benoit, 2005). One difference noted was with respect to candidate seat. This book's study found that challengers in the sample were more positive, while incumbents were more prone to feature a negative affective tone in their tweets. Past studies indicate the opposite is true for blog content (Bichard, 2006). Perhaps social media provides an outlet where incumbent candidates are more likely to take a risk and circulate negative information by way of hashtag, links, and direct quotes to soften the blow. Twitter allows candidates to highlight negative information while still maintaining a comfortable distance. More study is needed on the differences between how Republicans and Democrats tweet. The content analysis found that among the relative handful of 2010 candidates under study, Republicans were more apt to feature a positive tone when compared with Democrats. Future research should be done to find out if Republicans, as a whole, are more positive than their Democratic counterparts when tweeting about politics.

When assessing the dominant themes present, the campaign tweets stuck to a small number of frames to make the messages more coherent, a pattern that also has been found in framing studies not related to Twitter. The media validation frame used news media articles and editorials to discuss positive and negative information about candidates, a strategy that also has been employed in political advertisements (Parmelee, 2003). This use of media links and direct quotes is an ideal way to offer negative information while avoiding potential backlash (Bichard, 2006). The source frame presented candidates as purveyors of timely political information. The source frame corroborates content analysis findings in terms of the prevalence of tweet topics such as campaign trail and call to action.

The frames that were found do reveal several things about the candidates who sent them, in terms of their political perceptions and how they campaign. The heavy use of the media validation frame by such a politically diverse group of candidates suggests that most candidates believe that the news media is considered trustworthy. This implication is significant, because politicians are often quite critical in other forums (such as in their speeches) about the reliability of the news media. But as previous research indicates, campaigns use media validation because (despite occasional press-bashing) the campaigns believe that media validation gives candidates and their messages increased credibility and legitimacy (Parmelee, 2003, pp. 94–95).

The use of the source frame indicates that candidates were prepared to spend the time and effort required to provide a wide variety of information in an attempt to influence their followers (and anyone else who received the candidates' tweets) to volunteer, contribute, and vote. However, the source frame was focused on a one-way transmitting of information. This problem also can be seen in the fact that the candidates were followed by many more users than they themselves chose to follow. This lack of reciprocation of communication is indicative of a one-way communication style. Although the content analysis of tweets revealed a widespread use of interactive features, most tweets were used to simply pass along information; the tweets lacked a true feedback component (a component clearly indicative of two-way communication). Campaigns were not willing, or perhaps able, to engage with followers by answering their questions, sharing their comments, or soliciting their advice. This situation is unfortunate because in-depth interviews with political Twitter users found that they wished they could engage more with the politicians they follow. These findings further show a disconnect between what followers want and what politicians are giving.

When looking at the content analysis of tweets, engagement efforts (by way of interactive features) did differ with respect to the experience, party, and gender of candidates in the sample. Incumbent and male candidates used hashtags with more frequency. This situation is probably due to their prior established connections with support groups and followers. Challengers and Republican candidates preferred to reply/mention. Challengers also were more likely to retweet, as were female candidates. The use of URL links was most prevalent among the incumbent candidates.

As in past research, the use of URL links was the most popular attempt to encourage voters to interact with the campaign (Trammell, Williams, Postelnicu, and Landreville, 2006). These links most often featured opponent information or a specific call to action to get involved with the campaign. The use of URL links that focused on opponents strategically allowed candidates to showcase critiques of their competitors but also distance themselves from perceived negativity. The @reply/@mention and retweet functions were most prevalent when tweeting about specific endorsements or events on the campaign tail. These options were possibly used to spread the word about other supporters in hopes of encouraging voters to get more involved and further engaged with the campaign. One reason the @mention feature was found regularly in tweets that included endorsements was that candidates often mentioned the Twitter accounts of the endorsers in their tweets. These mentions, however, were not aimed at answering questions or addressing concerns from supporters or critics. So while Twitter considers replies to also be mentions (Twitter Help Center, 2011), mentions do not always facilitate feedback and engagement the way replies often do. As a result, future studies should look at the @mention and @reply features separately, because mentions can be less reflective of two-way conversations than replies.

The use of common hashtags by many campaigns is significant because this practice helps to guard against the negative effects of selective exposure and selective avoidance. Those people who practice selective exposure and selective avoidance expose themselves only to those political views that provide, as Sunstein (2001) says, "echoes of their own voices" (p. 49). However, those people who visited hashtags such as #cagov and #pasen were able to receive a wide variety of political information from the Democratic and Republican candidates. While much of the information found in hashtags (and in candidates' tweets that used the media validation and source frames) attacked a candidate's opponent, research has found that negative appeals are not necessarily a bad thing. There is no consistent evidence that negative political appeals decrease voter turnout or have other detrimental effects on society (Richardson, 2003, pp. 61–88). In fact, negative political advertisements have been shown to include more factual content than positive advertisements (Jamieson, 1992, p. 103).

Numerous seemingly nonpolitical campaign tweets were found. These tweets are still important because even tweets about sports or music can serve a useful political objective. This display of a more conversational rhetoric was apparent in many of the 2010 campaign tweets. The practice's prevalence offers support for prior research showing recent efforts by candidates to appear more personal (Trammell, Williams, Postelnicu, and Landreville, 2006). During the last 40 years, presidents have had to appeal to an electorate that is increasingly less loyal to any political party (Alvon, 2004; Oppenheimer, 1996; Cook, 1994). One way to appeal to the growing number of political independents is for candidates to display themselves as personally and professionally mirroring the society that they wish to represent, rather than spelling out specific policy positions (Parmelee, 2009b). Campaign tweets that, for example, were rooting a popular sports team on to victory are part of how a candidate tries to be a personification of society and win independent voters.

The use of a more personal or conversational tone was not a tactic all candidates found equally appealing. Republicans and females were more likely to tweet in this fashion and typically did so when they discussed topics of a more personal nature. These tweets were also typically positive and enthusiastic. Content analysis revealed that a conversational tone often was used when candidates featured a retweet, reply/mention, or a photo in their Twitter post. These tweets were typically very light and gave candidates the opportunity to appear more friendly and approachable, with informal dialogue concerning sports, entertainment, and even their family life.

The framing of Twitter content in the 2010 election did appear to have some influence on the election outcome. Analysis indicates that many of the tweets from campaign losers featured topics relating to campaign strategy, ideology, or personal issues. Perhaps voters are more interested in specific endorsements and information about how to get involved. The findings also suggest that tweets from winning candidates were more apt to feature replies/mentions and URL links. These tweets resonate with voters by offering at least some level of increased interactivity and engagement potential. Future study is needed that quantitatively captures the content in URL links to assess its true interactive quality.

The many facets of framing involved in elections necessitate a multidimensional examination in order to provide data on the topics, themes, and tones used to frame campaign rhetoric. Twitter content, while short, provides a unique social outlet to investigate the use of framing themes. This chapter used both quantitative and qualitative methods to reveal a variety of frames used strategically by the candidates in the 2010 campaign. The message tactics indicate an emphasis on campaign strategy and a positive tone. There is also a strong effort to appear credible, interactive, and even approachable. Successful candidates featured an appropriate mix of formal yet friendly rhetoric, often using strategic links or hashtags to highlight negative opponent information. Future elections will likely learn from these maneuvers and find ways to be even more appealing to voters.

Chapter 7

Conclusion

How Twitter Influences the Relationship between Political Leaders and the Public

According to Twitter's founders, the name *Twitter* was selected because the dictionary says it means: "a short burst of inconsequential information" (Sarno, 2009). The findings in the study for this book, however, show that Twitter is not inconsequential when it comes to politics. Data from the parts of the study (the survey, in-depth interviews, frame analysis, and content analysis) indicate that Twitter is a major player in terms of political discourse. Because of the number of people using the microblogging service for politics, how they use it, and how they are affected by it, Twitter influences how political leaders and the public relate in a number of crucial ways:

- The relationship that followers have with their leaders is quite powerful. Political leaders' tweets regularly cause followers to look up information and take other actions that the leaders request. In addition, the relationship that followers have with the leaders often influences followers' political views as much as or more than their family and friends.
- From the followers' perspective, the relationship goes beyond receiving information from leaders; it is about sharing leaders' information with others. Leaders tweet political information to followers, and followers pass that information along. Leaders' tweets give followers something to talk and tweet about with others, which is a popular activity among followers. This relationship is beneficial for followers and leaders. Followers now have access to more political information to share, and leaders have their views spread by followers to an increasingly wide audience.
- From the leaders' perspective, the relationship is based on using Twitter mainly as a one-way communication vehicle to transmit their policies and ideas. However, their followers want to use Twitter as a forum for two-way

communication with leaders and other politically interested individuals. As a result, many followers crave engagement with leaders but often are left disappointed.

- One of Twitter's great strengths is that it forces political leaders (and anyone else) to quickly get to the point. Politicians, for example, are notoriously longwinded in their speeches, press releases, and other forms of communication. Those followers who receive politicians' brief tweets, however, are able to see elected officials in a new light. The 140-character limit of tweets means that politicians and other leaders must be succinct in their writing, and that brevity is a refreshing change. As writing teacher William Zinsser (2001) noted: "Clutter is the disease of American writing. We are a society strangling in unnecessary words, circular construction, pompous frills and meaningless jargon. . . . The secret of good writing is to strip every sentence to its cleanest components" (p. 7). Twitter imposes that kind of brevity.
- While the average political Twitter user often seeks a politically diverse range of leaders to follow, those who are extremely ideological tend to avoid diverse viewpoints on Twitter. This practice may not be healthy.

To further explore the relationship between leaders and followers, Chapter 1 posed several questions concerning political Twitter use, including the following: Who follows political leaders on Twitter, and why? How influential are political tweets? Does political Twitter use increase exposure to diverse views? How significant is Twitter use as a political innovation? What is in the content of political tweets? Answers to these questions are summarized here.

REASONS FOR FOLLOWING POLITICAL LEADERS

Those people who use Twitter for politics are Internet-savvy and politically active. They have very high levels of political interest and political self-confidence. They are more highly educated than the general public, with 70 percent in the survey reporting a bachelor's or graduate degree. The typical political Twitter user is a white male in his 30s or 40s who has moderate-to-high household income and considers himself to be a political junkie. The typical user follows many political leaders: 43 percent of respondents follow 5 to 20 leaders, and 31 percent follow more than 20 leaders.

While people have many motives for using a new technology, a handful of key motives usually influence how that technology is used. In terms of Twitter, several motives drive users to follow political leaders. Social utility is the most popular of these motives. In order of importance, the other motives are entertainment, self-expression, information/guidance, and convenience. Those people with a social utility motive are following political leaders to obtain political information that can assist them in their social interactions, such as when they have political discussions with acquaintances in-person or on Twitter. This finding shows how willing followers are to spread leaders' views. The implications of the popularity of the motive of social utility become clear when this motive is compared with the motive of information/guidance. Those people with an information/guidance motive are following political leaders to obtain political information that will keep them informed and that will help guide their decisions about important issues. In the case of the motive of information/guidance, the material in political leaders' tweets travels just once (from leaders to their followers). As a result, the information being tweeted spreads only so far. With the followers' motive of social utility, however, leaders' tweets make multiple trips. Leaders' tweets go to followers, but in addition the information in the leaders' tweets then goes to a wide variety of others. The material spreads when followers talk about the information face-to-face with acquaintances or tweet about the information with their band of politically interested followers. The popularity of the social utility motive suggests that Twitter is a useful venue for political leaders, because leaders can inform and influence an audience that spreads far beyond their groups of followers.

Other motives also are telling in their implications. For example, those people with self-expression motives want to engage in dialog with the political leaders they follow. They wish to communicate support or criticism of those leaders and the leaders' tweets. Many people surveyed and interviewed had this motivation. The implication is that political leaders can better meet the needs of their followers when they make the effort to do two-way communication with followers. Leaders can engage with followers in several ways, such as replying to followers' comments, soliciting followers' advice on political matters, retweeting, mentioning followers in their tweets, and interacting on hashtags that their followers frequent. Many of these techniques are already used by businesses on Twitter to help with product development and to win consumer loyalty (Milstein, 2010a).

The relative popularity of the entertainment motive among respondents provides a glimpse into how Twitter is used politically. In-depth interviews with followers found that entertaining tweets from political leaders often serve as an antidote to all the serious political news that followers are exposed to on Twitter and elsewhere. It would be wrong to conclude that those people with this motivation find leaders' tweets to be trivial and, therefore, not influential. According to the interviews, entertainment is not the primary motive to follow political leaders, but it is a secondary motive to social utility, self-expression, or information/guidance. In other words, followers are primarily motivated to follow political leaders by factors other than entertainment; but followers still crave a healthy dose of entertainment from leaders. Based on these findings, political leaders' tweets should not be limited to serious political news, but occasionally could include satirical comments about issues or other leaders, and funny observations about politics and life. However, entertaining tweets should not predominate, because that is not the main reason political leaders are followed.

When compared with other ways to communicate politically, Twitter has several close cousins in the social networking sites of Facebook and MySpace. These sites are more like Twitter than blogs, such as *RedState* and the *Huffington Post*. This conclusion is based on past findings that social networking sites are used politically because of social motives, while information-seeking motives mainly drive political blog use (Ancu and Cozma, 2009; Kaye, 2005; Kaye and Johnson, 2006). Certainly Twitter shares some connections with blogs. For instance, both are used politically for self-expression motives, though to a greater degree on Twitter. Both are used for informational motives, though much more so on blogs.

In terms of informational motives, interviews with followers revealed what types of information they most want to get from political leaders. One major type is political insight. The study showed that followers are looking for more than mini press releases from leaders. Followers want leaders to give them an insider's perspective on political issues and what it is like to be involved in politics. As a result, political leaders should do more than tweet links to their latest press releases, position papers, and studies (though there is a role for that information). To satisfy followers' need for political insight, leaders could include tweets that provide a look behind the curtain of what it is like to be a political leader, what influences them, and how they make decisions.

The motives for following political leaders on Twitter are somewhat dependent on who followers consider to be political leaders. Followers with a narrow definition of a *political leader*, such as current elected officials only, are less likely than those followers with a broader definition to be driven by social, expressive, or entertainment motivations. The vast majority of followers, however, have a broad definition of a *political leader*, which includes such individuals as current elected officials, former elected officials, candidates for office, political appointees, political commentators, political parties, political action committees, and think-tanks. Some followers say that such individuals and groups are all leaders because all of these sources influence political discourse and alter the outcome of legislation.

THE PERSUASIVE POWER OF POLITICAL TWEETS

No matter what types of political leaders are being followed, leaders' tweets wield a lot of political power with followers. Almost 90 percent of those people in the survey said they look at least sometimes for information (such as websites, blogs, books, or articles) that is recommended and/or linked-to in leaders' tweets. More than 50 percent said that they do so either "often" or "always." These results reveal one reason why the 140-character limit of tweets does not hamper Twitter's ability to influence political discourse. The real power of political tweets often comes from the embedded links, which serve as a jumping off point to a vast amount of information.

In addition, more than 60 percent in the survey said that they retweet political leaders' tweets at least sometimes. That number is even higher for those people who follow a mix of elected, nonelected, and organizational leaders on Twitter. It is interesting to see how eager followers are to act upon leaders' tweets, rather than passively scan tweets and do nothing more. More than 60 percent reported taking action, such as signing a petition or contributing to a candidate, at least sometimes. The amount of activity that was measured is higher than what other studies have found regarding general Twitter use (Smith and Rainie, 2010; Sysomos, 2010b).

The findings also should clearly demonstrate to political leaders the value of using Twitter. Those leaders who invest the time and resources to tweet useful political information can be rewarded in a number of ways. Such tweets can influence followers to look at issues from the leaders' perspectives, as followers regularly click on leaders' recommended links. Thus leaders have the potential to persuade many others, each time their followers retweet the links.

So what makes political leaders' tweets so influential? Participants in the in-depth interviews said there are nine elements that cause leaders' tweets to be acted upon: clarity, a call to action, personal relevance, professional usefulness, helpful links and hashtags, including a political counterpoint, humor, interactivity, and outrageousness. Some of these elements are important for fairly obvious reasons; for example, tweets that are written clearly and include politically useful information have a better chance to persuade than tweets that are confusing or irrelevant. Other elements, however, deserve further discussion. The fact that participants said they were looking for political counterpoints indicates they are open to having their political views influenced by an ideologically wide range of leaders. The desire for humorous political tweets dovetails with the finding that many followers have an entertainment motivation in following political leaders. Also, other research has found humor to be quite persuasive. One study on why some e-mail messages are forwarded frequently found that humor was a key determinant because humor can "spark strong emotion" (Phelps et al., 2004, p. 345). Interactivity, as has been noted previously, is an important element because followers like to see their leaders engaging with their audiences (not merely transmitting to them). One form of interactivity happens when leaders solicit advice from their followers. The last element mentioned, outrageousness, underscores the point that leaders' tweets can have unintended consequences. A tweet that seems exaggerated or false often causes followers to react, sometimes by criticizing the leader who sent it.

Taken together, the findings add to what is known about the persuasiveness of word-of-mouth communication. While past research shows that companies can harness the power of WOM to create buzz marketing campaigns around their products (Godes and Mayzlin, 2009), far less is known about whether political leaders can use Twitter to create political buzz. Surveys and in-depth interviews with followers indicate that political leaders can be proactive in using their tweets to generate a lot of interest in an issue. What leaders want to avoid, however, is using Twitter to do political "astroturf" campaigns, which are "campaigns disguised as spontaneous, popular 'grassroots' behavior that are in reality carried out by a single person or organization" (Ratkiewicz, Conover, Meiss, Goncalves, Patil, Flammini, and Menczer, 2011, p. 1). Astro-turfers achieve this effect on Twitter by creating many fake user accounts to initially spread a leader's message. However, such a practice is not necessary on Twitter because followers seem quite willing to spread leaders' ideas without any deception needed.

Followers' motives play a major role in how influential political leaders' tweets can be. Those followers with social and self-expressive motives were the most likely to respond to leaders' tweets by retweeting, looking for recommended information, or taking suggested actions. With that knowledge in mind, it becomes even clearer why political leaders can benefit by interacting more with their followers. Those followers with social and self-expressive motives are the individuals who interact the most on Twitter and expect engagement with the leaders they follow. As a result, leaders who engage in two-way communication on Twitter stand the best chance of attracting and keeping those followers with social and self-expressive motives—the very individuals most influenced by leaders.

One big surprise of the study's results is how influential leaders' tweets are in shaping the political views of their followers. The survey found that certain demographic groups have their political beliefs influenced more by tweets from leaders with whom they usually agree than by anyone else in their social circle, including friends, family, and co-workers. These demographic groups include women, Hispanics, those people older than 40 years old, those making $100,000 or less, and those with less than a college degree. Even among all survey respondents, tweets from leaders with whom followers agree proved to be remarkably influential. Such tweets had the same score as family members for influence on respondents' political views. Only friends scored higher, but just barely. The results are surprising given the nonexistent nature of followers' relationships with political leaders. As the in-depth interviews confirmed, the vast majority of people have never met, talked to, or interacted in any way with the leaders they follow. The only connection most followers have with leaders comes when leaders send out their tweets, which usually resemble mini press releases. This finding might lead some to suggest that leaders need not bother interacting more with their followers, considering how much influence they already enjoy. However, in-depth interview comments suggest that leaders' tweets might be even more persuasive in shaping followers' political views if leaders were more interactive. That assumption comes from the fact that those participants who said leaders' tweets were not as influential as friends and family did cite the level of engagement as the main reason.

It is worth emphasizing that those people who said leaders' tweets were more influential than friends and family were talking about tweets from leaders with whom they share a similar ideology. In addition, friends and family were especially not influential when they differed politically from the participants, according to the in-depth interviews. These findings contribute to research into the distinctions between homophily and tie strength, which are separate, but related, concepts. *Homophily* is the degree to which two people share something in common (such as ideology), while *tie strength* refers to how much mutual involvement two people have in a relationship. In the case of leaders' tweets, homophily was often a more important factor than tie strength at influencing political views. This result matches other studies that have shown how homophily can trump tie strength in the age of the Internet and social media. Thus the factor of homophily gives virtual strangers the power to influence important decisions (Steffes and Burgee, 2009).

POLITICAL TWITTER USE AND DEMOCRACY

The evidence shows that it would be an oversimplification to say that using Twitter is either good or bad for democracy. The answer depends on which political Twitter users are being discussed. Among all survey respondents, the numbers were quite positive. More than 40 percent said they follow leaders they usually do not agree with politically. That number is nearly double the percentage of blog users who read blogs that challenge their views (Johnson et al., 2009).

Interview participants said that between 30 percent and 50 percent of the leaders they follow provide opinion-challenging information, with the rest supplying opinion-reinforcing information. They gave several reasons for following opinion-challenging leaders. Tweets from such leaders allow them to test their allegiance to a particular position, learn as much as possible about the "other side," and see what their opponents are thinking so that they can devise a response. Participants who had their views altered by opinion-challenging tweets also said that the detailed nature of the information that was linked to in the tweet made it influential.

Sunstein (2001) worries that users of new media such as Twitter merely "hear echoes of their own voices . . . to wall themselves off from others" (p. 49). Sunstein's view exemplifies two concepts: selective exposure and selective avoidance. Those followers who use Twitter to hear ideological echoes are practicing *selective exposure* (seeking opinion-reinforcing information). Those followers who use Twitter to wall themselves off politically are engaging in *selective avoidance* (avoiding opinion-challenging information). If a lot of the public used Twitter to concurrently practice *both* selective exposure and selective avoidance, then Twitter would be helping to develop a close-minded public. In contrast, a healthy democracy needs a well-informed public who can understand various sides of key public policy issues.

Thus it is crucial to find out how many political Twitter users concurrently engage in *both* selective exposure and avoidance. According to the study's data, the majority of political Twitter users are not using the microblog to simultaneously hear echoes of their political views and wall themselves off from political counterpoints. The percentage of those people who follow only leaders with whom they agree is 43 percent. The percentage of those people who follow leaders with whom they usually disagree is 41 percent. The percentage of those who follow a mix of leaders with whom they agree and disagree is 40 percent.

But when the study examined those people who were ideologically extreme, a different story was revealed. Those followers who are strong conservatives or strong liberals are more likely (than the less ideological) to avoid leaders with whom they disagree and to follow only leaders with whom they agree. The ideological strength of a respondent consistently emerged as a key predictor of who practices selective exposure and selective avoidance. These results are different from what Garrett (2009) and Johnson et al. (2011) found with regard to those who visit political websites. In both of those studies, the ideologically strong were not the most likely to avoid political websites that challenged their views.

So why is political Twitter use producing different results in this book's study, than in the website studies of Garrett (2009) and Johnson et al. (2011)? That question needs to be investigated further. Demographic differences between political website users and political Twitter users may be part of the reason. Perhaps the way Twitter is set up makes it too easy to avoid opinion-challengers. Maybe a differently worded survey question would change the results. In the survey of this book, followers were asked if they follow leaders with whom they "usually do not agree politically" (not leaders with whom they often or sometimes do not agree). The wording is important because the in-depth interviews found that opinion-challenging information sometimes comes from leaders with whom followers usually agree.

Whatever the reasons, the data of this book's study suggest that political Twitter use among the highly ideological does potentially harm their ability to understand opposing views. The evidence is mixed, however, on which political or ideological camp is the least open to diverse views. Strong liberals were the most likely to select only agreeable leaders to follow on Twitter, but moderate liberals were more likely than the more conservative to follow leaders who are politically moderate. Moderate liberals also were more likely than their conservative counterparts to follow at least one political leader with an opposing ideological viewpoint.

Ideology is not the only factor influencing selective exposure and selective avoidance. Those followers with high levels of political interest and political self-confidence were less likely to engage in selective avoidance, as were those followers who regularly reply to leaders. The results are not surprising, as other studies have found that there is a positive relationship between political interest and seeking diverse views (Knobloch-Westerwick and Meng, 2009). Also, the link between replying and seeking opinion-challengers can be explained by followers' desire to criticize political leaders. On the other hand, avoiding opinion-challengers is practiced more by those people who follow only elected officials, and by those who take actions, such as signing a petition or donating money, as the result of a tweet.

Selective exposure is practiced more by the young, by those people who have an entertainment motive for following political leaders, and by those people who regularly retweet leaders. The link between retweeting and selective exposure is similar to what Conover et al. (2011) found in an analysis of 250,000 tweets from the 2010 U.S. congressional elections: Political retweets exhibit "a highly segregated partisan structure" (p. 1). However, the same study found the opposite effect when analyzing tweets that included politically oriented hashtags and mentions, which are similar to replies. Tweets that included mentions were "dominated" by a "heterogeneous cluster of users in which ideologically-opposed individuals interact" (pp. 1, 7). This finding is similar to the connection that was found in the survey between replying and following opinion-challenging leaders. As a result, it is fair to say that certain features on Twitter, such as mentioning, replying, and hashtags, facilitate exposure to diverse viewpoints, while other features, such as retweeting, are less likely to aid exposure to different ideas.

In this book, the results in the chapters on selective exposure (Chapter 4) and word-of-mouth communication (Chapter 3) overlap and complement one another. For example, both chapters examined similar concepts from different angles: tweets from leaders with whom followers usually agree or disagree. In terms of selective exposure, survey findings showed that respondents overwhelmingly exposed themselves to opinion-reinforcing leaders. That finding makes sense, considering the influence some political tweets have as a form of word-of-mouth communication. WOM findings revealed that tweets from leaders with whom survey respondents usually politically agree (a homophilous social tie) were as influential as family members when it came to shaping respondents' political beliefs.

THE ROLES AND VALUE OF POLITICAL TWITTER USE IN FOLLOWERS' LIVES

Another way in the study to measure the importance of political Twitter use was to simply ask Twitter users how much the microblog has changed their lives politically. The answer was "quite a bit." According to the in-depth interviews, Twitter has caused a major shift in political behavior. Political Twitter use has increased activism, made users more inquisitive and knowledgeable, forced users to be more concise and clear, changed how political businesses interact with clients, and influenced how news travels on other media platforms. The magnitude of the political changes discussed puts Twitter in the same category as the most significant communication innovations of the last 30 years, such as the home computer and the DVR. That magnitude of political influence is because Twitter, personal computers, and DVRs are *discontinuous innovations*, which are innovations that "perform either a previously unfulfilled function or an existing function in a new way" (Robertson, 1971, p. 8).

Because those interviewed respondents were so adamant that Twitter has impacted their political lives, it is not surprising that they also said that they consider Twitter to possess the key characteristics of a successful innovation. Past research has found that widely adopted innovations have at least three characteristics: compatibility, relative advantage, and low complexity

(Tornatzky and Klein, 1982). Participants' comments indicate that Twitter is compatible with their political needs, has advantages over competing sources, and that it is easy to use. With its short messages delivered in real time, Twitter is compatible with people's fast-paced lives and need for instant information. Twitter's simple format also makes it easy to use even for those who are not technologically inclined.

In terms of relative advantage, the most interesting finding is how much of an advantage Twitter has over social networks such as Facebook. Even though almost all of the participants use Facebook, they said they prefer to use Twitter for politics because it is faster for receiving and distributing political information, has a more professional look, and is more secure. Participants said Facebook pages can get clogged with too much politically useless information, and that to them, the functions of Twitter and Facebook seem different. Participants' comments match the feelings of some political leaders. After holding virtual town hall meetings on Facebook and Twitter, Florida Governor Rick Scott concluded: "Twitter was way easier to respond," and "We got way more answers when we did the Twitter one" (quoted in Farrington, 2011).

A reoccurring theme from participants was that they use Facebook for their personal life but Twitter for their political life. Participants' comments point to the potential danger Twitter could face if it ever significantly changed its simple format and limited features. Twitter might destroy the very elements that make it unique in the political marketplace. Twitter's streamlined format also gives it advantages over newspapers, online news sites, television, radio, and blogs, which are considered difficult to scan for political updates. Participants said blogs and Twitter really serve different purposes because of the depth of information that blogs provide.

A few predictions now can be made because of participants' comments regarding Twitter's relative advantage, compatibility, and low complexity. Based on extensive research into many types of innovations that have enjoyed success over the years (Rogers, 2003; Tornatzky and Klein, 1982), Twitter seems to possess all of the right innovation characteristics that will allow it to survive well into the future. Furthermore, Twitter is likely to greatly increase in size and importance. After all, Twitter has plenty of room to expand because it has less than half as many users as Facebook and it makes up just 13 percent of American Internet users (Penner, 2010; Smith, 2011; Smith and Rainie, 2010; Weeks, 2010).

Those interviewed respondents clearly consider Twitter to have high political value. They also pointed to three main roles that the microblog plays in their political lives:

1. Twitter is a great way to get quick and unfiltered political information. In this role, Twitter's 140-character limit and simple format are strengths, not weaknesses. Twitter is a quick way to find interesting political information because a user can scan hundreds of political tweets in a few minutes and then decide which tweets deserve a deeper look by clicking on the tweets' links or hashtags.
2. Twitter is a soapbox on which to engage politically. Political Twitter users want to be more than mere receivers of information. They have a genuine desire to be part of the political process.
3. Twitter is a business tool for those people who work in politics or who cover politics. Those people who follow political leaders on Twitter are often political activists or leaders themselves.

When asked what they liked least about political tweets, the interviewed people mentioned the lack of any two-way communication with the leaders they follow. This disappointment is not surprising, given that so many participants have self-expressive motives for following leaders. One of the three most important roles for participants is using Twitter as a soapbox on which to engage politically. These findings provide more evidence that political leaders could benefit by replying to followers' questions and asking for their advice. This engagement would make those leaders seem more responsive to followers and more compatible with their political needs. Despite the weaknesses of Twitter mentioned, interview comments suggest that Twitter is a successful innovation for politics—up to the challenge of competing in a crowded field of social networking sites, blogs, traditional media, and other venues.

HOW CAMPAIGN TWEETS FRAME CANDIDATES

Because tweets can have a lot of political power, it is important to see what is in the contents of political leaders' tweets. What are leaders writing in tweets that make the messages so influential? To discover the content trends, an analysis was done on tweets from gubernatorial and senatorial candidates from the 2010 general election campaign. The examination included both a frame analysis and a content analysis to more accurately reveal trends in themes used to frame content. These analyses highlighted several topics that were emphasized in the campaign tweets during the 2010 election.

Content analysis revealed that the campaign trail was a dominant focus for many tweets. This finding supports past research asserting that the strategy frame is often a primary focal point in election dialogue (Bichard, 2006; Capella and Jamieson, 1997; Druckman, 2005). Candidates can easily keep voters aware and involved with the progression of daily campaign activities with Twitter. Tweets were also frequently focused on opponents. These messages often contained negative or critical information. More than 90 percent of tweets containing a negative tone were focused on opponents. This tactic is common among past research on online platforms (Bichard, 2006; Wicks and Souley, 2003) and allows candidates a quick and simple way to highlight their opponent's weaknesses.

A positive tone was apparent in many of the tweets analyzed, indicating that most candidates use Twitter as a tool for uplifting and personal acclaim (as past studies have suggested; Chambers and Bichard, in press; Cho and Benoit, 2005). One surprising finding was with respect to candidate seat. The current research indicated that challengers were more positive, while incumbents were more likely to feature a negative affective tone in their tweets. Perhaps the interactive tools on Twitter (hashtags, link features, mentions) make it less risky to highlight negative information. Candidates, even incumbents, can circulate critical information while still maintaining a comfortable distance from perceptions of negativity.

Results of the frame analysis indicate that campaign tweets make use of two main themes (with which candidates used to portray themselves). The first theme was one of *media validation*. In this frame, candidates' tweets had quotes from (and links to) news media articles and editorials that endorsed or included complimentary information about their candidacy. Candidates also used media validation in their tweets when attacking their opponents or when defending themselves against attacks. The second theme was *source frame*. This theme presented candidates' tweets as a valuable resource for timely political information. The source frame matched content analysis findings regarding the prevalence of tweet topics such as campaign trail and call to action.

The source frame, especially, shows why political tweets can be so influential. The frame analysis found candidates' tweets regularly included links to voter registration forms, position papers, ways to contribute, how to find polling places, polls, and news about the campaign. Candidates' Twitter accounts were a one-stop shop for interesting and "actionable" political information. The detailed policy and campaign information found in candidates' tweets is a far cry from the stereotype that Twitter users just talk about what they had for breakfast.

Although candidates maintained a focus on political information (in a formal rhetoric), personality was also evident in candidate tweets, especially in the final days of the campaign. Content analysis showed that a conversational style emerged in some tweets and focused on nonpolitical information such as sports, music, and family life. These tweets were likely used to portray a personal side to the candidates. This tactic has been noted in past research (Parmelee, 2009b; Trammell, Williams, Postelnicu, and Landreville, 2006). Republicans and females were more likely to take this approach and did so with a predominantly positive and enthusiastic tone. So, while Twitter serves primarily as a tool for users to obtain political information, followers do appreciate a limited amount of personal information tweeted by the leaders, because this information makes users feel that the political leaders are approachable and human.

The two frames used in the campaign tweets provide a window into the thoughts of the candidates who sent them. That situation is because frames do not exist in isolation but rather are created by—and are a reflection of—people who have their own preconceptions (called *schemata*) of the world (generally) and of politics (specifically). Smith (1997) clarifies this concept as "the individual frames issues within his or her established schemata" (p. 7).

So for example, campaign tweets show a lot about the candidates' preconceptions about politics (as politics relate to the news media and to Twitter). The extensive use of the media validation frame indicates that candidates believe that news media outlets are considered trustworthy. Apparently, candidates believe that citing such outlets gives them and their messages increased credibility and legitimacy. This finding is interesting because politicians on both sides of the political spectrum are famous for their public criticism of the media. However, candidates' tweets tell a different story. No matter whether the leaders are Democrats, Republicans, or independents, candidates' tweets link heavily to the media. For example, they linked to stories from traditional news outlets such as the *Los Angeles Times,* the *Washington Post,* the *Cleveland Plain Dealer,* the *Hartford Courant,* the *San Jose Mercury News*, CNN, and Microsoft/National Broadcasting Company (MSNBC).

Candidates value Twitter, based on the source frame and the heavy amount of tweeting that they do. Candidates spent a lot of time and effort to provide a wide array of political information in an attempt to influence their followers (and anyone else who receives the candidates' tweets) to volunteer, contribute, and vote. Candidates likely would not have invested the resources they did on Twitter had they believed it was not worth it.

The source frame also points to what is missing in the campaign tweets: a genuine sense of two-way engagement between candidates and their followers. The source frame was all about one-way communication of political information to followers and others on Twitter. Even attempts by the campaign tweets to seem interactive (such as retweeting, mentioning, and replying) were made in a way that simply broadcast a one-way message to followers that promoted the candidates. Candidates rarely interacted with followers by answering their questions or by soliciting their advice. The lack of engagement is unfortunate because many political Twitter users wish they could interact more with the politicians they follow. The frame analysis findings further confirm the disconnect between what followers want and what politicians are giving on Twitter.

Content analysis of the campaign tweets emphasizes an effort by candidates in the sample to appear interactive, even while they failed to genuinely engage. Although a variety of interactive features were coded, the most common by far was the use of URL links. More than 70 percent of the tweets analyzed featured a link to additional information. This result aligns with past research touting the popularity of such tactics (Trammell, Williams, Postelnicu, and Landreville, 2006). These links most often featured opponent information or a specific call to action to get involved with the campaign. The use of URL links that focused on opponents strategically allowed candidates to showcase critiques of their competitors while maintaining a safe distance. The reply/mention functions were used much less often in tweets (less than 26 percent), as was the retweet function (only 12.4 percent). The findings revealed a strategic effort to circulate information in a more one-way communication style, with less emphasis on engaging voters by asking for feedback or replying to their specific concerns. When used, replies/mentions most often showcased endorsements, or simply directed readers to get involved or donate to the campaign.

Another popular feature in the analyzed tweets was the hashtag. Approximately 60 percent of the tweets in the current sample featured a hashtag. This regular inclusion of hashtags in the campaign tweets is an important clue: Hashtags were most often used when discussing opponents. Over 77 percent of the tweets that mentioned an opponent also featured a hashtag. Many opposing candidates included the same state-specific hashtags in their tweets. For example, the Democratic and Republican candidates for California Governor and Pennsylvania Senate often used the #cagov and #pasen hashtags, respectively, when tweeting information about their records and those of their opponents. The significance of this finding is that such a practice can increase the amount of politically diverse views to which Twitter users are exposed. On Twitter, the tweets of anyone who includes a common hashtag are grouped together (and can be searched for). As a result, those users who regularly viewed hashtags such as #cagov, #pasen, #flgov, #nvsen, #ctsen, and #kysen during the campaign were able to see an ideologically diverse range of political information about the candidates. Common hashtags may help guard against the negative effects of selective exposure and selective avoidance (though only for those who make the effort to view such hashtags). Future studies should measure how often people visit political hashtags and how much time they spend at the linked information. In addition, content analysis should be done on political hashtags to precisely measure how diverse the linked-to views are and what types of individuals and organizations contribute.

The analysis of framing on Twitter allows candidates' tweets to be compared with more traditional forms of candidate communication, such as speeches and political advertising. Research into political advertising and speeches has found that successful politicians stick to a few main themes, such as change, values, freedom, and media validation (Devlin, 1994; Parmelee, 2002; Sing, 2010; Sloan, 1996). One of these themes, media validation, was used consistently in tweets, which suggests that candidates' tweets are crafted similarly to other forms of candidate communication.

LIMITATIONS AND IDEAS FOR FUTURE RESEARCH

This study has three limitations: the type of sampling done, the makeup of the samples, and the time period in which the sampling was conducted. For example, the survey used a nonrandom sample of followers of political leaders. This sampling type limits how much the findings can be said to represent the thoughts and actions of *all* followers of political leaders on Twitter. Future studies on this topic should strive for a larger sample size that is drawn randomly from the population being examined. Generalizability also is a problem with qualitative methods, such as in-depth interviews. In addition, there were political differences between those respondents in the survey and those respondents in the interviews. While there were about as many Republicans as Democrats in the interviews, Democrats outnumbered Republicans in the survey. Also, the surveys and in-depth interviews were conducted during the 2010 campaign, a time of intense political interest. Because of this timing, participants may have answered differently than if they had been contacted during a nonelection year.

Two other limitations exist with the survey, which was distributed via the Web. Those people who take Web surveys tend to differentiate less on rating scales than when they take face-to-face surveys (Heerwegh and Loosveldt, 2008). Also, survey respondents have been known to engage in "response substitution," which means their answers "might sometimes reflect attitudes that respondents want to convey but that the researcher has not asked about" (Gal and Rucker, 2011, p. 185).

The study's content analysis and frame analysis have sampling limitations. Both methods were conducted during a short time period right before the 2010 campaign, and the study focused on a relative handful of candidates for governor and the U.S. Senate. Results may have been different had these analyses been done on candidates for other offices or during a longer time-frame. Also, the messages found in campaign tweets may have little in common with tweets from politicians who are not up for election. More research is needed on how political leaders frame their tweets when they are not in the middle of a political campaign.

Another issue to consider is how users defined the concept of *political leader*. The conventional choice would have been to focus solely on elected public officials. However, today so many "others" (besides elected officials) wield genuine political power, especially in new media (such as blogs, Facebook, and Twitter). The decision was made for this study to let Twitter users define who they considered to be political leaders. The results were instructive. The vast majority of survey and in-depth interview participants said that many types of leaders are influencing them: current and former politicians, political appointees, commentators, and political organizations. Future scholars attempting research may find it useful to focus on one type of leader at a time to see if there are differences in how each type of leader influences followers. The chapters on uses and gratifications (Chapter 2), word-of-mouth communication (Chapter 3), and selective exposure (Chapter 4) compare followers by type of leader. These chapters compare followers of elected officials only, with those followers of a mix of elected officials, unelected individuals, and political organizations. Some differences were found, such as the motives of the two groups of followers. More research could define these differences further. For instance, there may be something unique about those Twitter users whose definition of the term *political leader* includes only elected officials. As a result, how those particular users are influenced by elected officials may be different than how followers of a mix of political leaders are influenced by elected officials.

More research could be done on the senders and receivers of political tweets, and the influence political tweets have on traditional media outlets. Elected officials and other political leaders should be interviewed to find out why they engage so little with their followers. The lack of engagement by leaders was one of the few problems participants talked about during the in-depth interviews. Is it mostly a logistical problem for leaders, of being unable to monitor and respond to the large volume of tweets coming in to them? Or do leaders feel that a two-way dialogue is not worth the effort? A survey of congressional staff members suggests that the answer is probably not the latter, as staffers say that Twitter is gaining political respectability. More than 40 percent of staffers said that Twitter is an important way to understand constituents' views (Congressional Management Foundation, 2011, p. 6). However, understanding constituents' views is not necessarily the same as interacting with followers and soliciting their input. It would be useful to ask political leaders how much effort they put into engagement on Twitter, how often they interact and solicit advice, and what would make them more likely to engage.

Those Twitter users who regularly receive and send political tweets should be interviewed to find out what they see as the "unwritten" rules of Twitter culture. In other words, what are the social norms and expectations of political Twitter users? Finding the answer could help political leaders and others who are trying to be influential on the microblog to play by the rules. A similar study has already discovered the social norms and expectations that are connected with Facebook culture (Vorvoreanu, 2009).

Also needed is further investigation of the various ways businesses successfully use Twitter for engagement with customers. Specifically, there may be several techniques that businesses use that could be transferred to the political world and help political leaders use Twitter to its full potential. What can political leaders learn from businesses that use Twitter to engage customers on how to improve products and services, and attract new customers who spread positive word-of-mouth about the brand? Such lessons could help political leaders use Twitter to get input from followers on what issues to focus on and attract new followers who will further spread leaders' views.

One technique used by businesses almost certainly would help political leaders increase their power and prominence without costing much time or effort. Some companies automatically track their customers' Klout scores. Klout is one of several firms that measures how much influence any given Twitter user has in the "Twitterverse." Businesses then make sure those users with the highest scores receive extra attention and are responded to quickly (Gerstner, 2011). Businesses track such scores so they can focus their efforts on keeping happy those customers who are the most likely to help or hurt the business with positive or critical tweets. Political leaders could use a similar strategy when interacting with their followers, or anyone else on Twitter. For example, when deciding which followers' questions or comments to reply to, leaders could focus mostly on those followers with high Klout scores. This tracking would allow leaders to efficiently engage in more two-way communication without being overwhelmed by trying to reply to every tweet. The added benefit is that the high-influence followers are the most likely to widely spread positive publicity about the leaders who replied to them.

Still another unexplored area of Twitter research involves the agenda-setting power of political tweets. Traditionally, *agenda setting* is said to occur when heavy news media coverage of an issue causes the public to see that issue as very important. There are several aspects of agenda setting that may apply to Twitter. Research has found that major media outlets (such as national newspapers) often play a leadership role in setting the agenda of smaller newspapers and TV news, which in turn set the public's agenda (Reese and Danielian, 1989). Political advertising, too, has been found to set the agenda of news media, which then sets the public's agenda (Roberts and McCombs, 1994). Perhaps a well-orchestrated campaign of tweets from a political leader about an issue could cause that issue to be covered heavily by the news media, thereby leading the public to think more about that issue. Such a process was suggested by several in-depth interview participants, including Nansen, who said, "Twitter has the ability to drive traffic across all platforms." In addition, Steve, who writes for a newspaper, said that political tweets generate story ideas. As a result, more research is needed to determine to what degree political tweets influence the agenda of news media outlets and the public. Agenda-setting effects also can be looked at from the opposite direction: Who (or what) sets the agenda of political tweets? Does news media coverage affect what issues are included in political tweets? What causes some issues to be top trending topics on Twitter?

Many of the findings presented from this study should be re-examined in the coming years. As Twitter continues to attract a wider audience, the demographic and political makeup of those people who follow political leaders is likely to change, causing some findings no longer to be true. This phenomenon has been seen before. For example, early Internet studies from the 1990s found that online users were quite different from the general population (Kraut, Patterson, Lundmark, Kiesler, Mukhopadhyay, and Scherlis, 1998) in several demographic and psychological ways. But later research contradicted these findings, as the continued popularity of the Internet meant that the average user was more mainstream (Kaye and Johnson, 2004; Tancer, 2008). In terms of who follows political leaders on Twitter, the surveys and in-depth interviews were conducted with people who were self-described "political junkies" with a higher level of political interest than the average American. In the future, those twitterers who follow political leaders may be more demographically and politically mainstream, which might mean that their motives for following and the effects of following might be different than it is with political junkies.

Finally, future studies will need to investigate how political Twitter use differs from the political use of other microblogs. While Twitter is the most popular microblogging service, other microblogs include Emote, Jaiku, Ping-Gadget, Plurk, and Tumblr. Each microblog is slightly different in its format and features. It is possible that a competing microblog will beat Twitter for political usefulness. If another microblog becomes dominant, it will be important to find out what aspects of its format and features made it so popular. Of course, it also is possible that all microblogging services will eventually become obsolete. Factors that might lead to Twitter's demise include excessive spam and the addition of too many extra features, both of which could detract from users' ability to easily access quick, timely information (Clay, 2009). In addition Twitter could fail to pay its way and go out of business, or be bought out by Google, Facebook, or another company that might alter Twitter in ways that would leave it unrecognizable. But current trends show Twitter is on the rise in terms of popularity, economic viability, and political influence. The study's findings indicate that Twitter is a powerful force that influences the relationship between political leaders and the public. Politically interested individuals and groups can no longer ignore the opportunities presented by Twitter to engage in political discourse and to influence the outcome of campaigns and legislation.

Bibliography

About this site (2010). Retrieved from http://tweetcongress.org/about.

Abraham, L. B., Morn, M. P., and Vollman, A. (2010). Women on the Web: How women are shaping the Internet. ComScore, Inc. Retrieved from www.comscore.com/Press_Events/Presentations_Whitepapers/2010/Women_on_the_Web_How_Women_are_Shaping_the_Internet.

Ammah-Tagoe, A. (2009, Sept. 8). Who's winning the Twitter wars? *Newsweek.* Retrieved from www.newsweek.com/2009/09/08/who-s-winning-the-twitter-wars.html.

Ancu, M., and Cozma, R. (2009). MySpace politics: Uses and gratifications of befriending candidates. *Journal of Broadcasting & Electronic Media, 53*(4), 567–583.

Anderson, R. L., and Ortinau, D. J. (1988). Exploring consumers' postadoption attitudes and use behaviors in monitoring the diffusion of a technology-based discontinuous innovation. *Journal of Business Research, 17*(3), 283–298.

Anderson, J., and Rainie, L. (2010, July 2). The future of social relations. Pew Research Center's Internet & American Life Project. Retrieved from http://pewinternet.org/Reports/2010/The-future-of-social-relations.aspx.

Ashley, C., and Oliver, J. D. (2010). Creative leaders: Thirty years of big ideas. *Journal of Advertising, 39*(1), 115–130.

Associated Press (2010, June 15). Some old politicos are getting their Web feet wet. Retrieved from www.npr.org/templates/story/story.php?storyId=127861578&sc=17&f=104.

Atkin, C. K. (1985). Informational utility and selective exposure to entertainment media. In D. Zillmann and J. Bryant (Eds.), *Selective exposure to communication* (pp. 63–92). Hillsdale, NJ: Lawrence Erlbaum.

Auter, P. J. (2007). Portable social groups: Willingness to communicate, interpersonal communication gratifications, and cell phone use among young adults. *International Journal of Mobile Communications, 5*(2), 139–156.

Avlon, J. (2004). *Independent nation: How centrists can change American politics.* New York: Three Rivers Press.

Balaban, D. C., and Baltaretu, C. M. (2010). Motivation in using social network sites by Romanian students: A qualitative approach. *Journal of Media Research, 1*(6), 67–74.

Banks, E. (2011, Feb. 11). Egyptian president steps down amidst groundbreaking digital revolution. *Mashable.* Retrieved from http://mashable.com/2011/02/11/egyptian-president-steps-down/.

Beck, P., Dalton, R., Green, S., and Huckfeldt, R. (2002). The social calculus of voting: Interpersonal, media, and organizational influences on presidential choices. *American Political Science Review, 96*(1), 57–73.

Benderly, J. (2011, March 14). Democrats look to Twitter to reverse fortunes for 2012. *Roll Call.* Retrieved from www.rollcall.com/issues/56_95/-204065-1.html.

Berry, E. (2009, April 8). Protests in Moldova explode, with help of Twitter. *New York Times.* Retrieved from www.nytimes.com/2009/04/08/world/europe/08moldova.html?_r=1.

Bichard, S. (2006). Building blogs: A multi-dimensional analysis of the distribution of frames on the 2004 presidential candidate web sites. *Journalism & Mass Communication Quarterly, 83*(2), 329–345.

Bimber, B. (1998). The Internet and political transformation: Populism, community, and pluralism. *Polity, 31*(1), 133–160.

Blair, M. E., and Hyatt, E. M. (1995). The marketing of guns to women: Factors influencing gun-related attitudes and gun ownership by women. *Journal of Public Policy & Marketing, 14*(1), 117–127.

Brown, T. J., Barry, T., Dacin P., and Gunst, R. (2005). Spreading the word: Investigating antecedents of consumer's positive word-of-mouth intentions and behaviors in a retailing context. *Journal of the Academy of Marketing Science, 38*(2), 123–128.

Brown, J. J., and Reingen, P. H. (1987). Social ties and word-of-mouth referral behavior. *Journal of Consumer Research, 14*(3), 350–362.

Brustein, J. (2011, March 21). On Twitter, conservative (or liberal) by association. *New York Times.* Retrieved from http://bits.blogs.nytimes.com/2011/03/21/on-twitter-conservative-by-association.

Bryant, J., and Miron, D. (2004). Theory and research in mass communication. *Journal of Communication, 54*(4), 662–704.

Buley, T. (2010, January 13). Republican's tweet revenge. *Forbes.* Retrieved from www.forbes.com/2010/01/13/congress-republicans-democrats-technology-personal-twitter.html.

Bumgarner, B. A. (2007). You have been poked: Exploring the uses and gratifications of Facebook among emerging adults. *First Monday, 12*(11). Retrieved from http://firstmonday.org/htbin/cgiwrap/bin/ojs/index.php/fm/article/view/2026/1897.

Capella, J., and Jamieson, K. (1997). *Spiral of Cynicism: The Press and the Public Good.* New York, NY: Oxford University Press.

Carlson, N. (2011). Chart of the day: How many users does Twitter really have? *Business Insider SAI*. Retrieved from www.businessinsider.com/chart-of-the-day-how-many-users-does-twitter-really-have-2011-3.

Catone, J. (2010, Aug. 3). A look back at the last 5 years of blogging. *Mashable*. Retrieved from http://mashable.com/2010/08/03/last-5-years-blogging.

Cha, M., Haddadi, H., Benevenuto, F., and Gummadi, K. P. (2010). Measuring user influence in Twitter: The million follower fallacy. *Proceedings of the International AAAI Conference on Weblogs and Social Media*. Retrieved from http://twitter.mpi-sws.org.

Chaffee, S. H., Saphir, M. N., Graf, J., Sandvig, C., and Hahn, K. S. (2001) Attention to counter-attitudinal messages in a state election campaign. *Political Communication, 18*(3), 247–272.

Chambers, B., and Bichard, S. (in press). Public opinion on YouTube: A functional theory analysis of the frames employed in user comments following Sarah Palin's 2008 acceptance speech. *International Journal of E-Politics*.

Cho, S., and Benoit, W. (2005). Primary presidential election campaign messages in 2004: A functional analysis of candidate news releases. *Public Relations Review, 31*(2), 175–183.

Chyi, H., and McCombs, M. (2004). Media salience and the process of framing: Coverage of the Columbine school shootings. *Journalism & Mass Communication Quarterly, 81*(1), 22–35.

Clay, J. (2009, April 26). Ten reasons why Twitter will eventually wither and die. Retrieved from http://elearningstuff.net/2009/04/26/ten-reasons-why-twitter-will-eventually-wither-and-die/.

Comm, J. (2010). *Twitter power 2.0. How to dominate your market one tweet at a time*. Hoboken, NJ: John Wiley & Sons.

Congressional Management Foundation (2011). *Communicating with Congress: Perceptions of citizen advocacy on Capitol Hill*. Washington, D.C.: The Partnership for a More Perfect Union. Retrieved from http://pmpu.org/wp-content/uploads/CWC-Perceptions-of-Citizen-Advocacy.pdf.

Conover, M. D., Ratkiewicz, J., Francisco, M., Goncalves, B., Flammini, A., and Menczer, F. (2011). Political polarization on Twitter. *Proceedings of the 5th International Conference on Weblogs and Social Media*. Retrieved from http://truthy.indiana.edu/site_media/pdfs/conover_icwsm2011_polarization.pdf.

Cook, R. (1994, May 7). A generation of voters is up for grabs. *Congressional Quarterly Weekly Report*, p. 1166.

Cook, C., Heath, F.M., and Thompson, R.L. (2000). A meta-analysis of response rates in Web- or Internet-based surveys. *Educational and Psychological Measurement, 60*(6), 821–826.

Coursaris, C. K., Yun, Y., and Sung, J. (2010). Understanding Twitter's adoption and use continuance: The synergy between uses and gratifications and diffusion of innovations. *SIGHCI 2010 Proceedings*. Retrieved from http://aisel.aisnet.org/sighci2010/3.

Creswell, J. W., Plano Clark, J. L., Gutmann, M. L., and Hanson, W. E. (2003). Advanced mixed methods research designs. In A. Tashakkori and C. Teddlie (Eds.), *Handbook of mixed methods in social & behavioral research* (pp. 209–240). Thousand Oaks, CA: Sage.

Devlin, L. P. (1994). Television advertising in the 1992 New Hampshire presidential primary election. *Political Communication, 11*(1), 81–99.

de Vise, D. (2009, Sept. 20). Tweeting their own horns. *Washington Post.* Retrieved from www.washingtonpost.com/wp-dyn/content/article/2009/09/19/AR2009091902389.html.

de Vreese, C. (2004). The effects of frames in political television news on issue interpretation and frame salience. *Journalism & Mass Communication Quarterly, 81*(1), 36–52.

DiMaggio, P. J., and Sato, K. (2003). Does the Internet Balkanize political attention? A test of the Sunstein thesis. Paper presented at the annual meeting of the American Sociological Association, Atlanta, GA. Retrieved from www.allacademic.com/meta/p106938_index.html.

Donia, L. (2010, March 23). A look at Cory Booker, the social media mayor. Center for Social Media. Retrieved from www.centerforsocialmedia.org/node/1386/node/7.

Driessens, O., Raeymaeckers, K., Verstraeten, H., and Vandenbussche, S. (2010). Personalization according to politicians: A practice theoretical analysis of mediatization. *Communications, 35*(3), 309–326.

Druckman, J. (2005). Media matter: How newspapers and television news cover campaigns and influence voters. *Political Communication, 22*(4), 463–481.

Dupagne, M., and Garrison, B. (2006). The meaning and influence of convergence: A qualitative case study of newsroom work at the Tampa News Center. *Journalism Studies*, 7(2), 237–255.

Economist (2010, May 6). Sweet to tweet: Twitter makes politicians seem more accessible. To matter, it needs to change their behaviour. Retrieved from www.economist.com/node/16056612?story_id=16056612.

Ehrlich, B. (2010, June 16). Many Facebook and Twitter users unhappy with Obama speech on BP oil spill. *Mashable.* Retrieved from http://mashable.com/2010/06/16/obama-speech-facebook-twitter-oil-spill.

Eisenstein, J., O'Connor, B., Smith, N. A., and Xing, E. P. (2010). A latent variable model for geographic lexical variation. *Proceedings of the 2010 Conference on Empirical Methods in Natural Language Processing*, pp. 1277–1287.Cambridge, MA: Association for Computational Linguistics. Retrieved from www.cse.ohio-state.edu/~fosler/emnlp2010-final/pdf/EMNLP124.pdf.

Entman, R. M. (1993). Framing: Toward clarification of a fractured paradigm. *Journal of Communication, 43*(4), 51–58.

Fabian, J. (2009, Aug. 24). Liberal activists flock to new website to organize on Twitter. *The Hill.* Retrieved from http://thehill.com/blogs/blog-briefing-room/news/other/56053-liberal-activists-flock-to-new-website-to-organize-on-twitter-.

Fabian, J., O'Brien, M., and Viebeck, E. (2010, Aug. 14). Recess is no rest for Hill's top tweeters: The 25 must-follow Twitter feeds. *The Hill*. Retrieved from http://thehill.com/homenews/house/114291-25-must-follow-twitter-feeds.

Fahrenthold, D. A., and Kane, P. (2011, June 16). Rep. Anthony Weiner resigns. *Washington Post*. Retrieved from www.washingtonpost.com/politics/anthony-weiner-to-resign-thursday/2011/06/16/AGrPONXH_print.html.

Farrell, M. B. (2009, June 6). Can Twitter help fix San Francisco's potholes? *The Christian Science Monitor*. Retrieved from www.csmonitor.com/USA/2009/0606/p02s01-usgn.html.

Farrington, B. (2011, March 23). Florida Gov. Scott holds Facebook "town hall." Associated Press. Retrieved from www.businessweek.com/ap/financialnews/D9M50UU80.htm.

Festinger, L. (1957). *A theory of cognitive dissonance*. Stanford, CA: Stanford University Press.

Finn, S., and Gorr, M. B. (1988). Social isolation and social support as correlates of television viewing motivations. *Communication Research, 15*(2), 135–158.

First, D. J. (2009, June 29). Restaurants using Twitter for cheap, effective marketing. *Boston Globe*. Retrieved from www.boston.com/ae/food/restaurants/articles/2009/06/29/restaurants_finding_twitter_a_cheap_effective_marketing_tool?mode=PF.

Fiske, S., and Taylor, S. (1991). *Social cognition*, 2nd Edition. New York, NY: McGraw-Hill.

Friedkin, N. (1980). A test of the structural features of Granovetter's "strength of weak ties" theory. *Social Networks, 2*, 411–422.

Gal, D., and Rucker, D. D. (2011). Answering the unasked question: Response substitution in consumer surveys. *Journal of Marketing Research, 48*(1), 185–195.

Gamson, W. A., and Modigliani, A. (1987). The changing culture of affirmative action. In R. G. Braungart and M. M. Braungart (Eds.), *Research in political sociology* (Vol. 3, pp. 137–177). Greenwich, CT: JAI Press.

Garrett, R. K. (2009). Politically motivated reinforcement seeking: Reframing the selective exposure debate. *Journal of Communication, 59*(4), 676–699.

Gerstner, L. (2011, July). How to complain and get results. *Kiplinger's Personal Finance Magazine*, p. 72.

Ghanem, S. (1997). Filling in the tapestry: The second level of agenda setting. In M. McCombs, D. Shaw, and D. Weaver (Eds.), *Communication and democracy: Exploring the intellectual frontiers in agenda-setting theory* (pp. 3–14). Mahwah, NJ: Lawrence Erlbaum.

Gilliam, J. (2009). Introducing act.ly—Petitions designed for Twitter. Retrieved from www.jimgilliam.com/2009/06/actly.

Gitlin, T. (1980). *The whole world is watching: Mass media in the making and unmaking of the new left*. Berkeley, CA: University of California Press.

Gladwell, M. (2000). *The tipping point: How little things can make a big difference*. New York, NY: Little, Brown.

Glaser, B., and Strauss, A. (1967). *The discovery of grounded theory*. Chicago, IL: Aldine.

Global Web Index (2010, July 23). Is Twitter a good marketing tool? *Trendstream*. Retrieved from www.trendstream.net/archives/1708.

Godes, D., and Mayzlin, D. (2009). Firm-created word-of-mouth communication: Evidence from a field test. *Marketing Science, 28*(4), 721–739.

Golbeck, J., Grimes, J. M., and Rogers, A. (2010). Twitter use by the U.S. Congress. *Journal of the American Society for Information Science and Technology, 61*(8), 1612–1621.

Golbeck, J., and Hansen, D. L. (2010). Computing political preference among Twitter followers. College Park, MD: Human–Computer Interaction Lab, University of Maryland. Retrieved from http://hcil.cs.umd.edu/trs/2010-20/2010-20.pdf.

Goldenberg, J., Libai, B., and Muller, E. (2001). Talk of the network: A complex systems look at the underlying process of word-of-mouth. *Marketing Letters, 12*, 209–221.

Goldsmith, R. E., and Horowitz, D. (2006). Measuring motivations for online opinion seeking. *Journal of Interactive Advertising, 6*(2), 1–16.

Gonsalves, A. (2010, Sept. 6). Twitter mobile use soaring. *Information Week*. Retrieved from www.informationweek.com/news/windows/reviews/showArticle.jhtml?articleID=227300209.

Granovetter, M. S. (1973). The strength of weak ties. *American Journal of Sociology, 78*(6), 1360–1380.

Granovetter, M. S. (1983). The strength of weak ties: A network theory revisited. *Sociological Theory, 1*, 201–233.

Grindley, L. (2009, March 11). How to win followers, gain influence on Twitter. *National Journal*. Retrieved from www.nationaljournal.com/njonline/no_20090311_6338.php.

Grossman, L. (2009, June 17). Iran protests: Twitter, the medium of the movement. *Time*. Retrieved from www.time.com/time/printout/0,8816,1905125,00.html.

Haridakis, P. M., and Rubin, A. M. (2003). Motivation for watching television violence and viewer aggression. *Mass Communication & Society, 6*(1), 29–56.

Havey, N. (2010, April 8). Can Act.ly keep Sen. Brown green? *Huffington Post*. Retrieved from www.huffingtonpost.com/nathan-havey/can-actly-keep-sen-brown_b_530470.html?view=print.

Heerwegh, D., and Loosveldt, L. (2008). Face-to-face versus Web surveying in a high Internet coverage population: Differences in response quality. *Public Opinion Quarterly, 72*(5), 836–846.

Hendricks, J. A., and Denton, R. E. (2009). *Communicator-in-chief: How Barack Obama used new media technology to win the White House*. Landham, MD: Lexington Books.

Hennig-Thurau, T., Gwinner, K., Walsh, G., and Gremler, D. (2004). Electronic word-of-mouth via consumer-opinion platforms: What motivates consumers to articulate themselves on the Internet? *Journal of Interactive Marketing, 18*(1), 38–52.

Hill, R. A., and Dunbar, R. I. M. (2003). Social network size in humans. *Human Nature, 14*(1), 53–72.

Hitwise (2011). Top 20 sites & engines. Retrieved from www.hitwise.com/us/data-center/main/dashboard-10133.html.

Howard, A. (2010, May 10). 5 ways government works better with social media. *Mashable.* Retrieved from http://mashable.com/2010/05/10/social-media-government.

Huberman, B. A., Romero, D. M., and Wu, F. (2009). Social networks that matter: Twitter under the microscope. *First Monday, 14*(1). Retrieved from http://firstmonday.org/htbin/cgiwrap/bin/ojs/index.php/fm/article/viewArticle/23/7/2063.

Iyengar, S., and Hahn, K. S. (2009). Red media, blue media: Evidence of ideological selectivity in media use. *Journal of Communication, 59*(1), 19–39.

Iyenger, S., Hahn, K. S., Krosnick, J. A., and Walker, J. (2008). Selective exposure to campaign communication: The role of anticipated agreement and issue public membership. *The Journal of Politics, 70*(1), 186–200.

Iyengar, S., and Simon, A. F. (2000). New perspectives and evidence on political communication and campaign effects. *Annual Review of Psychology, 51*(1), 149–169.

Iyengar, S., and Simon, A. (1993). News coverage of the gulf crisis and public opinion: A study of agenda-setting, priming, and framing. *Communication Research, 20*(3), 365–383.

Jamieson, K. H. (1992). *Dirty politics: Deception, distraction, and democracy.* New York, NY: Oxford University Press.

Jansen, B. J., Zhang, M., Sobel, K., and Chowdury, A. (2009). Twitter power: Tweets as electronic word of mouth. *Journal of the American Society for Information Science and Technology, 60*(11), 2169–2188.

Jerome, S. (2010, Nov. 18). GOP members more influential than Dems on Twitter, study finds. *The Hill.* Retrieved from http://thehill.com/blogs/hillicon-valley/technology/130003-gop-members-more-influential-on-twitter-study-finds.

Jin, B., and Park, N. (2010). In-person contact begets calling and texting: Interpersonal motives for cell-phone use, face-to-face interaction, and loneliness. *Cyberpsychology, Behavior, and Social Networking, 13*(5). Retrieved from www.liebertonline.com/doi/abs/10.1089/cyber.2009.0314.

Johnson, T. J., Bichard, S. L., and Zhang, W. (2009). Communication communities or "cyberghettos"? A path analysis model examining factors that explain selective exposure to blogs. *Journal of Computer-Mediated Communication, 15*(1), 60–82.

Johnson, T. J., Kaye, B. K., Bichard, S. L., and Wong, W. J. (2007). Every blog has its day: Politically-interested Internet users' perceptions of blog credibility. *Journal of Computer-Mediated Communication, 13*(1), Retrieved from http://jcmc.indiana.edu/vol13/issue1/johnson.html.

Johnson, T. J., Zhang, W., and Bichard, S. L. (2011). Voices of convergence or conflict? A path analysis investigation of selective exposure to political websites. *Social Science Computer Review.* Retrieved from http://ssc.sagepub.com/content/early/2010/09/08/0894439310379962.abstract.

Johnson, T., Zhang, W., Bichard, S., and Seltzer, T. (2010). United we stand? Online social network sites and civic engagement. In Zizi Papacharissi (Ed.), *Networked self: Identity, community, and culture on social network sites* (pp. 185–207). New York, NY: Routledge.

Johnson, T., Bichard, S., and Zhang, W. (in press). Revived and refreshed: Selective exposure to blogs and political websites for political information. In Francesca Comunello (Ed.), *Networked sociability and individualism: Technology for personal and professional relationships.* IGI Global Publishers.

Johnson, T., Bichard, S., Zhang, W., and Kaye, B. (2010). Shut up and listen: The influence of selective exposure to blogs on political tolerance. In Frank Columbus (Ed.), *Blogs and blogging: Types, impact and future directions.* Hauppauge, NY: Nova Science Publishers, Inc.

Jones, B. (2010, Jan. 13). More governors finding Twitter tweets sweet. *USA Today.* Retrieved from www.usatoday.com/tech/hotsites/2010-01-13-governors-tweet-Twitter_N.htm.

Kahneman, D., and Tversky, A. (1984). Choice, values, frames. *American Psychologist, 39*(4), 341–350.

Katz, E., and Lazarsfeld, P. (1955). *Personal influence: The part played by people in the flow of mass communications.* Glencoe, IL: The Free Press.

Kayahara, J., and Wellman, B. (2007). Searching for culture—high and low. *Journal of Computer-Mediated Communication, 12*(3). Retrieved from http://jcmc.indiana.edu/vol12/issue3/kayahara.html.

Kaye, B. K. (2005). It's a blog, blog, blog, blog world: Users and uses of weblogs. *Atlantic Journal of Communication, 13*(2), 73–95.

Kaye, B. K. (2007). Web site story: An exploratory study of blog use motivations. In M. Tremayne (Ed.), *Blogging, citizenship, and the future of the media* (pp. 127–148). New York, NY: Routledge.

Kaye, B. K., and Johnson, T. J. (2002). Online and in the know: Uses and gratifications of the Web for political information. *Journal of Broadcasting & Electronic Media, 46*(1), 54–71.

Kaye, B. K., and Johnson, T. J. (2004). A Web for all reasons: Uses and gratifications of Internet components for political information. *Telematics and Informatics, 21*(3), 197–223.

Kaye, B. K., and Johnson, T. J. (2006). The age of reasons: Motives for using different components of the Internet for political information. In A. P. Williams and J. C. Tedesco (Eds.), *The Internet election: Perspectives on the Web in campaign 2004* (pp. 147–167). Lanham, MD: Roman & Littlefield.

Kennamer, J. D. (1990). Political discussion and cognition: A 1988 look. *Journalism Quarterly, 67*(2), 348–352.

Kinder, D. R. (2003). Communication and politics in the age of information. In Sears, D. O., Huddy, L., and Jervis, R. (Eds.), *Oxford handbook of political psychology* (pp. 357–393). New York, NY: Oxford University Press.

Klout. (2010, Aug. 3). Klout score. San Francisco, CA. Retrieved from http://klout.com/jimdemint.

Knauer, V. (1992). *Increasing customer satisfaction*. Pueblo, CO: United States Office of Consumer Affairs.

Knobloch-Westerwick, S., and Meng, J. (2009). Looking the other way: Selective exposure to attitude-consistent and counterattitudinal political information. *Communication Research, 36*(3), 426–448.

Ko, H., Cho, C. H., and Roberts, M. S. (2005). Internet uses and gratifications: A structural equation model of interactive advertising. *Journal of Advertising, 34*(2), 57–70.

Kraut, R., Patterson, M., Lundmark, V., Kiesler, S., Mukhopadhyay, T., and Scherlis, W. (1998). Internet paradox: A social technology that reduces social involvement and psychological well-being? *American Psychologist, 53*(9), 1017–1031.

Krippendorff, K. (1980). *Content analysis: An introduction to its methodology*. Beverly Hills, CA: Sage.

Krugman, D. (1985). Evaluating audiences of the new media. *Journal of Advertising, 14*(4), 21–27.

Lazarsfeld, P. F., Berelson, B. R., and Gaudet, H. (1948). *The people's choice: How the voter makes up his mind in a presidential campaign*. New York, NY: Duell, Sloan, & Pierce.

Lee, M., and Youn, S. (2009). Electronic word of mouth (eWOM): How eWOM platforms influence consumer product judgement. *International Journal of Advertising, 28*(3), 473–499.

Leung, L. (2007). Stressful life events, motives for Internet use, and social support among digital kids. *CyberPsychology & Behavior, 10*(2), 204–214.

Liu, I. L. B., Cheung, C. M. K., and Lee, M. K. O. (2010). Understanding Twitter usage: What drives people to continue to Tweet. *PACIS 2010 Proceedings*. Retrieved from http://www.pacis-net.org/file/2010/S21-04.pdf.

Lombard, M., Snyder-Duch, J., and Bracken, C. (2002). Content analysis in mass communication: Assessment and reporting of intercoder reliability. *Human Communication Research, 28*(4), 587–604.

Lotan, G., and Gaffney, D. (2011). Breaking Bin Laden: Visualizing the power of a single tweet. SocialFlow. Retrieved from http://blog.socialflow.com/post/5246404319/breaking-bin-laden-visualizing-the-power-of-a-single.

Matthes, J. (2009). What's in a frame? A content analysis of media framing studies in the world's leading communication journals, 1990–2005. *Journalism & Mass Communication Quarterly, 86*(2), 349–367.

McCombs, M., and Ghanem, S. (2001). The convergence of agenda-setting and framing. In S. Reese, O. Gandy, and A. Grant (Eds.), *Framing public life* (pp. 67–81). Mahwah, NJ: Lawrence Erlbaum.

McCombs, M., Llamas, J., Lopez-Escobar, E., and Rey, F. (1997). Candidate images in Spanish elections: Second-level agenda setting effects. *Journalism & Mass Communication Quarterly, 74*(4), 703–717.

McCracken, G. (1988). *The long interview*. Thousand Oaks, CA: Sage Publications.

McGhee, E., and Krimm, D. (2009). Party registration and the geography of party polarization. *Polity, 41*, 345–367.

McLeod, J. M., Scheufele, D. A., and Moy, P. (1999). Community, communication, and participation: The role of mass media and interpersonal discussion in local political participation. *Political Communication, 16*(3), 315–336.

Milian, M. (2009, Nov. 16). President Obama: "I have never used Twitter." *Los Angeles Times*. Retrieved from http://latimesblogs.latimes.com/washington/2009/11/obama-never-used-twitter.html.

Millard, J. (2009). Performing beauty: Dove's "real beauty" campaign. *Symbolic Interaction, 32*(2), 146–168.

Miller, C. C. (2009, July 23). Marketing small businesses with Twitter. *New York Times*. Retrieved from www.nytimes.com/2009/07/23/business/smallbusiness/23twitter.html?_r=&pagewanted=print.

Milstein, S. (2010a). Twitter 101. Case studies: Pepsi. Retrieved from http://business.twitter.com/twitter101/case_pepsi.

Milstein, S. (2010b). Twitter 101. Case studies: Dell. Retrieved from http://business.twitter.com/twitter101/case_dell.

Mislove, A., Lehmann, S., Ahn, Y. Y., Onnela, J. P., and Rosenquist, J. N. (2010). Pulse of the nation: U.S. mood throughout the day inferred from Twitter. Retrieved from www.ccs.neu.edu/home/amislove/twittermood.

Morozov, E. (2009, June 17). Iran elections: A Twitter revolution? *Washington Post*. Retrieved from www.washingtonpost.com/wp-dyn/content/discussion/2009/06/17/DI2009061702232.html.

Morreale, J. (1991). *A new beginning: A textual frame analysis of the political campaign film*. Albany, NY: State University of New York.

Mutz, D. (2006). *Hearing the other side: Deliberative vs. participatory democracy*. Cambridge, UK: Cambridge University Press.

Nemeth. C. J., and Rogers, J. (1996), Dissent and the search for information. *British Journal of Social Psychology, 35*(1), 67–76.

Nielsen Wire (2010). Social networks/blogs now account for one in every four and a half minutes online. Retrieved from http://blog.nielsen.com/nielsenwire/online_mobile/.

O'Brien, M. (2010, Aug. 4). Pelosi says on Twitter she'll reconvene House to vote on state aid bill. *The Hill*. Retrieved from http://thehill.com/blogs/twitter-room?start=10.

O'Connor, B., Balasubramanyan, R., Routledge, B. R., and Smith, N. A. (2010). From tweets to polls: Linking text sentiment to public opinion time series. Washington, D.C.: *Proceedings of the International AAAI Conference on Weblogs and Social Media*. Retrieved from www.cs.cmu.edu/~nasmith/papers/oconnor+balasubramanyan+routledge+smith. cwsm10.pdf.

O'Dell, J. (2010, June, 8). Twitter hits 2 billion tweets per month. *Mashable*. Retrieved from http://mashable.com/2010/06/08/twitter-hits-2-billion-tweets-per-month.

Okazaki, S. (2009a). The tactical use of mobile marketing: How adolescents' social networking can best shape brand extensions. *Journal of Advertising Research, 49*(1), 12–26.

Okazaki, S. (2009b). Social influence model and electronic word of mouth: PC versus mobile Internet. *International Journal of Advertising, 28*(3), 439–472.

Oliphant, J. (2009, March 5). Politicians using Twitter in growing numbers. *Chicago Tribune*. Retrieved from www.physorg.com/news155481820.html.

Oppenheimer, B. I. (1996). The importance of elections in a strong congressional party era: The effect of unified vs. divided governments. In B. Ginsberg and A. Stone (Eds.), *Do Elections Matter?* 3rd Edition, (pp. 120–139). Armonk, NY: M. E. Sharpe.

Ostermeier, E. (2009, July 15). How do politicians use Twitter? A case study of Rep. Laura Brod. *Smart Politics*. Retrieved from http://blog.lib.umn.edu/cspg/smartpolitics/2009/07/how_do_politicians_use_twitter.php.

Ostrow, A. (2010a, July 31). Twitter hits 20 billion tweets. *Mashable*. Retrieved from http://mashable.com/2010/07/31/twitter-hits-20-billion-tweets.

Ostrow, A. (2010b, July 20). A look back at the last 5 years in social media. *Mashable*. Retrived from http://mashable.com/2010/07/20/last-5-years-social-media.

Palka, W., Pousttchi, K., and Wiedemann, D. G. (2009). Mobile word-of-mouth—A grounded theory of mobile viral marketing. *Journal of Information Technology, 24*(2), 172–185.

Pan, Z., Shen, L., Paek, H.-J., and Sun, Y. (2006). Mobilizing political talk in a presidential campaign. *Communication Research, 33*(5), 315–345.

Papacharissi, Z. (2002). The self online: The utility of personal home pages. *Journal of Broadcasting & Electronic Media, 46*(3), 346–368.

Papacharissi, Z. (2004). Democracy online: civility, politeness, and the democratic potential of online political discussion groups. *New Media & Society, 6*(2), 259–283.

Papacharissi, Z., and Rubin, A. M., (2000). Predictors of Internet use. *Journal of Broadcasting & Electronic Media, 44*(2), 175–196.

Park, N., Kee, K. F., and Valenzuela, S. (2009). Being immersed in social networking environment: Facebook groups, uses and gratifications, and social outcomes. *CyberPsychology & Behavior, 12*(6), 729–733.

Park, C., and Lee, T. M. (2009). Information direction, website reputation and eWOM effect: A moderating role of product type. *Journal of Business Research, 62*(1), 61–67.

Parker, A. (2011, Jan. 30). Twitter, as helpmate, goes to Capitol Hill. *New York Times*. Retrieved from www.nytimes.com/2011/01/30/us/politics/30twitter.html?_r=1.

Parmelee, J. H. (2002). Presidential primary campaign videocassettes: How candidates in the 2000 U.S. presidential primary elections framed their early campaigns. *Political Communication, 19*(3), 317–331.

Parmelee, J. H. (2003). *Meet the candidate videos: Analyzing presidential primary campaign videocassettes*. Westport, CT: Praeger.

Parmelee, J. H. (2006a). Understanding symbolism in magazine coverage of President Reagan. *Florida Communication Journal, 34*(2), 54–69.

Parmelee, J. H. (2006b). Examining "meet the candidate videos" at the gubernatorial level. *Florida Communication Journal, 34*(2), 82–93.

Parmelee, J. H. (2009a). Media pluralism by default: The case of Moldova. *Central European Journal of Communication, 2*(2), 279–293.

Parmelee, J. H. (2009b). "A better man for a better America:" Presidential campaign films as a mirror of society. *Atlantic Journal of Communication, 17*(2), 88–100.

Parmelee, J. H., Davies, J., and McMahan, C. (2011). The rise of non-traditional site use for online political information. *Communication Quarterly, 59*(5), 1–16.

Parmelee, J. H., and Perkins, S. C. (2012). Exploring social and psychological factors that influence the gathering of political information online. *Telematics and Informatics, 29*, 90–98.

Parmelee, J. H., and Perkins, S. C. (in press). Discourse: Mixed methods. In Carol A. Chapelle (Ed.), *Encyclopedia of applied linguistics.* Hoboken, NJ: Wiley Blackwell.

Parmelee, J. H., Perkins, S. C., and Sayre, J. J. (2007). "What about people our age?" Applying qualitative and quantitative methods to uncover how political ads alienate college students. *Journal of Mixed Methods Research, 1*(2), 183–199.

Parr, B. (2010a, June 23). Twitter lets you automatically follow your Facebook friends. *Mashable.* Retrieved from http://mashable.com/2010/06/23/huge-twitter-lets-you-automatically-follow-your-facebook-friends/.

Parr, B. (2010b, July 7). The first thing young women do in the morning: Check Facebook. *Mashable.* Retrieved from http://mashable.com/2010/07/07/oxygen-facebook-study.

Pauly, J. J. (1991). *A beginner's guide to doing qualitative research in mass communication* (Journalism Monograph No. 125). Columbia, SC: Association for Education in Journalism and Mass Communication.

Penenberg, A. L. (2010, July 1). Social networking affects brains like falling in love. *Fast company.* Retrieved from www.fastcompany.com/magazine/147/doctor-love .html.

Penner, C. (2010). Discovering who to follow. Retrieved from http://blog.twitter .com/.

Perez, S. (2010, Sept. 14). Twitter is not a social network, says Twitter exec. *New York Times.* Retrieved from www.nytimes.com/external/readwriteweb/2010/ 09/14/14readwriteweb-twitter-is-not-a-social-network-says-twitte-85900.html ?partner=rss&emc=rss.

Pew Research Center. (2010, May 23). New media, old media: How blogs and social media agendas relate and differ from traditional press. Retrieved from http:// pewresearch.org/pubs/1602/new-media-review-differences-from-traditional-press.

Pew Research Center. (2003, Jan. 5). Political sites gain, but major news sites still dominant. Retrieved from http://people-press.org/report/169/political-sites-gain-but-major-news-sites-still-dominant.

Phelps, J. E., Lewis, R., Mobilio, L., Perry, D., and Raman, N., 2004. Viral marketing or electronic word-of-mouth advertising: Examining consumer responses and motivations to pass along email. *Journal of Advertising Research, 44*(5), 333–348.

Pinkston, M. (2009). CPAs embrace Twitter: Brief messages leave powerful impressions. *Journal of Accountancy*, Aug. Retrieved from www.journalofaccountancy .com/Issues/2009/Aug/20091828.

Podoshen, J. S. (2008). The African American consumer revisited: brand loyalty, word of-mouth and the effects of the Black experience. *Journal of Consumer Marketing, 25*(4), 211–222.

Postelnicu, M., and Cozma, R. (2008). Befriending the candidate: Uses and gratifications of candidate profiles on MySpace. Paper presented to the *National Communication Association Convention*, San Diego, CA, November.

Price, V., Cappella, J. N., and Nir, L. (2002). Does disagreement contribute to more deliberative opinion? *Political Communication, 19*(1), 95–112.

Price, V., and Tewksbury, D. (1997). News values and public opinion: A theoretical account of media priming and framing. In G. A. Barnett and F. J. Boster (Eds.), *Progress in communication sciences: Advanced in persuasion* (pp. 173–212). Greenwich, CT: Ablex.

Raacke, J., and Bonds-Raacke, J. (2008). MySpace and Facebook: Applying the uses and gratifications theory to exploring friend-networking sites. *CyberPsychology & Behavior, 11*(2), 169–174.

Radick, S. (2010, July 2). How social media is changing the way government does business. *Mashable.* Retrieved from http://mashable.com/2010/07/02/social-media-government-business.

Ratkiewicz, J., Conover, M., Meiss, M., Gonçalves, B., Patil, S., Flammini, A., and Menczer, F. (2011). Truthy: Mapping the spread of astroturf in microblog streams. *Proceedings of the International World Wide Web Conference, Hyderabad, India.* Retrieved from http://portal.acm.org/citation.cfm?id=1963301.

Raymond, M. (2010, April 28). The library and Twitter: An FAQ. Library of Congress Blog. Retrieved from http://blogs.loc.gov/loc/2010/04/the-library-and-twitter-an-faq.

Reese, S. D., and Danielian, L. H. (1989). Intermedia influence and the drug issue: Converging on cocaine. In P. J. Shoemaker (Ed.), *Communication campaigns about drugs: Government, media, public* (pp. 29–46). Hillsdale, NJ: Lawrence Erlbaum.

Richardson, G. (2003). *Pulp politics: How political advertising tells the stories of American politics.* Landham, MD: Rowman & Littlefield.

Roberts, M., and McCombs, M. (1994). Agenda setting and political advertising: Origins of the news media. *Political Communication, 11*(3), 249–262.

Robertson, T. (1971). *Innovative behavior and communication.* New York, NY: Holt, Rinehart, Winston.

Rogers, E. M. (1958). Categorizing the adopters of agricultural practices. *Rural Sociology, 23*(4), 345–354.

Rogers, E. M. (2003). *Diffusion of innovations.* 5th Edition. New York, NY: The Free Press.

Rubin, A. M. (1993). The effects of locus of control on communication motivation, anxiety, and satisfaction. *Communication Quarterly, 41*(2), 161–171.

Ruggiero, T. E. (2000). Uses and gratifications theory for the 21st century. *Mass Communication & Society, 3*(1), 3–37.

Saleem, M. (2010, March 18). The current state of Twitter. *Mashable.* Retrieved from http://mashable.com/2010/03/18/twitter-infographic/.

Sarno, D. (2009, Feb. 18). Twitter creator Jack Dorsey illuminates the site's founding document. *Los Angeles Times.* Retrieved from http://latimesblogs.latimes.com/technology/2009/02/twitter-creator.html.

Schaefer, R. J., and Avery, R. K. (1993). Audience conceptualizations of "Late night with David Letterman." *Journal of Broadcasting & Electronic Media, 37*(3), 253–273.

Scheufele, D. A. (1999). Framing as a theory of media effects. *Journal of Communication, 49*(1), 103–122.

Scheufele, D. (2000). Agenda setting, priming, and framing revisited: Another look at cognitive effects of political communication. *Mass Communication & Society, 3*(2), 297–316.

Schindler, R. M., and Bickart, B. (2005). Published word of mouth: Referable, consumer generated information on the Internet. In C. P. Haugtvedt, K. A. Machleit, and R. F. Yalch (Eds.), *Online consumer psychology: Understanding and influencing consumer behavior in the virtual world* (pp. 35–61). Hillsdale, NJ: Lawrence Erlbaum Associates.

Shear, M. D. (2010, June 25). High-tech Obama makes "Twitters" gaffe. *Washington Post.* Retrieved from www.washingtonpost.com/wp-dyn/content/article/2010/06/25/AR2010062503015.html.

Shen, F. (2004). Chronic accessibility and individual cognitions: Examining the effects of message frames in political advertisements. *Journal of Communication, 54*(1), 123–137.

Shumow, M. (2010). "A foot in both worlds": Transnationalism and media use among Venezuelan immigrants in South Florida. *International Journal of Communication, 4*(1), 377–397.

Sills, S. J., and Song, C. (2002). Innovations in survey research: An application of Web surveys. *Social Science Computer Review, 20*(1), 22–30.

Silverman, M. (2010, June 9). How political campaigns are using social media for real results. *Mashable.* Retrieved from http://mashable.com/2010/06/09/political-campaigns-social-media.

Sing, C. S. (2010). "Yes we can"—framing political events in terms of change: A corpus-based analysis of the "change" frame in American presidential discourse. *Belgian Journal of Linguistics, 24,* 139–163.

Sloan, J. W. (1996). Meeting the leadership challenges of the modern presidency: The political skills and leadership of Ronald Reagan. *Presidential Studies Quarterly, 26*(3), 795–804.

Smith, A. (2011, June 1). Twitter update 2011. Pew Internet & American Life Project. Retrieved from www.pewinternet.org/Reports/2011/Twitter-Update-2011.aspx.

Smith, J. (1997). The framing context model. Paper presented at the Conference for the Center for Mass Communication Research, "Framing the New Media Landscape," Columbia, SC, October 13–14.

Smith, T., Coyle, J. R., Lightfoot, E., and Scott, A. (2007). Reconsidering models of influence: The relationship between consumer social networks and word-of-mouth effectiveness. *Journal of Advertising Research, 47*(4), 387–397.

Smith, S. M., and Krugman, D. M. (2010). Exploring perceptions and usage patterns of digital video recorder owners. *Journal of Broadcasting & Electronic Media, 54*(2), 248–264.

Smith, A., and Rainie, L. (2010, Dec. 9). Who tweets? Pew Internet & American Life Project. Retrieved from http://pewresearch.org/pubs/1821/twitter-users-profile-exclusive-examination.

Stafford, T. F., Stafford, M. R., and Schkade, L. L. (2004). Determining uses and gratifications of the Internet. *Decision Sciences, 35*(2), 259–288.

Steffes, E. M., and Burgee, L. E. (2009). Social ties and online word of mouth. *Internet Research,19*(1), 42–59.

Sternberg, J. (2009, Oct. 19). How local politicians are using social media. *Mashable.* Retrieved from http://mashable.com/2009/10/19/social-media-local-politics.

Stewart, M., and Rohrs, J. (2010). Twitter X-factors: A research series from ExactTarget, CoTweet. Retrieved from http://email.exacttarget.com/uploadedfiles/resources/SFF4_Twitter_Final.pdf.

Stromer-Galley, J. (2003). Diversity of political conversation on the Internet: Users' perspectives. *Journal of Computer-Mediated Communication, 8*(3). Retrieved from http://jcmc.indiana.edu/vol8/issue3/stromergalley.html.

Stroud, N. J. (2008). Media use and political predispositions: Revisiting the concept of selective exposure. *Political Behavior, 30*(3), 341–366.

Sun, T., Seounmi, Y., Guohua, W., and Mana, K. (2006). Online word of mouth (or mouse): An exploration of its antecedents and consequences. *Journal of Computer-Mediated Communication, 11*(4). Retrieved from http://jcmc.indiana.edu/vol11/issue4/sun.html.

Sunstein, C. R. (2001). *Republic.com.* Princeton, NJ: Princeton University Press.

Sysomos (2010a, June). Judging a Twitter user by their followers. Retrieved from http://www.sysomos.com/insidetwitter/followers.

Sysomos (2010b, Sept.). Replies and retweets on Twitter. Retrieved from www.sysomos.com/insidetwitter/engagement.

Sysomos (2010c, July 14). Exploring the use of Twitter around the world. Retrieved from http://blog.sysomos.com/2010/01/14/exploring-the-use-of-twitter-around-the-world.

Tancer, B. L. (2008). *Click: What millions of people are doing online and why it matters.* New York, NY: Hyperion.

Tankard, J. W. (2001). The empirical approach to the study of media framing. In S. D. Reese, O. H. Gandy, and A. E. Grant (Eds.), *Framing public life* (pp. 95–106). Mahwah, NJ: Lawrence Erlbaum.

Tapscott, D. (2009). *Grown up digital: How the net generation is changing your world.* New York: McGraw-Hill.

Taylor, C. (2011, Feb. 14). Twitter CEO: Why there won't be a "Twitter phone." *Mashable.* Retrieved from http://mashable.com/2011/02/14/twitter-ceo-why-there-wont-be-a-twitter-phone/.

Taylor, M. (2009, June 15). Twitterers protest #CNNFail on Iran coverage. *Wall Street Journal.* Retrieved from http://blogs.wsj.com/digits/2009/06/15/twitterers-protest-cnn-fail-on-iran-coverage/.

Tessler, J. (2010, June 24). Twitter settles with FTC over data security lapses. *Associated Press.* Retrieved from www.washingtonpost.com/wpdyn/content/article/2010/06/24/AR20100623231_pf.html.

Thelwall, M. (2009). Homophily in MySpace. *Journal of the American Society for Information Science and Technology, 60*(2), 219–231.

Thorson, K. S., and Rodgers, S. (2006). Relationship between blogs as eWOM and interactivity, perceived interactivity, and parasocial interaction. *Journal of Interactive Advertising, 6*(2), 34–44.

Tornatzky, L. G., and Klein, R. J. (1982), Innovation characteristics and innovation adoption-implementation: A meta-analysis of findings. *IEEE Transactions on Engineering Management, 29*(1), 28–45.

Trammell, K., Williams, A., Postelnicu, M., and Landreville, K. (2006). Evolution of online campaigning: Increasing interactivity in candidate web sites and blogs through text and technical features. *Mass Communication & Society, 9*(1), 21–44.

Traylor, M. B., and Mathias, A. M. (1983). The impact of TV advertising versus word of mouth on the image of lawyers: A projective experiment. *Journal of Advertising, 12*(4), 42–47.

Twitter Help Center. (2011). What are @replies and mentions? Retrieved from http://support.twitter.com/articles/14023-what-are-replies-and-mentions.

Van Grove, J. (2010, June 3). Google launches new tools for political campaigns. *Mashable.* Retrieved from http://mashable.com/2010/06/03/google-campaign-toolkits.

Ventsias, T. (2009, September 15). UM study shows congressional use of Twitter falls short. University of Maryland Newsdesk. Retrieved from www.newsdesk.umd.edu/culture/release.cfm?ArticleID=1964.

Viebeck, E. (2010, July 19). Texas lawmaker solicits questions for forum via Twitter. *The Hill.* Retrieved from http://thehill.com/blogs/twitter-room?start=40.

Vorvoreanu, M. (2009). Perceptions of corporations on Facebook: An analysis of Facebook social norms. *Journal of New Communications Research, 4*(1), 67–86.

Walker, J., Wasserman, S., and Wellman, B. (1994). Statistical models for social support networks. In S. Wasserman and J. Galaskiewicz (Eds.), *Advances in Social Network Analysis* (pp. 53–78). Thousand Oaks, CA: Sage.

Wall, M. (2006). Blogging Gulf War II. *Journalism Studies, 7*(1), 111–126.

Wee, C. H., Lim, S. L., and Lwin, M. (1995). Word-of-mouth communication in Singapore, HK: With focus on effects of message-sidedness, source, and user-type. *Asia Pacific Journal of Marketing and Logistics, 7*(1), 5–36.

Weeks, L. (2010, June 9). In your Facebook: Social sites are everywhere. NPR. Retrieved from www.npr.org/templates/story/story.php?storyId=127527648.

Weimann G., Tustin D. H., Vuuren D., and Joubert, J. P. R. (2007). Looking for opinion leaders: Traditional vs. modern measures in traditional societies. *International Journal of Public Opinion, 19*(2), 173–190.

Wicks, R., and Souley, B. (2003). Going negative: Candidate usage of Internet web sites during the 2000 presidential campaign. *Journalism & Mass Communication Quarterly, 80*(1), 128–144.

Wojcieszak, M. (2010). "Don't talk to me": Effects of ideologically homogeneous online groups and politically dissimilar offline ties on extremism. *New Media & Society, 12*(4), 637–655.

Wojcieszak, M. (2008). False consensus goes online: Impact of ideologically homogeneous groups on false consensus. *Public Opinion Quarterly, 72*(4), 781–791.

Wojcieszak, M. E., and Mutz, D. C. (2009). Online groups and political discourse: Do online discussion spaces facilitate exposure to political disagreement? *Journal of Communication, 59*(1), 40–56.

Yang, C., Wu, H., Zhu, M., and Southwell, B. G. (2004). Tuning in to fit in? Acculturation and media use among Chinese students in the United States. *AsianJournal of Communication, 14*(1), 81–94.

Yoo, K. H., and Gretzel, U. (2008). What motivates consumers to write online travel reviews? *Information Technology & Tourism, 10*(4), 283–295.

Zaller, J. R. (1992). *The nature and origins of mass opinion.* Cambridge, UK: Cambridge University Press.

Zhang, W., Johnson, T., Seltzer, T., and Bichard, S. (2010). The revolution will be networked: The influence of social network sites on political attitudes and behaviors. *Social Science Computer Review, 28*(1), 75–92.

Zinsser, W. (2001). *On writing well.* New York, NY: Harper Collins.

Index

About the Authors

John H. Parmelee is an associate professor of communication at the University of North Florida. He has a doctorate from the University of Florida and a master's degree from Columbia University's Graduate School of Journalism. His academic research interests include political communication as well as how journalism works in emerging democracies. He has published research in various academic journals, including *Political Communication, Communication Quarterly, Communication Studies, Journal of Mixed Methods Research,* and *Telematics and Informatics.* He also is the author of *Meet the Candidate Videos* (Westport, CT: Praeger).

Shannon L. Bichard is an associate professor of advertising in the College of Mass Communications at Texas Tech University where she has served since 2001. Her research interests focus on public opinion and consumer behavior, with an emphasis on online communication and political engagement. Her research has appeared in journals such as *Journalism & Mass Communication Quarterly, Journal of Computer-Mediated Communication, Social Science Computer Review, International Journal of E-Politics,* as well as book chapters regarding social networking in politics. Her teaching area is advertising; she currently advises the AAF National Student Advertising Competition team. Bichard received her B.A. and master's degree from the University of Central Florida and her doctoral degree from the University of Florida.